ESSAY

Advance Praise for Literary Writing in the 21ˢᵗ Century

Literary Writing in the 21ˢᵗ Century is a remarkable collection of writings by one of the boldest and most incisive critics writing today. Anis Shivani is determined to throw open the shutters and force us to take a look at our culture and our books in a new way. He deserves our serious attention.
—**James L. Magnuson, Director of the James A. Michener Center for Writers at UT Austin, and author of *Ghost Dancing and Windfall***

Literary Writing in the 21ˢᵗ Century is a brimming cornucopia of literary thinking. Interviews, reviews, essays, symposia: they are all here—fresh, edgy, incisive. Shivani is a bodacious critic committed to bursting through barriers of all kinds. As you read his work, prepare to be challenged, skewered, delighted, and in the end, transformed.
—**Alyson Hagy, author of *Boleto* and *Ghosts of Wyoming***

Literary Writing in the 21ˢᵗ Century is a grab bag compendium of critical provocations, and Shivani is its principal provocateur. A writer who knows the canon but is not of it, he takes cosmopolitan sightlines on his array of subjects. If criticism were a game of high-stakes poker, Shivani would be the man across the table looking to raise every bet. He doesn't win every hand, but he does manage to keep things interesting.
—**Sven Birkerts, editor of *AGNI*, and author of *The Gutenberg Elegies: The Fate of Reading in an Electronic Age* and *American Energies: Essays on Fiction***

For the past few years, I have enjoyed the provocative and insightful essays and reviews of Shivani in a number of leading literary periodicals published throughout the United States. In *Literary Writing in the 21ˢᵗ Century*, he has gathered a large number of his conversations which continue his cogent analysis of the contemporary literary landscape. I know of no current literary critic who matches Shivani in courage, breadth of careful reading, and erudition.
—Larry D. Thomas, Member, Texas Institute of Letters, 2008 Texas Poet Laureate, and author of *As If Light Actually Matters: New and Selected Poems*

Shivani is both blunt and bold; on top of it all, he writes with admirable verve. Anis Shivani is the Thelonious Monk of contemporary criticism, and this book is his "Ruby My Dear."
—Larry Fondation, author of the novels *Angry Nights and Fish*, *Soap and Bonds*, and the story collections *Common Criminals* and *Unintended Consequences*.

From essays on the current state of contemporary fiction and poetry, to interviews and conversations with today's authors and publishers, *Literary Writing in the 21ˢᵗ Century* encourages an energetic conversation about the literary community in which we should all be glad to participate.
—Anne Sanow, author of *Triple Time*, winner of the PEN New England/L. L. Winship Award for Fiction

Literary Writing in the 21st Century

Conversations

ALSO BY ANIS SHIVANI

Anatolia and Other Stories

Against the Workshop: Provocations, Polemics, Controversies

The Fifth Lash and Other Stories

My Tranquil War and Other Poems

Karachi Raj: A Novel

Whatever Speaks on Behalf of Hashish: Poems

Soraya: Sonnets

Literary Writing in the 21st Century

Conversations

Anis Shivani

Texas Review Press
Huntsville, Texas

FIRST EDITION
Requests for permission to acknowledge material from the work should be
sent to:

Permissions
Texas Review Press
English Department
Sam Houston State University
Huntsville, TX 77341-2146

Cover Design: Nancy Parsons, Graphic Design Group

Library of Congress Cataloging-in-Publication Data
Names: Shivani, Anis, author.
Title: Literary writing in the 21st century : conversations / by Anis Shivani.
Other titles: Literary writing in the twenty first century
Description: First edition. | Huntsville, Texas : Texas Review Press, [2017]
Identifiers: LCCN 2017000906 (print) | LCCN 2017008592 (ebook) |
ISBN
    9781680031294 (pbk.) | ISBN 9781680031300 (ebook)
Subjects: LCSH: American literature--21st century--History and criticism. |
    Contemporary, The, in literature. | Literature publishing--United
    States--History--21st century. | Authors and publishers--United
    States--History--21st century.
Classification: LCC PS229 .S55 2017 (print) | LCC PS229 (ebook) | DDC
    810.9/006--dc23
LC record available at https://lccn.loc.gov/2017000906

For Paul Ruffin (1941-2016), in memoriam

Table of Contents

Preface

My aim in this book is to present a sustained series of dialogues amongst leading figures in the publishing industry—fiction writers, poets, essayists, critics, editors, publishers, booksellers, even book designers—about the state of the industry: how and why different kinds of writing is being produced in this country, what are the means by which it's getting into readers' hands, and how both production and distribution are changing and what is good and bad about those changes.

Of course, the rise of new technologies in the last several years, since the arrival of what we call Web 2.0 (and now whatever comes after that), has radically altered our modes of consuming culture, including writing, and of course the parallel ascendancy of MFA programs as almost the sole generator of legitimized creative writing is the other factor to contend with, but I have tried in these interlocutions to ground the debate in larger questions of literary value.

Who among our fiction writers and poets are worthy of emulation and why? Should we classify writing into different sub-genres, with distinct parameters, and when does this hurt and when does this help? Should we focus on quantity over quality, and are we perhaps shortchanging readers by creating bubbles where different literary elites find their prejudices confirmed but where there is not much of a populist impetus? Who, in fact, are the readers—not just of creative writing but of writing about writing, i.e., criticism—and who are the authors, and what kind of relationship exists between them, in this second decade of the twenty-first century? Should readers be guided to read better? Likewise, should writers let go of institutional resources as the primary means to validate their work, or should they try to reform institutions from within, if we can even agree that reform is required in the first place?

In short, this is a story—told through the voices of the most diverse array of participants from the entire spectrum of the literary world I could assemble over a sustained period of time—about not only the state of literary authorship and readership at the present moment, including how we got here from the recent past and what the immediate future looks like, but this is also a fearless discussion about what is worth aspiring to in the throes of ambition and what classifies as mere fads of the moment.

I am, of course, a critic, and not hesitant to use judgment, but you will note that this is true of all the strong writers and readers presented in this book: they all have firm criteria by which to measure the quality of exchanges in the day-to-day constitution of the literary sphere, and they are not afraid to speak their minds.

My big hope for this book is that it will help open the doors of conversation between teachers and students, between students of writing at different levels in the academy and outside it, and between readers and everyone else professionally engaged in writing, to air out the questions that need to be addressed more publicly.

Are you, wherever you find yourself on the literary spectrum, doing the best you can, according to whatever standards you have constructed to measure your sense of well-being and improvement?

If you are an apprentice writer, how can you chart a sustainable yet fulfilling path beyond the confines of the academy, beyond your limited time of relative privilege and security, to see you through to the ultimate ends of your writing journey?

If you are involved in any of the different spheres of the writing industry, and you want to move from where you are to wherever you think might be a better position of service and endurance, how can you do so in light of what others are contemplating and visualizing as the present and future of writing?

The participants in this book gave their most deeply felt answers to these questions—or rather questions opening up other questions—and I truly hope that as a result this book might become a standard resource for students both inside formal creative writing programs and those pursuing writing independently, to reduce the sense of loneliness that constitutes the DNA of the writing vocation but also to encourage forms of community that are geared above all to improvements in the quality of writing.

If you notice that this book studiously avoids discussion of what seem to me any of a number of peripheral contemporary distractions, often predominant on the internet, that get us away from this most essential of values—the quality of writing itself—then that is how I have always functioned as a critic. It may be a bit old-fashioned, but I hope it is avant-garde too for the same reason: to keep the discussion focused on writing itself, even while accounting for and fully comprehending the material infrastructure of writing, seemed to me the best way to proceed with these conversations that have developed over the long duration.

I wanted this to be an honest book seeking honest answers, and I hope you'll see it the same vein.

Anis Shivani
Houston, Texas
April 24, 2017

Authorship in Contemporary American Literature

1.

Who is the author? Is he even around anymore? Can we ascribe texts to authors, or is the author well and truly dead? To authors, these questions might sound a little silly—authors are, after all, invested in being authors—but there has been a lively modern debate around them for at least fifty years, sparked in particular by two seminal post-structuralist essays, one by Roland Barthes called "The Death of the Author" (1967)[1] and another by Michel Foucault called "What Is an Author?" (1968).[2] Barthes and Foucault posed extremely provocative questions that have lost none of their urgency with the passage of time and seem perfect starting points for any discussion of the status of the author under current conditions of technology, readership, politics, patronage, and mass culture.

New Criticism sought to banish the author from research, the text being all that mattered. In many ways Derridean deconstruction perpetuated this indifference or even disrespect toward the autonomy of the author. Ironically, the peak of this assault, in the late 1960s, was also the moment when the author, as the object of study, began her long march back to the center of critical consciousness. The death of the author was attached to the death of man and of course also the death of god (who had been killed off by Nietzsche long ago but was due for a fresh beheading). Indeed, Foucault's work is a close genealogical relative of Nietzsche's, as both remove man (and, by association, god) as the object of interest. For Foucault, discourse is everything: discourse produces its own conditions of analysis and study, discourse produces authors, discourse produces

1. Roland Barthes, "The Death of the Author," in *Image—Music—Text*, ed. and trans. Stephen Heath (London: Fontana, 1977).

2. Michel Foucault, "What Is an Author?" in *Language, Counter-Memory, Practice: Selected Essays and Interviews*, ed. and trans. Donald F. Bouchard (Ithaca, N.Y.: Cornell University Press, 1977).

scholars who study authors, as well as readers who abide by the conditions of reading. Yet this simplified version of Foucault's thought ignores the crucial fact that in that very essay he allows room for authors who alter the nature of discourse. The same goes for Barthes, who, in later books like *The Pleasure of the Text* (1975) and *Sade, Fourier, Loyola* (1976), brought the author back in.

In recent years, under the sign of New Historicism, a tremendous amount of scholarship has been generated that focuses on the emergence of the author in modernity, allying that emergence with the invention of print technology and the concomitant rise of the private bourgeois individual pursuing self-mastery. Reams of scholarship probe the development of the profession of authorship, from the Renaissance to the Enlightenment to the Romantic era to modernism. Looking particularly at authors like Erasmus, Milton, and Johnson, scholars have drawn links between authors' self-fashioning and the conditions of their financial survival, as the nature of patrons and readers underwent dramatic transformation over time.

In the Middle Ages, the author was secondary to the canonical text, his contribution taking the form of glosses and commentaries. Further, his writing was subject to additional commentary from other authors, and the resulting constant state of flux, anchored in the canonical text, prevented the emergence of the freestanding author we have come to know since then. Though the preferred medieval term was *auctores*,[3] the label was provisional and not indicative of the free agency we ascribe to authors today. In careful prefaces, authors fashioned images of continuity and derivation, rather than originality or creativity. Their intention was to honor the work of forebears, or to dispute it as the case might be, but not to set themselves up as authorities ab initio. It was in the Renaissance, with the proliferation of print technology, that the author came into his own. The ease of reproducing texts meant that authors no longer had to depend on the support of individual patrons; the sheer quantity of reproduction allowed a readership that would indirectly subsidize the author's labors. A great deal of research has been done on the social conditions under which copyright emerged

---

3. "The word 'author' derives from the medieval term *auctor*, which denoted a writer whose words commanded respect and belief. The word auctor derived from four etymological sources: the Latin verbs *agere*, 'to act or perform'; *auieo*, 'to tie'; *augere*, 'to grow'; and from the Greek noun *autentim*, 'authority.'" Donald A. Pease, "Author," in Sean Burke, *Authorship: From Plato to Postmodernism: A Reader* (Edinburgh: Edinburgh University Press, 1995). See also A. J. Minnis, *Medieval Theory of Authorship: Scholastic Literary Attitudes in the Later Middle Ages* (London: Scolar, 1984), Lisa Jardine, *Erasmus, Man of Letters: The Construction of Charisma in Print* (Princeton, N.J.: Princeton University Press, 1993), and Jane Chance Nitzsche, *The Genius Figure in Antiquity and the Middle Ages* (New York: Columbia, 1975).

as a necessary condition, allowing authors to feel proprietary about their writing, and how this new sense of ownership altered the relationship between authors and readers.[4] With the rise of copyright in the seventeenth and eighteenth centuries, authors began to address a vast, amorphous readership hungry for both information and enlightenment. The case has also been made that privacy in its modern formulation arose as a direct result of this development, which in turn is the foundation of modern liberalism.[5] Print created readers who became introspective during the solitary practice of reading. It remains an open question whether liberalism can survive the foreseeable end of print. In any event, the nexus between print, copyright, readership, privacy, and the author is clear and well-defined.

It has also been prolifically noted that the emergence of copyright had everything to do with the desire for censorship. Censorship provided a means by which the state could get hold of out-of-control discourses, assign responsibility and authority, and control dissemination of texts by means of granting proprietary rights to stationers (booksellers) and later publishers.[6] Property leads inevitably to a punitive regime, and it was no different in the case of authorship. We cannot lose sight of this central reality as we try to grapple with authorship today.

In the American context, various segments of the nineteenth-century readership, both antebellum and postbellum, have been the subject of an explosive amount of research, examining how Emerson, Thoreau, Whitman, Dickinson, Poe, Melville, Hawthorne, and, not least of all, Twain, constructed themselves as authors according to changing circumstances. Twain—much like David Sedaris today—was conscious of his positioning within the marketplace and used every device of publicity and marketing to establish the well-known persona that has come down to us. Similarly, we are apt to think of the modernists as

---

4. On copyright, see Mark Rose, *Authors and Owners: The Invention of Copyright* (Cambridge, Mass.: Harvard, 1993), Benjamin Kaplan, *An Unhurried View of Copyright* (New York: Columbia University Press, 1967), and Paul Goldstein, *Copyright's Highway: From Gutenberg to the Celestial Jukebox* (Stanford, Calif.: Stanford Law and Politics, 2003).

5. Among others, Cecile M. Jagodzinski has made this point well in *Privacy and Print: Reading and Writing in Seventeenth-Century England* (Charlottesville: University Press of Virginia, 1999). Jagodzinski quotes Alan Westin that individual privacy's four basic functions include "personal autonomy, emotional release, self-evaluation, and limited and protected communication." The rise of social media is clearly altering each of these elements, as authors are keenly responsive. As Jagodzinski explains, "Authors play a crucial role in this creation of the private self, for they are originators of the text, authoring and authorizing the readers represented within their works. At the same time, they are readers themselves, and so are perhaps the first negotiators of the distance between the public and the private life."

6. See, for instance, Annabel Patterson, *Censorship and Interpretation: The Conditions of Writing and Reading in Early Modern England* (Madison, Wisc.: University of Wisconsin Press, 1984).

indifferent to public opinion, but research has shown that they took assiduous care to elaborate their self-presentation for the public, patrons, and posterity. Publicity has never been a stranger to any form of authorship, and authors have always been eager to seize upon the little space allowed them by literate culture to constitute themselves as authorities to the extent that it is possible. Otherwise, what is the point of being an author?

Authorship is extremely relevant today because around this conception many of the major issues—intention, originality, creativity, genius, influence, authenticity, plagiarism, selfhood, free agency, subjectivity, causality, and ownership—revolve in an endless gyre. There is no getting away from this protean concept, in connection with which we can pose questions key to today's literary culture, such as: What is the author's status in a rapidly consolidating publishing industry with sharp declines in literary readership? What about the almost complete integration of literary writing within the academy, arguably the biggest change in writing in recent decades? What about the rise of social media and new technologies of writing and reading that take direct aim at the old monopoly of print? To speak of the author is always to speak of the reader, and the forms of influence that work in both directions immediately come into play. It has been held since Barthes and Foucault that the death of the author means the birth of the reader, but can it be that the death of the author also means the death of the reader? This is the central question the notion of authorship allows us to explore.

Let's consider first exactly why Barthes and Foucault remain so germane to any debate about authorship today. In their essays, Barthes and Foucault said both less and more than what is generally made of them: less because their concept of the demise of the author was more of a wish or fantasy than a declaration of a fait accompli, and more because their very modesty tempers a resounding epitaph to the project of the human that only seems to have accelerated in the ensuing years of postmodern spectacle.

In "The Death of the Author," Barthes holds that when the author starts writing, he disappears: "As soon as a fact is narrated no longer with a view to acting directly on reality but intransitively, that is to say, finally outside of any function other than that of the very practice of the symbol itself, this disconnection occurs, the voice loses its origin, the author enters into his own death, writing begins." He raises the question with respect to the voice in Balzac's story "Sarrasine," wondering who exactly is speaking, whose psychology, whose worldview is being represented in the narratorial voice. (In 1970 Barthes would publish *S/Z*, a book breaking down the entire story into codes, a bravura act of criticism that took the author out of the equation entirely and focused only on the semiotics of narration.)

What Barthes is positing here is a more intelligent way of reading, giving the reader the authority to make sense of the text as he will. Barthes would go on to elaborate the concept of *jouissance* (translated by Richard Howard as "bliss"), the variety of pleasure that the reader experiences when the text opens itself to her without the author imposing predetermined meaning. Reader-reception theory was alive and well before Barthes, but he certainly contributed one of the most fruitful ideas to come out of the post-structuralist movement in crediting the reader as the primary arbiter of meaning.

Barthes says he understands that in popular culture the author is still the focus of biographies and the imputation of motives, but all this ought to be irrelevant to the ideal of readership (which also means authorship) that he is putting forward. In effect, Barthes is outlining a new way of doing criticism. Modernist authors had long prescribed their own death, but criticism never took them up on this radical idea. Reiterating Stéphane Mallarmé's well-known thoughts on authorship, Barthes says, "It is language which speaks, not the author; to write is, through a prerequisite impersonality (not at all to be confused with the castrating objectivity of the realist novelist), to reach that point where only language acts, 'performs,' and not 'me.'" This accords with Jacques Lacan's idea that *language* thinks us into existence or Foucault's idea that *discourse* thinks us into existence—ideas that I, for one, find increasingly convincing. Barthes holds Proust in high regard for not just "putting his life into his novel" but making "of his very life a work for which his own book was the model." The writer should be reframed as the "scriptor," who is "born simultaneously with the text," without "preceding or exceeding the writing."

This resembles to some extent New Criticism's banishment of the author, but it is a more radical project. Barthes sounds a lot like Foucault when he says that writing "has no other origin than language itself, language which ceaselessly calls into question all origins." The writer merely gives expression to a web of intertextuality, borrowing and stealing from other texts, from language already in existence, mixing it up according to his needs. This is a profound undermining of the traditional notion of the author as creative genius, manufacturing works ex nihilo, as though he were a god. Instead, Barthes holds, "the text is a tissue of quotations drawn from the innumerable centers of culture," and, as a result, the scriptor "no longer bears within him passions, humors, feelings, impressions, but rather this immense dictionary from which he draws a writing that can know no halt." We reduce the complexity of texts when we assign all-knowing singular authors to them. In a sense, this also means for Barthes the end of criticism as we know it, since "historically the reign of the Author has also been that of the

Critic." Instead, the reader is the figure that matters, "the space on which all the quotations that make up a writing are inscribed without any of them being lost."

Barthes is not proposing the end of reading. Rather he is proposing a rebirth such as has never been seen before. His own "autobiography," *Roland Barthes by Roland Barthes* (1977),[7] puts the onus of expectation on the reader, decentralizing the author, even though it appears that the author is all there is in photographs and fragments of autobiographical texts. For a rebirth of reading of the kind Barthes idealizes, authors are needed who are so big that they get swallowed up in their writing, authors capable of effacing themselves in the language of their work to such an extent that they become radical threats to the community of readers, posing unbearable challenges—Barthes offers Mallarmé, Valéry, and Proust as examples. This view of writing is said to be anti-humanist, because it kills off man as the object of study, man in the abstract or the universal, the summum bonum of modernity. But it is also humanism taken to the nth degree, because in place of the decipherable, automotive, representative author, it creates a void into which the reader may step and create the text of his choosing, according to his own context and inclination.

I think the paradigmatic modern author who took on Barthes's challenge was Salman Rushdie in *The Satanic Verses* (1988). He showed that an author's authority could still be so important that it could shake the whole world, set into motion political cataclysms and clashes of civilization far exceeding anything mere politicians could conjure up. He took the Barthesian philosophy of *jouissance* to heart, leaving everything up to the reader, eliminating himself by way of excessive presence. It wasn't just a few blasphemous lines that riled his opponents, but the fragmented narrative style that threw doubt on conventional notions of revelation, newness, inspiration, rebellion, and obedience: all of the novel's diverse strands, both ancient and modern, revolved around these axes. The great chronological span was emptied of determinate historical meaning, which is another way of saying that Rushdie wrote a novel illustrating the author's absence precisely as Barthes envisioned. *The Satanic Verses* is a text above all about the (fraudulent) nature of inspirational writing, in which Muhammad's divine revelation is reduced to a web of intertextuality and Rushdie's (and Muhammad's companion Salman's) intervention transforms the paradigmatic readerly text, i.e., the Qur'an, into a writerly text. It is a great irony that popular culture immediately proceeded to resurrect the body of the author by designing to kill him, when he had done everything

---

7. *Roland Barthes by Roland Barthes*, trans. Richard Howard (New York: Hill and Wang, 1977).

he could to throw interpretive authority over to the reader, not the maker of texts (himself or Muhammad).

We're familiar with the Iranian fatwa as the source of the trouble. At the time, however, the arbiters of official literary culture—it's all too easy to forget now—were split between those who stood for the author's right to ruffle any community he chose and those who thought Rushdie a troublemaker who had it coming to him. From this perspective, Rushdie's memoir *Joseph Anton* (2012) represents a triumphant rescue of the author from all the forces that would belittle him—the parallel, for our times, of Voltaire and Rousseau's efforts at the inception of the enlightenment. Rushdie's unforgivable offense—in the eyes of many in the literary community at the time of the fatwa, and among some disgruntled reviewers of *Joseph Anton*—was his lack of repentance at writing a text overloaded with *jouissance*, rather than a text providing what Barthes called *plaisir*, or comfortable pleasure: the sort of text that the publishing industry is organized to disseminate. *Plaisir* corresponds with *texte lisible* (the readerly text), whereas *jouissance* relates to *texte scriptible* (the writerly text), which few authors have the courage to invent.

Ironically, by constructing so massive a conception of the author—as moral legislator for the culture at large, in the way Shelley would have it in his defense of poetry, and in the way Plato forbade it in *The Republic*, excluding the rhapsodes from his republic of reason, as he also did in *Ion*—Rushdie in his memoir is returning us to a project of reading as *jouissance* as advocated by Barthes. Only middling authors interfere with their readership's rightful ascendancy. Another layer of irony revealed in Rushdie's memoir is that Jacques Derrida was not as supportive of Rushdie in his years of hiding as he could have been, speaking instead of the responsibility of the author toward the beliefs of particular communities, though not going so far as to place him in the category of troublemaker—just as Henry James, though he refused to sign a petition in support of Oscar Wilde when he was arrested, never went so far as to condemn Wilde. The handful of negative reviews of *Joseph Anton* reveal an acute discomfort with the legislative/high priest function that Rushdie ascribes to the author, preferring the typical American novelist's false modesty as a point of departure.[8]

Foucault was in some senses responding to Barthes's essay, though his brief was more historical, or rather genealogical, to use his preferred term. His purpose

---

8. The two most petty reviews were Isaac Chotiner's in *The Atlantic*, http://www.theatlantic.com/magazine/archive/2012/12/how-the-mullahs-won/309170/, and Zoe Heller's in *The New York Review of Books*, http://www.nybooks.com/articles/archives/2012/dec/20/salman-rushdie-case/?pagination=false.

was the same as in *The Order of Things: An Archeology of the Human Sciences* (1970), where he elaborated the conditions for the emergence of various formative discourses. How do discourses come into being? Who authorizes them? How do they gain currency, how can we judge their power and influence over people, and how can we recognize the moments of transition from one discourse to another? It's been commonly noted of Foucault that he posits a radical rupture in discourses from one era to another, rather than a gradual development of ideas as is the wont for progressive thinkers. Rupture poses a threat to reason and progress; it suggests that other factors besides the autonomy of intellectual disciplines may be in play. Rupture makes scholars deeply uncomfortable.

In "What Is an Author?" Foucault wanted to show just how ruptures in the notion of the author have taken place in history. In contrast to both structuralists and phenomenologists, Foucault was interested in the historical conditions that determine the relationship between the author and the text. Samuel Beckett's plaintive cry "What matter who's speaking, someone said, what matter who's speaking?" is the leitmotif of Foucault's essay, and the presumed death of the author only makes the question more urgent. Echoing Barthes, Foucault holds that "the essential basis of writing is not the exalted emotions related to the act of composition or the insertion of a subject into language. Rather, it is primarily concerned with creating an opening where the writing subject endlessly disappears."

Post-structuralism can be interpreted as the philosophy of absence rather than the classical Western norm of presence. (This is Derrida's signature move.) Foucault takes this one step further by speaking of *death* instead of mere absence. The author, as in *The Arabian Nights*, was compelled to keep narrating in order to forestall death. But "where a work had the duty of creating immortality, it now attains the right to kill, to become the murderer of its author." Foucault adds that "writing is now linked to sacrifice and to the sacrifice of life itself; it is a voluntary obliteration of the self that does not require representation in books because it takes place in the everyday existence of the writer." Further, "if we wish to know the writer in our day, it will be through the singularity of his absence and in his link to death, which has transformed him into a victim of his own writing."

These enigmatic remarks signify not just the modernist aesthetic of the self-sufficiency of the text, but the more radical notion of writing having become antithetical to life itself, because it is invested in the processes and meanings of death, or rather, alienation from the text. The extreme professionalization of the author within the contemporary popular discourse of authorship has killed him, is always killing him, especially when he feels he is most alive. Rushdie's fight, to return to that archetypal example, is both to exterminate himself as the author whom popular culture constructed in reaction to his intransigence in the face of the fatwa and to regain immortality for himself as the author of *The Satanic Verses*, the text that was all but forgotten in the heat of the moment.

Foucault points to many problems in the conventional definition of the author. It is difficult, for one thing, to determine exactly which texts belong to a particular author. Should we include everything? The fashion of publishing an author's letters, diaries, unfinished works, and uncollected fragments is aimed at rounding out our impression of the author's historical existence, but sometimes that goal can detract from the author's literary legacy. One thinks of Susan Sontag's journals, some of which are banal in the extreme, or of David Foster Wallace's unfinished last novel, *The Pale King* (2011), a piece of inchoate writing that fed into the need to canonize the author upon his death. Should these have been published, and are these texts we should ascribe to the author Susan Sontag or the author David Foster Wallace? And if they are not, then what are we to make of Vladimir Nabokov's *The Original of Laura*, which his son Dmitri published in the form of index cards, or E. M. Forster's letters, which J. R. Ackerley preserved—and published—against the wishes of their author, or—perhaps the most radical example—Kafka's instructions to his executor, Max Brod, to destroy all his work, a trafficking in death that somehow feels all too appropriate? Authors always have to face the risk of unintended consequences, and, in these cases, the authors in question may have been trying to interfere unfairly with *ecriture* (writing), taking away from the reader any opportunity to fill in the space left by the author's absence. If *scriptor* is Barthes's helpful notation, then *ecriture* is Foucault's contribution, signifying "the conditions of any text, both the conditions of its spatial dispersion and its temporal deployment."

There are other problems with respect to the stability of the author. Foucault starts using the terminology of the "author-function" to designate "the existence, circulation, and operation of certain discourses within a society." The author-function is closely related to the dispensation of punishment that arose with the responsibilities of ownership. Not all discourses require authors: Foucault notes that in the Middle Ages, scientific texts required authorship whereas literary texts did not, while the opposite holds true today. It's difficult for us to think of authorship without intention, and modern criticism evokes Christian exegesis when it "employs devices…to prove the value of a text by ascertaining the holiness of its author." Foucault breaks down the various "I's" of the author in the text, in terms that evoke Wayne Booth's precise formulations in *The Rhetoric of Fiction* (1983).

But just when we think we have the author-function within our grasp, Foucault seemingly undermines the entire notion by offering the concept of the "transdiscursive author." This refers to authors who are "initiators of discursive practices," authors like Freud and Marx, who, unlike scientific authors, create discourses that lead to further discourses that only elaborate, never overturn, their foundational discourses. The nineteenth century was particularly rich in foundational discourses. Foucault notably excludes novelists from transdiscursive authorship because according to him they do not have the same potential to authorize future discourses in line with their founding texts. This would seem to herald the return of the author in a big way, after Foucault has just gone to great pains to demolish him, but Foucault seems to want to set up different terms of critical analysis when looking at discourses (such as economics or psychology) as a whole, rather than at texts or series of texts by the same author. When he says that "we can easily imagine a culture where discourse would circulate without need for an author," he sounds very Barthesian, elevating this as the ideal for authorship and readership.

Both Barthes and Foucault give us a less authoritarian, monopolistic, determinate way of looking at texts and their authority and reception. They equip us with a new critical vocabulary with which to judge writing. Do some texts, more than others, create openings wherein the author disappears and assigns the responsibility of reading to the reader? How do such texts come into being? How can we get away from simplistic notions of intention and sincerity, which do little to promote the practice of *ecriture*—or *texte scriptible*? Are there more fruitful ways of thinking about the ownership of texts—and discourses—than we are used to? Who can lay claim to originality, and why is it important to understand its preconditions? From technology to economics to culture, the tendency today ought to be for the supremacy of *ecriture*, the reduction of the author to *scriptor*, whereas in fact the literary industry pushes hard for exactly the opposite, the transcendence of the author and the negation of the reader.

2.

The questions of creativity, originality, free will, selfhood, psychology, causality, subjectivity, and ownership all revolve around the agency of the author versus the reader. To the extent that we believe in the romantic idea of genius, we ascribe agency to the author. But if we ascribe potency to discourse or language, in the post-structuralist vein, then we give agency to the reader. Authorship is always a question about readership. Does the independent author produce the text, or is the author himself the product of discourse? How far is the author free of culture and history, and how much is he part of it? Both premodern divine inspiration and postmodern intertextuality undercut the agency of the author.

In contemporary American literature, the author, once a strictly liberal/ bourgeois creation, is being both straitjacketed (under corporatization) and put on a pedestal (hyper-authorship). These tendencies are taking place simultaneously, creating much of the confusion between conventional and postmodern concepts of the author. Corporate publishing doesn't want to end the concept of the author as Barthes and Foucault would have it, but instead wants to elevate and revise it for its own purposes. Impersonalization of the work is back in force, breaking the circuit between the author and the conditions of production, which can never be part of the official discussion—hence the popular "craft interview," devoid of economic content. At the same time, the personality of the author is back, but only a certain kind of personality, which has been preapproved for publicity purposes—the author as cheerleader for the publishing industry's general health and vitality.

The author (in the sense of how he is allowed to think of himself) has in effect become an appendage to the Author (the version promoted in public). Regardless of genre, the Author must be at the forefront of self-promotion, in his appearances as teacher, reader, mentor, conference-goer, blogger, and social media enthusiast. The stabilization of the author-function in the midst of the potential chaos dictated by Web 2.0 is one of the great accomplishments of corporate publishing, resulting in the refutation of postmodernist conceptions of the author. For example, in a recent PBS interview, Jennifer Egan, often heralded for the "postmodern" techniques employed in *A Visit from the Goon Squad* (2010), went out of her way to present herself as a conventional author interested mainly in depth of character, as is typical of other authors questioned about similar tendencies.[9] She also made a big point of the fact that she writes by hand rather than on a computer. And what, today, is more "old school" than handwriting?

How does biography fit into this picture? While New Historicism has of late been busy investigating the conditions of authorship, the trend in popular biographies has been the opposite: to read the author as an extension of his writing.

---

9. See http://www.youtube.com/watch?v=pZGXILewUSQ. Alternating points of view in Egan's book pass for the height of experimentation in mainstream literary fiction today, without any of the charge of destabilizing ways of knowing and perceiving the world.

Thus Blake Bailey on John Cheever, or Tracy Daugherty on Donald Barthelme, present authors who are of a piece with their oeuvres: dysfunctional suburbanite in the case of Cheever, postmodern avatar in the case of Barthelme.[10] Nor is this tendency to visualize the work in the biography and the biography in the work entirely unjustifiable. The trouble is that too often today biographers overreach in making these connections. Biography wants to regard the body of work as autobiographical, since to ascribe romantic genius to the author would be to leave inexplicable gaps. A recent manifestation of this tendency is D. T. Max's biography of David Foster Wallace, which must simultaneously exalt the author of *Infinite Jest* (1996), supposedly the greatest avant-garde modern American text, and map the tortured life of its author, who failed to produce a follow-up.[11] What Joyce Carol Oates has memorably termed the "pathography" is clearly the genre under which many recent literary biographies fall—the exemplary instance being Blake Bailey's summation of Richard Yates as a tortured, self-destructive alcoholic. Such pathographies equate the hidden monstrosities of the writer with the transparent pathologies of the writing, in order to reduce author to realist transcriber of the facts of his own life—a memoirist, in other words.

With the exception of some avant-garde writers, most American authors today deny all knowledge of post-structuralism on the public record, either because they don't know what it is (which is astonishing in itself) or because they want to pretend naiveté about the development of criticism in the last fifty years in order to preserve an image of innocence that predates the claims of Barthes and Foucault, as though theory were a rumor in distant ramparts that had nothing to do with them personally. This habit is democratic to the degree that it allows aspirants to work their way assiduously into the club through hard work, the benefits of mentorship (and writing programs), and acceptance of the codes of publishing. At the same time it results in the phenomenon of authors such as Zadie Smith, or James Wood at *The New Yorker*, writing criticism that, because it is uninformed by theory, prohibits them from engaging with the substance of literary criticism for the past half-century—and separates them entirely from the discourse of academic criticism. Unlike European authors, American authors are uncomfortable taking on public roles, except in a mode that denies postmodern realities. It is difficult to imagine a figure like Umberto Eco, whose work effortlessly straddles literature and theory, being taken seriously as a public figure in

---

10. See Blake Bailey, *Cheever: A Life* (New York: Vintage, 2010), and Tracy Daugherty, *Hiding Man: A Biography of Donald Barthelme* (New York: St. Martin's, 2009).

11. D. T. Max, *Every Love Story Is a Ghost Story: A Life of David Foster Wallace* (New York: Viking, 2012).

America, where readers are addressed in the commonest language possible to confirm the validity of their empirical experiences and to root authorship in the same muck. To be a politically aware author, which in turn would mean mastery of theory, conflicts with corporate publishing's mandate of faux naiveté.

The movement in authorship has been from anonymity in the Middle Ages (the author as provider of gloss or commentary with no proprietorial ownership of ideas) to biography as confirmation of individual genius in the early modern age (as with Samuel Johnson or other giants of the eighteenth and nineteenth centuries) to the attempted separation of biography from text in the modernist early twentieth-century (as with James Joyce and William Faulkner) to the situation today, where an excess of memoir-like detail, originating both from the author and his supporters, blurs any distinction between the author's biography and the text, in effect merging the two. Corporate publishing prefers a cleaned-up image of the efficient, driven, rule-bound author—very much like the ideal parent in contemporary liberal parenting discourse—so the apparent excess of biographical details is deceptive, because the movement is always a purgative one, toward a fulfilled author in line with the desires and aspirations of neoliberal society. The author today is supposed to have no independent personality. He may not be wild, unruly, drunk, addicted, etc., at least in his finished presentation. In memoir, these deviances function as personality disorders to be overcome on the road to becoming a corporate writer. *Memoir as a genre formally expunges the deviances of authorship.* (It is important, of course, to note the difference between the contemporary genre known as memoir, given to redemptive struggle against self-generated misery, and the now-outmoded genre of literary autobiography, of which Nabokov's *Speak, Memory* and Rushdie's *Joseph Anton* are examples; these are not forms of purging but embellishments of the author's self-conception in mythical, intellectualized, historical dimensions.)

The construction of authorship is also integrally connected with notions of ideal citizenship. At times, the ideal citizen may be at war with the militant aims of the state; such was often the case during the 1960s, and earlier during the 1930s: Henry Miller as foulmouthed blasphemer, Hemingway as stoic Übermensch, Updike as dissenting suburbanite. Yet even rebelliousness is circumscribed when it must fit into an ideal of citizenship. John Cheever lived what appears to have been a double life, repressing his homosexuality in order to match the image of citizenship he was propagating through his *New Yorker* platform. He was publicly questioning suburban proprieties, but not the very foundation of gender relations, so crucial aspects of his life could not be part of his fiction. The form taken by the idealization of authorship at any given time provides important clues about the condition of politics. Today, under circumstances of indirect state patronage, particularly through employment in universities, the ideal is, not surprisingly, a condition separating the personal from the political. The author respectfully carries on with her "humanist" mission, giving the state a wide berth. Going back to Foucault's notion of the discourse that the author inhabits at any given time, the discourse inhabited by American authors today is that of neoliberalism, even if authors often lack any knowledge of political economy or the desire to express it in those specific terms. The end of the Cold War in 1989 was an important marker in this development. The quintessential Cold War authors (Updike and Roth, with feet firmly planted in PEN citizenship), classically liberal in their opposition to communist tyranny (which requires a belief in liberalism's power to extend happiness to growing numbers of people), have given way to neoliberal authors who deny any great political ambitions beyond a certain procedural effectiveness. Today's ideal of citizenship is politically passive, beholden to consumerism, globally translatable.

We might view this as a culminating stage in the death of the author, with authors voluntarily placing themselves in a matrix of political helplessness, and thereby reduced to observers rather than participants. Consider Dave Eggers, Generation-X literary activist par excellence, author of books that identify with victims of war and oppression, often in faraway lands beyond his immediate reckoning. In retrospect, *Zeitoun* (2009), his indictment of post-Katrina discrimination in New Orleans, appears not so much a declaration of war against the authoritarian state as a tender note of resignation, ascribing blame to individuals rather than systemic failures. The frame of reference to explain the torture inflicted on his protagonist Zeitoun is Milgram's experiments in collective psychosis, not Adorno and Horkheimer's indictment of the enlightenment as containing the seeds of its own destruction. In his novel *A Hologram for the King* (2012), Eggers visits his sincerity (years of good citizenship having expunged the irony for which he became famous after his first book) upon young Saudi hepcat Yousef, who would be right at home in the milieu of irony for which the McSweeneys became famous before they became Believers.

The acknowledgments sections of books—now veritable encyclopedias of references—provide yet another way to kill the author writ large, the author as romantic genius, creator of new discourses. Rachel Toor, for example, finds the new practice of extensive acknowledgments perfectly justifiable and gratifying.[12]

---

12. See her essay, "I'd Like to Thank the Academy," *Chronicle of Higher Education*, May 3, 2013: http://chronicle.com/article/Id-Like-to-Thank-the-Academy/138873/.

Yet acknowledgments are often so extreme in their extensiveness that they become another way to seek anonymity. Thus, *Hologram* comes with thanks to an array of benefactors, social workers, and ideal citizens totaling one hundred and twenty-six people. This is entirely typical: acknowledgments for nonfiction books can easily run into the many hundreds, the author recognizing not only every form of institutional support she ever got, but also her entire professional and social Rolodex. Eggers's sweeping acknowledgments create a shield against personal responsibility for the text published under his name. The ideal citizen has no personality of his own, no unmandated eccentric quirk that cannot be resolved by group therapy.[13]

The enclosure of the author within the discourse of neoliberalism might be seen as the final nail in the coffin. The author in his historical context began to be superseded with the rise of New Criticism, an approach that gathered steam with post-structuralism and is achieving completion in the post-theory age. For authors to be free of public responsibility is for them to be part of the materiality of neoliberal discourse without answering for it. Exemption from political life has been a pervasive demand of authors since the late twentieth-century, a reaction intensified by the autonomy that MFA culture demands from political responsiveness. Authors may take up certain safe positions—such as criticism of the Bush administration after the Iraq war proved to be a disaster, or after the Katrina debacle—but as a rule, political opinion is not a key preoccupation, and is limited to conventional positions well after the fact. The writing program's very rationale is to establish authors free of financial exigencies—or at least that is the promise, for those few who reach the finish line—while authors outside academia who write for popular audiences have no place in the economy of prestige. The proportion of literary authors—aside from genre writers—seeking livelihoods outside academia has declined to negligibility, since academia tries to rope in any writer at the first signs of success to enhance its own prestige. There are few literary authors more commercially viable than Jonathan Lethem today, yet even he recently accepted the position of Disney Professor of Writing at Pomona College in California, a position for which Junot Diaz, even more commercially omnipresent than Lethem, was also in the running. Academic positions offer authors these days a kind of security that no amount of commercial success provides; not just health insurance and a pension, but a secure position within a larger institution, complete with title and business card.

Another explanation for this mass exodus is that academia constrains

---

13. Watch Eggers being himself, the self-pronounced virtuous citizen of the republic of letters, at http://www.youtube.com/watch?v=jXg958I4IKQ.

discourse within familiar bounds (teaching compels this), and authors actively yearn for this further restraint. So with the uniformity of self-conception that comes with joining academia, the bigger question that arises is what kind of national tradition is being created by such pervasive affiliation. The answer these days seems to be American exceptionalism in an age of tense globalism, a proclamation of national innocence in the midst of inescapable national crimes, with the author keeping safe distance from the new authoritarianism and committing to the regime of doctrinaire innocence. That's the national tradition that's being authorized without explicit recognition per se, and authors from Chad Harbach to Jonathan Franzen to Jhumpa Lahiri fully participate in this project.

What happens to the author's prestige in this mode of institutionalization? One answer is that, with the rise of social media and mass creativity, we have *all* become authors. This seems the logical endpoint of the democratic process that started with the invention of the printing press, but to take it to its conclusion means the complete victory of authorship as well as its complete annihilation. Again, the progression has been from the *auctor* (the Middle Ages) to author (eighteenth century) to genius (romanticism) to attenuated author (twentieth century and thereafter). Total democracy means the end of the author. No author has the authority anymore to transcend even lowbrow culture. The author's prestige, such as it is, derives precisely from his *inability* to transcend, to demarcate the moral dimensions of the reigning discourse of political economy, even as commercial publishing holds on to the romantic idea of genius as a marketing tool.

Thus the consistent need to construct a stable/knowable/marketable/niche identity for each reputable author, a singular self that is artificially limited in scope, a perfectly devourable subject for the consumer society, a hypocritical project eliciting the passive collaboration of authors. Think again of Salman Rushdie's attempted discontinuous persona (for which he continues to face a backlash from the literary establishment) as opposed to the verifiable, unmystified, continuous persona of an author like Meghan O'Rourke, whose poetry of grief and memoir of grief never attempt any transcendence but limit themselves to what (popular) culture is allowed to understand. O'Rourke's memoir *The Long Goodbye* (2011), about her mother's death from cancer at a relatively early age, raises the discomfiting question of the author's intention to write the memoir about the impending death actually altering her thoughts and behavior; the death in question derives its authenticity from its democratic leanings, its coherence from the author's academic authority, its metaphors of confession from the commoditization of grief. Another paradigmatic recent example is the instant hagiography that arrived with Chad Harbach's overhyped novel *The Art of Fielding* (2011) from his close friend and associate Keith Gessen, a transparent attempt to resolve the contradictions between literary aspirations and the debased state of corporate publishing; in this dynamic Harbach emerges as an author who derives his prestige from being able to straddle both worlds effortlessly.[14]

This brings us to copyright. Is copyright a democratic gesture anymore or an elitist one? Does it protect the author or the publisher? Is it different now than it was in the past? Copyright's origins in the first age of liberal property rights point to its simultaneous exclusive and inclusive nature. Copyright began as a means of monetizing the text—in the process fixing the identities of all involved in publishing—and new forms of commoditization always exert pressure on copyright. The vigorous assertion of copyright in the face of the electronic challenge is concordant with the virtues of the earliest model of literary citizenship but is out of touch with new realities. One of these is the idealization of *uncreativity*, above all by Kenneth Goldsmith, who, in his recent appearances at the White House (May 11, 2011) and on *The Colbert Report* (July 23, 2013), has made a virtue of the sheer unreadability of his uncreative texts, completing the collapse from *jouissance* to *plaisir* to sheer boredom.[15] *Flarf*—a form of poetry produced through random internet searches, or google sculpting, yielding odd juxtapositions and unharmonious mixtures of high and low registers—is indeed a form of uncreative creativity, a return to pre-Gutenberg folklore, repeating what the people have already said unpoetically, finding in it the only poetry possible these days. Goldsmith has correctly argued that conceptual writing employs intentionally self- and ego-effacing tactics, taking uncreativity, unoriginality, illegibility, appropriation, plagiarism, fraud, theft, and falsification as its precepts, but it is unfortunate that he must then kick the reader out of the equation and focus only on what the author "learns" during composition. At least conceptual poetry admits to the lack of incentives to create revolutionary poetry. Copyright, on the other hand, is institutional dogma that affirms the writer's genuine creativity under new forms of duress. It is in direct confrontation with the internet's tendency to want to redefine the author—where the text begins and ends, how author and reader interact—by devising new means

---

14. Keith Gessen, *Vanity Fair's How a Book Is Born: The Making of The Art of Fielding* (Kindle Edition, 2011): http://www.amazon.com/Vanity-Fairs-Book-Born-ebook/dp/B005LEWYYU/ref=sr_1_1?ie=UTF8&qid=1367787813&sr=8-1&keywords=HARBACH+GESSEN.

15. "Conceptual writing obstinately makes no claims on originality. On the contrary, it employs intentionally self and ego effacing tactics using uncreativity, unoriginality, illegibility, appropriation, plagiarism, fraud, theft, and falsification as its precepts." Kenneth Goldsmith, "Conceptual Poetics," http://sibila.com.br/poetry-essays/conceptual-poetics/2701.

of feedback, reinforcement, disputation, and commentary. New forms of fan fiction, collaborative writing, remix, and sampling reflect the uncreativity that is natural to digital space, even as traditional publishing and its allied writing program infrastructure tries harder than ever to sustain the idea of the author as intellectual property.

Copyright claims to be the sufficient incentive that will produce and protect creativity, but it can be argued that today its liberal authoritative function incorporates a moribund tradition of authorship. Jonathan Lethem's *Harper's* magazine essay "The Ecstasy of Influence" (Feb. 2007), endorsing plagiarism and made up mostly of borrowed texts, created considerable anxiety among believers in copyright. John Updike was apoplectic on numerous occasions that the assault on copyright meant the death of writing. David Shields, in creating his anti-fiction manifesto *Reality Hunger* (2010) from borrowed texts (Knopf compelled him to acknowledge his source texts at the end of the book, whereas he'd wanted to skip them), created the same sort of anxiety. Earlier copyright controversies, such as Alice Randall's appropriation of Margaret Mitchell's *Gone with the Wind* in *The Wind Done Gone* (2001), seem almost quaint by comparison.

Yet all this represents a futile diversion from the question which the institutions of authorship don't want readers to ponder, namely, How do authors forge authenticity? Is anything left over beyond the rational consumer or informed voter of social science, and is that the sphere of authenticity? If so, is it dangerous, and does the author see himself as playing a dangerous role? Hollywood sci-fi of the 1950s addressed this disquietude in a previous age of conformism. The constant barrage of public relations—publishing being fully caught up in this—allays the uneasiness toward the post-human (inaugurated by Marx, Freud, Lacan, Derrida, and Foucault) by reauthenticating the capitalist human subject swayed by rational needs and desires. The author-persona created for public consumption (such as Dave Eggers's good citizen getting around over the course of his maturity to slay his earlier ironic tendencies, or Jhumpa Lahiri limiting her multicultural investigations to issues of interpersonal relationships) is *imitable*, designed for the reader to copy. Imitability necessitates repetitiveness and standardization. This also explains the contemporary American author's inordinate modesty and passivity. We have returned to the medieval condition of authors' authority deriving from the ability to gloss, as free will is again circumscribed by overweening institutional protection. The reader in turn acts his circumscribed part by limiting himself to procedural inquiries about the craft of writing, as one witnesses in the questions habitually rehashed at any literary reading. Here readers model themselves on fledgling authors of the kind they've just heard. Uninstitutionalized originality has no place in this scheme. The question of originality is sidestepped, even disallowed, as mechanical issues take over the pseudo-critical space.

It is common to see authors today actively *excluding* creative readers from interpretation, as transcendent questions arising from texts are determinedly redirected toward the writer's prosaic, even humble, intentions. Their own authenticity deriving in large part from the academic discourse of diversity, authors must blend into this discourse if they are to have any authority in the marketplace of texts. Authority is extracted ultimately from the community of novice writers, rather than freestanding critics, again evoking medieval conditions. Active readership, which may take interpretation in stray directions, becomes a hindrance to the author's establishment of authenticity, which rests on constraining the possible range of interpretations.

Authorship always seeks specific writing spaces wherein to perform its theatricality, but theatricality today is often narrowed to sincerity. How is sincerity staged, in what language, using what metaphors? Sincerity—whether in Meghan O'Rourke's recent memoir of grief, or Jonathan Franzen's fulminations against social media and his expressed aspiration to write the great social novel, or the vigorous efforts of David Foster Wallace's friends to cast him as a compassionate figure after his death—is the prevalent coin of authorship today. It is what permits disingenuousness toward the savagery of neoliberalism, as the author's sincerity becomes tantamount to the only authentic aesthetic viewpoint allowed.

Whereas the internet propels the logic of inconsistent personas—precisely the source of cultural discomfort, whenever disjunctions are revealed between the public and the private—the printed book rebels against the notion of anti-fixity. The rearguard movement in favor of print now taking place doubles down on defining the narrow interpretability of authors in all their public and private functions, which are supposed to be one and the same. The seemingly infinite expansion of acknowledgments in recent books is a sign of this phenomenon—solitude doesn't lend itself to knowability, whereas community does—even as it provides evidence of the domestication of the internet's suggestion that every person and every thought is a potential link, merely a click away. The way to contain the internet's threat against accountability, its infinite potential for readerly interpretation, very much as Barthes and Foucault had idealized, is for the author to be spirited away to a realm of old-fashioned authenticity.

Electronic space is a demon that conventional authorship is always trying to slay. As in medieval times, there has arisen an indispensable function for reader commentary which makes texts flexible, dynamic, and fluid. Richard A. Lanham explains that "the strategic self-denials of print, its linear, black-and-white transparency, bias expression toward the disembodied concepts of Platonic philosophy," whereas the "computer world was born under the opposite star of game and play, and its playful humor and game-centered characteristic structures have endured."[16] Conventional authorship doesn't want to rise to this challenge, whereby Foucault's notion of the death of the author and the birth of the reader, and Barthes's idealization of the pleasures of intertextuality, are coming close to realization. Electronic texts are dynamic in the manner of oral, Homeric poetry, but conventional authorship tries to put the genie back in the bottle. To the extent that the reader makes the text, the author's intentions don't matter, which in turn undermines authority. And authority today is directly confined to sincerity, heading off the fissures between the public and the private self. Insincerity, as with James Frey's transgressions, is the ultimately punishable crime of authorship today. Authors who feel differently toward sincerity are intolerably frightening specters whose existence is denied by mainstream channels and who are refused the full fruits of authorship. Whereas Frey always sought to come closer to the ideal of sincerity, his mea culpas escalating in intensity, an author like Laura Albert, who turned sincerity on its head through the invention of J. T. Leroy and never repented for her sin, is denied any claim on literary status. A vigorous effort is always underway to assimilate fledgling independent authors within academic discourses of specialized diversity and neoliberal notions of personal responsibility. Attenuated liberal bourgeois norms penetrate the author-persona in all his appearances, allying the author with his "sympathetic" and "relatable" book club-oriented creations. The sexless, passive, benign, hyper-innocent male has become a staple of American fiction, founded on a false picture of masculinity that seeks to be endearing and non-threatening to the presumed female readership. The author projects this same persona, seamlessly transporting sincerity from the page to the stage. Television, in its blundering way, has tried to address this crisis of masculinity, in notable series of the last decade such as *The Sopranos*, *Mad Men*, and *Breaking Bad*, featuring vigorous antiheroes. In this regard, television seems ahead of literary authorship, which has reduced the crisis of masculinity to the bumbling figure of the neutered male—an archetype closely aligned with the harassed academic of the writing program.

Print versus spectacle is the all-important battle because in it issues of national- and individual identity get resolved. The relationships among print, literacy, readership, copyright, privacy, authorship, and the self are in tremendous flux.

---

16. Richard A. Lanham, *The Electronic Word: Democracy, Technology, and the Arts* (Chicago: University of Chicago Press, 1993). Consult also George P. Landow, *Hypertext 3.0: Critical Theory and New Media in an Era of Globalization* (Baltimore: Johns Hopkins University Press, 2006).

All of these divisions are dissolving as print is dissolving. The attempt to present the serious author as highbrow, opposing mass culture, has been jettisoned in favor of a false democracy of creativity and authenticity. The truth is that "self-made" authors like Twain—or our leading authors until the ascendancy of writing programs—are no longer legitimate because today's democracy rests on false premises, being a class-determined expression of institutional formations. The hyperbolic listing of authors' diverse manual occupations (bartender, carpenter, roofer, etc.), which used to be a staple of book jackets, has given way to a listing of grants, fellowships, and institutional affiliations. In the first age of American realism, William Dean Howells wanted authorship to be a legitimate profession like law or medicine. This matched the institutional biases of the Progressive Era. For the first time ever, there now exists a transparent, dominant, well-trodden, salaried path toward authorship, via the writing program and employment as a teacher. Authors' faux humility, always on display, deflects suspicion that writing produced through this track is elitist. The electronic text becomes an enemy, a threat to copyright and its delusions of permanence and originality. The dread has been channeled into safe forms of collaboration—or publicity—where the author retains supremacy, even as the reader is allowed to make her harmless contribution: "feedback."

Fewer and fewer readers are not necessarily a regrettable development from the point of view of authorship's prestige, and the sought-after ideal may in fact be a perfect correspondence between readers and authors, so that only authors are readers of literary writing. This process is aided by redefining authorship as craft-inspired rather than stemming from the romantic genius heralded in the nineteenth century, so that the potential of authorship can be expanded to include nearly all readers. What ought to have happened with the ascendancy of the digital is that plagiarism should again have been overlooked (as was the case until the predominance of copyright in the eighteenth century) and copyright should have declined, but organized publishing is orchestrating the opposite reaction. The possibilities for true author-reader collaboration are being spurned, while the desire to elicit a constricted audience is influencing writing in turn. Essentially, this is the realization of New Criticism's conservative manifesto of killing off the author, but it is ironic that it's happening in a post-postmodern setting, as refined authorship settles for a stable though limited audience, and shows little interest in catering to a wide public. Like computing, writing is tending toward becoming free (since literary authors get the bulk of their remuneration from sources other than writing), especially since the costs of professional training are now front-loaded and must be paid back, like student loans, over an extended period of dedicated citizenship.

If one compares the conditions of creativity, ownership, and intention now versus the turn of the last century, everything is moving in the direction of the end of authorship. For authorship to move forward, it would have to interrogate how texts produce the author, taking up Barthes and Foucault's unanswered challenge. Superseded modes of authorship are put on steroids in the corporate dispensation, as deceit comes in the form of false impersonalization, whose technological habitat has ceased to exist. Whenever the author takes the stage these days to present himself as avatar of ideal pseudo-liberal citizenship, he reveals himself as the product of a discourse beholden to false authority.

3.

Audiences are always changing, and the status of authorship at any given time can only be understood by looking at responses to current audiences. The nature of the audience is in turn dependent on writing technologies, and as these allow more anonymity and interactivity (private coteries produced by new forms of self-publishing, the DIY ethic behind the resurgence of much innovative publishing as well as an unprecedented quantity of dross), authors are forced to redefine their incentives. Acceptance within the academic community becomes more important than praise (and profit) in the marketplace, breaking the connection between author and paying reader, a tendency exacerbated by the intimate-yet-distant nature of public readings today. If medieval authorship was ethical in responding to theological dictates, authorship today (in contrast to the modernist era) is becoming ethical again in responding to the specific psychological needs of coterie communities. The paradox is that universal ethics are dependent on communicating with the anonymous mass, whereas a provincial ethics (limited to community self-esteem) results from the author identifying with the reader (who is tantamount these days to another potential writer).

The perceived relationship today between impersonality and creativity has led to an impasse in authorship. Should the author make himself visible within his text? Or does empathy require invisibility? This goes back to T. S. Eliot's strictures on the poetry of impersonality, when he held that "the progress of an artist is a continual self-sacrifice, a continual extinction of personality."[17] If the author can't be seen, he is presumed to be free; his invisibility becomes the measure of his

---

17. T.S. Eliot, "Tradition and the Individual Talent," in *The Sacred Wood: Essays on Poetry and Criticism* (London: Methuen, 1932). In the same essay, Eliot writes, "Poetry is not a turning loose of emotion, but an escape from emotion; it is not the expression of personality, but an escape from personality."

autonomy. This is the dominant tendency in publishing today, the ideal toward which authors strive. Revelations of self are actually quite uninformative, as they forestall any fissures between the author's private and public selves. Thus, apparent intimacy becomes an obstruction to understanding authorial motivation. What Foucault meant by the death of the author turns out to be quite the opposite of the present coy maneuvering whereby Flaubert and George Eliot have become the ultimate models of the impersonal author despite technological innovations that demand the erasure of impersonality. These two, in particular, have become the idols of a resurgent social realism that seeks documentary effects, minus the visible presence of the author, in an act of massive critical misrepresentation; Flaubert and George Eliot, via Henry James, are said to have proposed the removal of the author in a way that critical analysis can't support.

Authors today are attempting to put themselves beyond critique by formalizing the terms of impersonal discourse: if discourse is seen as stemming from the indisputable reality of one's community, and if that community is put beyond the pale of criticism, then writing becomes immune to criticism because it is supposed to be objective discourse rooted in immutable sympathy. As Kenneth Dauber expresses it, "American writing is democratic rather than truthful. Its poetics, in effect, is a rhetoric. It is 'making'—poesis—conceived of as neither imitating nor creating, but negotiating."[18] This is political strategy disguised as aesthetic ideal. Creativity is circumscribed, allowed to speak only of what is personally known, and Beckett's question of "who speaks" is eliminated from consideration by the propagation of the false notion of disinterestedness. The first function of poetry that Shelley described in "A Defense of Poetry," namely that it "creates new materials of knowledge," is avoided when authorship becomes only a matter of transcribing alleged objective reality. Such a resurgence of naive realism would have been difficult to forecast for the technologically disorienting early twenty-first century, but it is indeed where we have landed.

In short, authorship today is in conflict with two centuries of literary history. The Wordsworthian "egotistical sublime" is being reduced to fiction and memoir that support outdated nineteenth-century objectivist notions of reality. Eliot's modernist ideal of impersonality has become an unassailable political tool in the service of disengagement and passive citizenship. Barthes and Foucault's idealizations of the death of the author have led not to the ascendancy of the reader amidst a proliferating web of intertextualities but to the reader's

---

18. Kenneth Dauber, *The Idea of Authorship in America: Democratic Poetics from Franklin to Melville* (Madison, Wisc.: University of Wisconsin Press, 1990).

strategic placement within a web of marketing strategies. The movement toward uncreativity in some experimental poetry actually represents the force of anonymity-seeking, as was true of premodern authorship. A wealth of spurious self-generated anecdotes constitutes the false intimacy created by contemporary authors like Junot Diaz and the like, reducing creativity to a determinate function of biographical circumstance. Originality is explained away in the context of institutional incentives. The function of literary autobiography today is to preempt investigation into the author's discrepant real life (to avoid the messiness), and to make any biography (beyond institutional involvement) beside the point as far as literary creation is concerned. Authors are required to be exemplary liberal citizens—witness Dave Eggers, and legions of others—so there are no dark secrets to know anyway. The merger between memoir and all other literary forms eliminates the need for philosophical investigation into the predicaments of authorship, since the author has preemptively satisfied any burgeoning curiosity by making intention foreseeable from the beginning.

Another way to put it is to say, with Jeffrey Mehlman, that authors are no longer attuned to the possibility of being alive to themselves, because they can't construct autobiographies separate from their productive labors.[19] A more radical way to frame it is that authors today deny their social role—they refuse any outside skepticism toward it—and thereby seek to endow their texts with an authority of presence, albeit with a democratically modified form of charisma and enlightenment. *Life writing*, the pervasive genre today, rests on the author not seeking new liberties but working within realist constraints. The hard-fought autonomy of authorship, won over centuries of struggle, has come down to freedom from postulating cultural alternatives. In America, most pieces of writing have become interchangeable (mass-produced within an artificially limited scale) to the extent that the author's signature has become redundant. This represents a form of demystification that is actually mystification. The life of the author today is the substance of his work, but his life must not be political. He must work vertically rather than horizontally, digging deeper and deeper inside himself with each book and becoming the reader's best friend. The author's authority is consumed in the new patronage as the return to the text-in-itself is compelled by a predictable lineage of self-representational moves.

The death of the author could have been politically liberating. Instead, American authors are collaborating in eliminating the newly opened critical

19. Jeffrey Mehlman, *A Structural Study of Autobiography: Proust, Leiris, Sartre, Lévi-Strauss* (Ithaca, N.Y.: Cornell University Press, 1974).

space by denying the possibility of criticism. Criticism *is* politics; without it, it is hard to imagine political responsibility. When the author seeks escape from political responsibility by becoming dependent on explicable biographical circumstances, he reappears on the public stage as a known quantity and eschews a public role. The answer today is a resounding no to the question of whether any kind of politics can emerge from creativity. Creativity, if it arises from genius, theoretically frees the author of responsibility to drudgery. But creativity, if it arises from institutional patronage, immerses the author into indentured labor. Quite different kinds of authority emerge from these different conceptions. If the author is a contractual laborer (as writing professors are today), he is not obligated to rethink political relations but merely to work within them. If the author is a genius, however, he is free from the debilitating logic of self-referentiality and can potentially think beyond economic constraints. The genius is more at liberty to abolish various divisions of labor, whereas the laboring author is compelled to work within a narrow niche. The laborer, rather than the genius, is a unified self, opposing Barthes and Foucault's views on discourse that splinters off in unforeseeable directions

Aside from rebellious authors like Rushdie, who don't seem to have gotten the memo, authors have disappeared from culture—they have in fact died, except that they themselves seem not to have noticed that they have died. Nor has the institutional apparatus that supports them noticed that they have died. They have died not the natural, joyous, liberating death Barthes and Foucault foresaw, but a death that has activated the old writing game all over again. They have stopped signing their names to their own texts, much as was the case before the revolution in printing. Authorial presence is being vigorously reasserted in all the ways inimical to the political revolution embodied in the thought of Barthes and Foucault.

Symposium: How Can Book Reviewing Be Made Relevant for the New Generation?

With rapid changes in the status of the print medium and the pervasiveness of new technologies, what is the state of book reviewing today? Is it a moribund art, or is it still a worthwhile cultural aspiration? I asked several American critics and reviewers—a good mix of young and old, established and emerging, writer-critics and dedicated critics—this question: "How can book reviewing be made relevant for the new generation of readers?" The respondents came at this question from many different angles, based on their expertise and background in criticism, addressing the question of technology head-on. What is the future of criticism in the world of the internet? Will the younger generation need to be addressed differently or will the old verities do?

Jay Parini has written biographies of John Steinbeck, William Faulkner, Robert Frost, and Gore Vidal, and his books of criticism include *The Art of Teaching,* *Why Poetry Matters,* **and** *Promised Land: Thirteen Books that Changed America.*

There is a crisis in reviewing, in part produced by graduate education in literature, with its emphasis on theory and the lack of regard in the academy for good and clear writing. In the past—perhaps before 1970—one could find any number of serious scholars who wrote decent criticism in the form of book reviews. That source of reviewers has more or less vanished, so the few publications that still review books must rely on a decreasing pool of well-informed critics. There is also the fact that novelists and poets themselves rarely spend much time reviewing books, and the best critics have often been writers themselves, from Ben Johnson and Dr. Johnson through Coleridge, Matthew Arnold, T.S. Eliot, Virginia Woolf, D.H. Lawrence, and so forth. I recently read a biography of

Sinclair Lewis, and the writer mentioned that Lewis—like any novelist of his time—could expect over two hundred reviews of a novel. This meant that no single review mattered much but that the public could expect a wide variety of opinions. Many of these reviews were quite long, too. Today the newspapers print badly argued, often showy, and usually brief takes on a book. The quality of a reviewer's prose, and the quality of sympathy brought to the book itself, seems not to matter, to editors or readers. How can literary culture survive in such a world?

Ron Charles is the editor of *The Washington Post*'s Book World.

I love the optimistic premise of this question! Book reviewers who hope to be relevant to a new generation of readers will have to: 1. Review books that young people want to read. This will require us to drop our "Eat your peas" attitude and stop concentrating on books about the morose musings of middle-age. 2. Publish reviews that are shorter, punchier, and less self-indulgent. Does that mean we have to dumb down review coverage? The opposite: We have to be smarter, sharper, wittier, and more efficient. 3. Put those reviews in places where young people are looking. Get over it: They don't subscribe to newspapers, and they're not going to. Aggregate book reviews with other entertainment news that young people are interested in and make those reviews accessible on mobile devices. Find ways to blend book reviews with social media that young people are using. None of this will work, of course, but it may keep us employed till we can all get jobs as SEO content managers.

Steven G. Kellman's many books of criticism include *The Self-Begetting Novel, Loving Reading: Erotics of the Text, Redemption: The Life of Henry Roth,* and *The Translingual Imagination.*

To be "relevant" (compelling and enlightening), book reviewing has to be what, at its best, it has always been: attentive, informed, articulate, and true. As long as new generations are indeed readers, Aristotle, Samuel Johnson, and Edmund Wilson continue to teach us how to read. That is not to deny that new books demand new ways of reading. It was ever thus, and the digitalization of language is not necessarily more disconcerting than was its dissemination on printed pages in a culture based on vellum. Accuracy and honesty remain urgent. Shunning taural-fecal rhetoric, reviews should be at least as gracefully written as what they describe. A new generation conducts its reading in an altered universe, in which books have been shoved to the peripheries occupied by ballet and lacrosse. Editors now more readily commission coverage of restaurants and movies. At the same time, opinions about books as commodities proliferate. Anyone contemplating buying a book—or lawnmower—can retrieve dozens of ratings. The situation is liberating. For too long, critics have practiced litigation without a gavel, reducing reviewing to the Siskel-Ebert recipe of plot summary and thumbs-up/thumbs-down. The new dispensation frees critics for more important work.

Kelly Cherry's many books of nonfiction include *The Globe and the Brain: On Place in Fiction, Girl in a Library: On Women Writers and the Writing Life,* and *History, Passion, Freedom, Death, and Hope: Prose about Poetry.*

To judge from what is happening now, reviewing on the internet, whether by blog or for e-zines, will continue to increase. The real question is whether internet reviewing will be insightful and well-written, though one might also ask whether internet reviews can command an audience large enough to prove significant for authors and publishers. The internet is commodious but for that very reason tends to collapse into fiefdoms. How much do internet reviews really affect readers' choices? Maybe a lot. Reader reviews have led me to and away from a number of books. It is easier to believe that a reader review is unbiased, whereas too many print reviews are hostage to preconceived opinions or to business decisions. That's the nature of the New York literary community. Of course, not knowing anything about the author of the internet review, I may be ignorant of the pressures on that review; for the nonce, it's a happy ignorance. I love print. I love letterpress. Creamy linenish pages with a font that understands the text are irresistible and to die for. But the conversation carried on by literary criticism and literary reviews is now helpfully augmented by the internet and will be pursued online by the next generation of readers.

Rigoberto Gonzalez is a poet, fiction writer, and critic whose nonfiction books include *Autobiography of My Hungers, Red Ink Retablos: Essays,* and *Butterfly Boy: Memories of a Chicano Mariposa.*

Since print reviews are falling by the wayside because of the diminishing number of newspapers and literary journals, readers and writers will have to rely more on the internet and social networking media—blogs, Facebook, webzines, Twitter—to distribute and locate information (opinions, buzz, reader responses) about books. Like many reviewers, I bemoaned the compromised quality of editing and fact-checking on the internet, but I believe that will change as it becomes clear that these entries are part of a critical dialogue and not just opportunities for book publicity or reviewer showboating. Poets have been taking advantage of these outlets for some time now since poetry books are typically excluded from print coverage. A few sites, like *The Constant Critic*, have been upholding high standards in poetry reviewing since they first hit cyberspace. Another site I usually turn to is *Fogged Clarity*. The next generation of readers will continue to absorb and process information through the use of technology, and as long as literary e-conversations reflect our ethnically and aesthetically diverse culture—in ways that book reviewing has not been in the past—we shouldn't fear that the book review will become obsolete or irrelevant.

Jane Ciabattari is an author of short story collections and a former president of the National Book Critics Circle.

From my perspective as a reviewer it boils down to a couple of basics. First is voice. No matter what the platform—print, online, podcast, video—an engaging, witty, passionate, knowledgeable, and distinctive voice is crucial. This may be why there is such a rage for the hybrid personal essay/criticism form. It helps if reviews give some context (the book as it fits into the writer's work, or into the literature of a particular country or genre). If possible, I think it's also helpful to give a sense of what it feels like to read the book (and perhaps comparisons to other books). And to offer as fluid a range of cultural references as feels right. (For instance, in the course of a day I've been playing Angry Birds on an iPad, listening to Kanye West's new album, and tracking down a 1964 recording of Frank O'Hara reading his "Lana Turner Has Collapsed" poem to post in a comment thread on Facebook. How does that play into my experience of reading Sharifa Rhodes-Pitts's engrossing memoir *Harlem Is Nowhere*? All are immersive experiences. Weaving those experiences together in some way might be more interesting than simply sticking to the text of the book.) Another example: I just reviewed the new Charles Baxter collection, *Gryphon*. On the snowy weekend when I was working on that review, I was also rereading Jonathan Franzen's *Freedom*, toggling between the two. I liked the Baxter better, for a lot of reasons. A review that explained why might be more interesting than a straightforward review of the Baxter. In both cases, a longer form review might be necessary. And I think that may be where we are headed next.

Sven Birkerts's books of criticism include *An Artificial Wilderness: Essays on Twentieth-Century Literature, The Electric Life: Essays on Modern Poetry, American Energies: Essays on Fiction,* and *The Gutenberg Elegies: The Fate of Reading in an Electronic Age.*

If book reviewing is to survive beyond being niche-centered product rating it needs to keep alive the context of the literary, which means discussing books (I assume we're talking about serious, aspiring sorts of books) in terms of their relation to the cultural situation, which means owning that there is such a situation and that it is shaped in a thousand scrutable and inscrutable ways by history—which is a long-winded way of saying that those who write about books cannot abandon the idea of continuity, cannot abandon the assumption of the tradition's mattering, cannot stop being intelligent across as wide a front as possible. How easy it is for a reviewer to just say some observant things about a work and leave it at that, and how hard to take the next step, which is to discuss it with reference to the culture. This has been one of the subtle, seldom remarked ways in which book reviewing has promoted the larger picture against which we take our collective measure. For any of this to be possible we will need more than a few venturesome and widely-referenced venues (print or online) and a strong stable of reliably reflective writers. They are out there.

Laurie Hertzel is senior editor for books at the *Minneapolis Star Tribune.*

Broadly speaking, our reviews serve the same purpose they always have—that is, we bring a thoughtful, critical eye to new books, and we try to make readers aware of books they might not otherwise see. We review the "big books"—King, Franzen, Moore—but we also keep an eye on smaller publishers, regional titles, debut novels, and poetry. A careful selection of books keeps us relevant—we also review popular fiction, graphic novels, and books for children and teens. Our pages abhor snootiness. While our critics are deeply well-read, their reviews are not ponderous or scholarly. They do not go on and on. Their reviews are short and interesting, they get to the point, they answer the questions "what does this book feel like" and "what is this author trying to accomplish?" But reviews cannot be relevant if nobody sees them, so I spend time on the internet—on Twitter, and Facebook, and blogs, posting links and making noise. More and more, we need to reach out beyond the printed newspaper to tap readers on the shoulder and say, "Look, here's something you might like. Here's a book you might want to read. And this is why."

Stacy Muszynski is a book reviewer who publishes in many venues.

This "new generation of readers" includes us all, from young readers new to the genre to those familiar with the book review's former form, its inky smells and inky ink (easily and oopsily pressed into fingertips, clean white shirts and foreheads as if every day were Ash Wednesday). Then as now as forever, history presses form and content to march on, mingle, find their own best selves. From paper editions searchable by microfiche to the interactive, immediately available, the relevant reviews will always be written by the one who, according to Alfred Kazin in 1960, "write[s] out of a profound inner struggle between what has been and what must be"; who, according to Randall Jarrell in 1952, can be the instrument through which the art is seen, as "[c]riticism demands of the critic a terrible nakedness"; who, according to Lionel Trilling in 1950, understands that "literature is the human activity that takes the fullest and most precise account of variousness, possibility, complexity, and difficulty"; who, according to Sugar in 2010, can "write like a motherfucker." Then there's my friend Franklin, of the new generation of readers, who told me yesterday via IM, "When I walk away from a book I want to see the world differently. I look for hints of this in a review. I know I can read old novels and get blown away, so why would I waste time on some new novels?" Indeed. Short answer: To be relevant, yesterday, today, forever, be catalytic.

Troy Jollimore is a philosopher and poet whose collections include *Tom Thomson in Purgatory, At Lake Scugog,* and *Syllabus of Errors.*

What the new generation of readers will have in common with previous generations is more important than what will set them apart. So book reviewing, to be relevant to these readers, should resist the urge to change in order to be relevant. In particular, it should resist the temptation to dumb down and simplify, to model itself after the customer "reviews" one finds on Amazon.com and elsewhere, or on the depleted and tiresome discourse that dominates talk radio, cable TV, and the blogosphere. It should remember that the job of the critic is not to give a thumbs-up or thumbs-down verdict on yet another disposable consumer product, but rather to help us as individuals be adequate to the best work of our time. And it should resist the view of the nonreading majority that books are better when they are less like books and more like DVDs or video games. The new generation of readers, like every generation of readers, will know that books are not like other media, that they have special and unique powers.

They will want honest and serious critics who are less interested in current trends than in enduring values and who know that books, unlike most of the things that one can trade money for today, are made to matter and to last.

Ange Mlinko has won the Randall Jarrell Award in Criticism, has been poetry editor for *The Nation*, reviews poetry widely, and has written five books of poetry including *Shoulder Season* and *Marvelous Things Overheard*.

I'm not sure what you mean by "relevant." Book reviews are intellectual candy; they are written, and read, because they engage us in a living communal discussion about ideas. Right now there is an explosion of reviewing, amateur and otherwise, on the internet. Most of it is unpaid. I'm all for the democratization of reading, writing, studying, and thinking. But the pragmatist in me wonders how long it will last.[1] What does all this surplus free writing say about the real productivity of the average educated person? Some questions: 1. Where is all this leisure to read and write coming from? Where is it leading to? Will it expand or contract as wealth drains away from the United States? Are we going to be too busy planting potatoes for our survival, or is the status quo of under-employment—and all the surplus free writing it generates—going to continue indefinitely? 2. What happens when we no longer have cheap, unlimited online access, and start paying for our time on the internet on a metered basis? That constraint will have consequences for both ends of the bell curve—the really, really dumb reviews and the really, really smart reviews. Even songbirds, I'm told, needed leisure to evolve their complicated repertoires. What is going to sustain our leisure?

Roxana Robinson, the author of four novels and three short story collections, is a scholar of nineteenth and early twentieth-century American art, and a frequent book reviewer.

Well, who is the new generation of readers? Do they read only vampire books? Have their brains been devoured by the internet? Have the seductions of short-form transmissions—tweets and texts—sucked the vital juices from their minds? Are they unable to follow a thought, or an argument, or a premise? Will they read only short and shallow reviews, unedited and uninformed, written only

---

1 Mlinko raises an important point, about surplus intellectual labor in the neoliberal economy, which I address in the concluding essay in this book.

by their peers? I don't think so. Every generation has its share of thoughtful, intelligent, demanding minds, just as every generation has its share of heedless and ignorant ones. It's the former, strong and dedicated, who will transmit the literary culture, and it's for them that the reviewer writes. Every generation both alters and absorbs the culture it confronts: each new generation will change some things, but not all. They were formed by what we are. We are both part of the changing continuum; we depend on each other for insight and understanding. So our responsibility as reviewers is to show new readers that reading great books hasn't changed, no matter how it's done. Our reviews should celebrate the beauty and power of literature; we should remind every generation that reading good writing is one of the great pleasures of being alive.

Colette Bancroft is the book editor of the _Tampa Bay Times_.

I think there's no question that book reviewing is indeed relevant to the new generation of readers. A look at any online book review site (Goodreads, etc.) will prove that old saw that everybody's a critic. Readers love the opportunity to write about books they've read and to read other people's critiques (and argue with them). The challenge is to sort through that overload and find reliable voices. If the question is whether the old gatekeeper model of reviewing—of books or anything else—is relevant, especially for younger readers, that's another matter. I think the days when having the title "book critic" and working for a print publication granted one authority are gone, and critics have to find ways to earn readers' respect and engage them in the conversation about books. It's not one-sided anymore.

Brian Henry is the author of many books of poetry, a translator of Slovenian poetry, the editor of _Verse_ magazine, and poetry critic for many publications.

I'm actually not sure it can! As someone who used to do a lot of reviewing for newspapers and literary magazines, I don't think traditional book reviews matter beyond academic and professional circles as much as they used to. They still matter to the reviewers and the authors being reviewed, of course, and to their publishers, hiring/tenure committees, friends of the author, etc., but not as much to readers—partly because people are reading less (not just poetry, but also literary fiction), and also because there are so many places to get opinions about books—blogs, sites like Goodreads, social media sites like Facebook—without the filter of an editor or the constraints of a word limit. That said, book reviews can be more relevant to any generation of readers by being honest, fair, humble, and immune to reputations and trends. Reviews are always secondary to the work being reviewed, but some reviewers seem desperate to upstage the author. And why write the tenth review of a book when you could write the first or second review of another book? Why let prize committees (a group of three to five people) determine what gets reviewed?

Greg Barrios is a poet, playwright, and journalist, serves on the board of directors of the National Book Critics Circle, and is the former book editor of the *San Antonio Express-News*.

While alarmists have huffed and puffed over the decline in newspaper book review sections as the end of discourse about books, the bottom line remains that book reviewers and newspapers have paid little attention to—much less reviewed—popular fiction written for young people. Writers like J.K. Rowling and Stephenie Meyer were never reviewed until young readers made them into megasellers. Now that e-books are outpacing sales of hard copies, the *New York Times* has announced plans for an interactive e-book best-seller list. Yet the *Times* hardly ever reviews any of the genre fiction series (graphic novels, manga, sci-fi, and horror) that young readers line up to buy at bookstore events. While book review sections may marginalize young readers, they have been secretly nourished by some of our finest children's and young adult book authors: Toni Morrison, Oscar Hijuelos, Madonna, and Barack Obama. (The President's book, *Of Thee I Sing,* is the number one children's picture book on the *Times* list, but it still hasn't been reviewed). So what makes anyone think new readers will flock to the gray old lady to learn more about their fave books or e-books? The internet is the new bookstore, library, and book review section. They can chat or text about a favorite on Facebook, blogs, Amazon, and discourse with the diverse customer's reviews. They can now access most any new or classic book instantly as an e-book and at a lower price. They are an empowered new generation of readers.

Michael Washburn is a book critic for many publications.

In a culture that all but prides itself on its refusal to read or engage critically, Americans who read books, let alone book reviews, inhabit a permanent minority. And it's that minority that we should focus on. Nobody, least of all a book critic, can achieve a mass conversion to a culture of arts and letters. For those with ears to hear, honest, smart criticism will endure; even if hunted to the brink of extinction the critical impulse will remain strong enough to linger indefinitely on that brink. But to remain as relevant as possible to our beloved minority, we must disenthrall ourselves from technology. A contrarian's argument, probably. If novelists write what they know, then the critics' corollary should be to write about one's interests—and ideas, however delivered or draped in content, are the preoccupation of the best critical minds. They're also why one reads criticism. We've been battered so long by distressed chatter about the decline of book culture that we often forget that innovations in content delivery do not diminish our craving for narrative or our appreciation for the ingenuity of argument. Don't evolve, I say. Inasmuch as user-generated reviews on Amazon don't undermine the integrity of the critical endeavor, neither do the iPad or the e-book. Write for new platforms, yes, but remember that the pleasure, the value, and the relevance of reviewing remain vested in the exercise of our premodern minds. The sizzle shall always remain quite distinct from the steak, and one will always leave you hungry.

Rebecca Oppenheimer, a member of Generation Y, is a freelance book reviewer.

Book reviews should be more relevant than ever to multitasking, overscheduled teenagers and young adults. Professional reviews can bring worthy books to the attention of people who have little time to spend in a bookstore or library and who find the online browsing experience too impersonal or overwhelming. Of course, the operative word in that first sentence is "should." How can we get this natural audience interested in book reviews? First, go where the young people are, both online and in person. Acknowledge them as readers, and show interest in them as an audience. Second, don't assume that certain books are beyond their intellectual abilities or the scope of their interests. A book that attempts to shed light on any aspect of the human condition will be relevant to at least some young people. Third, keep it short. A several-page essay, however compelling, will not attract a distracted young person who has never read book reviews before. But a brief review that points such a reader to a memorable book may convince him or her to give those longer pieces a try in the future.

What Should Be the Function of Criticism Today?

The premise of this essay is that criticism needs to play a central role in the revival of literature. At present, criticism, in the form of academic "theory," is in the curious position of simultaneous self-exaltation and self-marginalization, being a highly esoteric affair that makes no effort to reach the mass of readers. For much of the history of literary criticism, writer-critics, especially poet-critics, have been the most important figures—Dryden, Sidney, Shelley, Coleridge, Eliot, Tate, Jarrell, to name just a few. Two things have happened since the beginning of the second half of the twentieth century to make this breed all but extinct.

First, "creative writing" has swallowed up poets and fiction writers into a new formulation of writing, which thrives on narrow specialization (thus, poets can't be fiction writers or playwrights, let alone critics) and frowns on traditional literary criticism. In America, this process is the farthest advanced, but other Anglo-Saxon countries are following suit. As a result, instead of criticism what we are seeing from practicing creative writers is a narrow form of appreciation of mentors or workshop masters in journals and online forums, a form of empty praise that doesn't deserve the name criticism.

Second, theory has gone through various phases of resistance and counter-assault, but it is far from being disestablished in any way, despite the claim of some that we are already in a "post-theory" era. The problem with theory is also that it is not criticism in any form as we have known it throughout history; the theorist is interested not in evaluating literature qua literature, but in imposing a set of familiar operations on any text, arriving at familiar results. Derridean deconstruction, which ought to have been a temporary fad when it arrived on the American scene in the mid-1960s, has instead monopolized departments of literature—and many of the other humanities. This form of "criticism," like its creative writing counterpart, is not interested in reaching a broad audience, speaking only to like-minded theorists. It is best seen as a deflection of frustrated political instincts, in the only realm permitted free play to academics—the domain of language and text, rather than practice and application.

What is missing, then, is a vital criticism that is neither theory, a mundane exercise in proving, over and over, that all texts are unstable because of inherently contradictory meanings, nor the renewed form of aesthetic criticism emanating from workshop writers, which recalls the state of criticism before the establishment of "scientific" principles of objectivity by New Criticism in the 1930s. My proposed criticism is a form of humanist criticism, though the term unfortunately recalls the conservative and anti-democratic criticism of the 1920s, under the rubric of the New Humanists associated with Irving Babbitt.

With the proliferation of "creative writing," there is currently a mass pool of potential critics, trained in close reading of a diluted New Criticism variety, graduates of MFA programs (estimated at seventy-five thousand about fifteen years ago, and by now presumably much larger) who survive in various forms of under- or unemployment, or are unable to realize the literary goals to which they aspired when they enlisted in such programs. There are many informed readers in America who could turn to criticism as a vital act, using the internet as an unprecedented platform; they already do, to some extent, but criticism unfortunately tends to follow established patterns and it is a matter of habituating oneself and the reader to new expectations.

The internet is the most important new public sphere. Jürgen Habermas has explained that eighteenth-century English coffeehouses and other public spaces allowed the formation of middle-class taste in opposition to aristocratic and feudal values, constituting a revolution in ideals that still fuels whatever is left of political and social liberalism. Although the internet, as it currently stands, is only in a rudimentary form as far as the potential for humanist criticism is concerned, nonetheless our hopes must rest on it.[1] Whereas eighteenth-century taste was genteel and bourgeois, and that proposed by the nineteenth-century version of the "man of letters" was perhaps even tamer, until the concept petered out altogether in the academic critic of the second and third decades of the twentieth century, the new public sphere will be neither genteel nor mildly reformist. Radical, chaotic, uncontrollable energies are on the loose, and the critic must equip herself to contest on this hot terrain with all the rhetorical means at her disposal.

---

1 I have developed serious doubts about the potential of the internet, because I no longer think technology can compensate for the structural reasons causing the deficit in the public sphere. Moreover, every medium seems to compel its form of politics, and the internet has been no exception.

The literary product—by which I mean assembly-line writing, in tune with sales results and committee thinking, rather than the idiosyncratic creation of the individual genius—today is manipulated, propagandized, and hyped, and, as a result, unattractive to mass audiences, indifferent to fundamental issues of class and politics, and pretty much in its death throes. This holds true above all in America, where conglomerate publishing has reached its most advanced state, and different genres of writing are the brainchildren of marketing geniuses and corporate analysts, creating a doubtful product as far as literary values are concerned. Why is this phenomenon not being scrutinized to the degree it needs to be? Why is the lack of quality not more transparent?

The theorists don't care. They hardly pay attention to contemporary literature, and, besides, they are not in the business of evaluation and judgment; their interest is only in exploding the contradictions of the classic text in question, showing how it reveals Western biases toward logic and rationality and patriarchy and empire and leave it at that. The successful creative writers can't afford to offend anyone in authority who may withhold rewards and opportunity in the future—a necessary consequence of most of America's literary writers having become, in essence, state employees, upholding a collective aesthetic of bourgeois realism and individualized confessionalism, leaving the state's politics and policies well enough alone for the sake of job security. Somehow, separate from these two black holes of critical nothingness, a new criticism needs to arise to take on the honest evaluation of the literary merchandise.

Without such blunt assessment, we cannot know who is doing worthwhile writing and who is not, amidst the flood of hyped authors being published. We cannot separate the fads and fashions from the durable and classical. Without outspoken criticism reaching the vast potential audience, writing itself cannot be returned to a central position in culture, since the output is immense in volume and drowns out any thought process about its relevance or importance or meaning. Without discerning humanist critics beholden neither to "theory" nor to "creative writing," intelligent readers cannot come into being.

Without a criticism following new principles—not going back to the condition before post-structuralism, structuralism, or New Criticism, since this is neither desirable nor possible—we shall remain in a vacuum of analysis, readers continuing to inhabit a hazy state of mind about the true state of writing: there is much worthwhile writing being produced, even if it is not on the radar screen of the publicity mavens, and, moreover, such writing would increase in quantity and quality if there were a new critical force propagating its value to large numbers of potential readers.

Criticism should be conceived as the absolute fulcrum of a revived literary culture, because only it can advance good writing and create new readers, while relegating the boilerplate writing to the trash heap where it belongs.

We face a situation in the middle of the second decade of the twenty-first century where the critical landscape is almost completely vacant. Such a crisis in criticism is undoubtedly a reflection of the crisis of political legitimacy; yet this very crisis holds the promise of a new beginning. The economic landscape is fundamentally changing, and there is no going back to the verities of the New Deal, the minimal decencies provided by a reactive welfare state fending off the more generous welfare states of Western Europe or addressing Communist orthodoxy.

What will the writer of the future look like, how will she fit into new social institutions and collective expectations, what will be her status as an entrepreneur or employee or a mix of the two? We don't yet know, but it is against this vast empty panorama that the drama of criticism will play out in the near future. Randall Jarrell wrote of the 1950s that it was an age of criticism; in some ways, as far as highbrow minority culture (of the *Partisan Review* kind) was concerned, that was true. We are currently in an age that gives the false appearance of being also an age of criticism, indeed hypercriticism, but the principles animating post-structuralism (very much rooted in the quaint objectivities of formalism, New Criticism, and structuralism) are drained of passion and vitality. Literature and criticism have stopped speaking to each other, driving both to irrelevance and bankruptcy.

The literary critic of the future must be a giant. She cannot think of herself as providing gloss or commentary against huge bureaucratic forces beyond her ken, a mere commentator or assimilationist or sometimes wily antagonist to a machine that discounts her very essence. The writer of the future should think of criticism as her first and only real training ground, regardless of her branch of literary specialization. Indeed, conditions are such that without breathing the air of the kind of criticism I am expounding, the writer's effort will remain marginal and irrelevant, her fame stillborn, her aspirations to greatness so much illusion.

The writer's very survival is at stake. Criticism, far from an additional onerous task she must take on as pro bono service to the literary field, is the very soil in which her most individualized dreams and ambitions must be rooted. Both the peril and the promise are at their peak. Present institutions are rapidly crumbling, or at least their legitimacy is in unprecedented doubt. The alleged transition from a print to a post-print culture is in fact a red herring. The real potential of transformation is from a post-critical to a critical culture.

Into the breach, then! Here are some speculations about what a revived humanist criticism for the twenty-first century would look like, the pitfalls it would have to avoid and the faint grooves it would have to follow to the very ends, if we are to save literature itself from extinction.

1. Provide Deep Context.

How deep? Deeper than any form of literary criticism known today. Deep enough to include investigations of the author's relationship to her specialty, the connections between her and others like her and unlike her, the evolution of her thought process both in an individual and collective manner, and every available insight from philosophy, psychology, sociology, economics, art, and science to shed light on the work in question.

Readers today have quite discounted newspaper reviews, which are almost without exception worthless as criticism; editors generally impose a silence over rigorous critical standards, and reviewers know they must accede to the demands of the editors or find themselves out of an assignment. The general tendency of shallowness pervades all review forums, including those online, even among avant-garde publications from which one would expect differently.

The problem is that the review has gelled into a predictable form, a genre with its own conventions and formulas, offered to the public for ready consumption. Each and every one of this genre's conventions must be smashed and reconstructed if reviewing is to become relevant again. The review, instead of being a closed form with summary assessments, must become speculative, generalized, a mere tip of the iceberg for the knowledge contained within it. It must be so erudite as to destabilize the veracity of the work under consideration. It must set itself up as an equal and opposing force against the work of imagination.

If this sounds like theory's claims to superiority over creative work, it is only superficially so. Theory is invested in specific niches—psychoanalysis, feminism, New Historicism, queer studies, etc.—closeted within their individual parameters and following the rules of their sub-disciplines. I have nothing like this in mind. A creative work, if it is to be worth anything in the twenty-first century, must compel consideration of the vast edifices of knowledge underlying the author's worldview. It is these constructions that need to be brought into the open as the critic's most valuable function. Every piece of criticism in this vein becomes an open-ended, demanding, ferocious, relentless investigation of morality at a structural level. If I read Orhan Pamuk's *My Name Is Red*, I ought to be intrigued, as a critic, about any number of fundamental questions of art as a reflection of national culture and phases of enlightenment. A work like that begs the critic to pull herself out of the immediate needs of the book and the author, and revert to formative discipline.

If criticism performs in this suggested manner, anti-intellectual authors—who unfortunately dominate American letters today—would receive second-class treatment, as they deserve. Criticism should explore the depth of underlying ideas, and authors found wanting should be devalued. Shallowness quickly reveals itself. The tendency of writing in the twenty-first century, with the barrage of new information technologies, is to drive the reader toward a metaphysical receptivity where everything indeed does become apparently illuminated; but this effect, because of present social conditions, can in reality only be achieved by entering the darkest of labyrinths, the deep marrow of ideas in their origins and complexities. Authors who spurn their own narrow intellectual origins—every author starts with a limited base, but the successful ones exceed it—deserve heavyweight consideration.

Deep context means tackling the work of art at a level of complexity greater than its own, rather than retreating in the face of apparent self-containment. The critic must pry open books in a radically new manner, because such openness is both technologically more possible than ever and because readers don't need to hear mere readerly opinions or even technocratic lectures about what makes a work of art click. In short, expose shallowness, rather than back off in the face of marketing hype about an author's credentials. Readers need this clarity from the strong critic.

2. Merge Disciplines.

Again, there is superficial resemblance between this principle and a reigning shibboleth of the academy: interdisciplinarity. I don't mean anything like the debased academic notion of, say, putting economics and literature together. I mean the fluid merger of every known discipline that the critic can bring to bear on the analysis of individual works or groups of works. There should be no boundaries between forms of inquiry. If theory is in disrepute outside the academy, then so are the social sciences, particularly economics and political science, but also anthropology, sociology, psychology, and, on the humanist side, history. There are a number of reasons for this decline in legitimacy, which the critic should take advantage of.

The social sciences, in their modern form, began with the positivism of the mid-nineteenth-century, reached their heyday in the generally progressive political climate of the early twentieth century, then faced a crisis of articulation when confronted with worldwide economic, political, and social upheaval in the 1930s and thereafter. Fascism and global depression, not to mention genocide, total war, and atomic annihilation, were not exactly subjects amenable to social science verities. The disciplines became after-the-fact justifications of much human irrationality manifested in mass global actions, predicted already by Sigmund Freud, Émile Durkheim, Max Weber, Georges Sorel, Vilfredo Pareto, Gaetano Mosca, and other perspicacious thinkers of the early twentieth century. Nineteenth-century Comtean positivism became an irreconcilable historical anomaly in the midst of the vast technological and social transformations of the twentieth century.

All of the social science and humanities disciplines are in need of reconstitution, or reimagination, in the twenty-first century. As with literary studies, they have followed a path of ironic reflexivity in an attempt to make themselves more lucid and relevant, but have only succeeded in making themselves more obscure and irrelevant.

Economics, for instance, began as a science of human happiness in the midst of industrialization in the late eighteenth-century, but by the middle of the twentieth century had become a branch of mathematics, whose inner deliberations only the higher mathematicians could pursue. It needs to become a science of human fulfillment again. At the end of World War II, as American power assumed worldwide hegemony, all of the social sciences and humanities got corrupted as the post-war zeal for empire infected whatever remained of the myth of objectivity. Psychology rests on foundations that have tottered so precipitously in the wake of mass irrationalism that today it is without a base altogether. Anthropology flourished early in the twentieth century when optimism about the human race and honest belief in moral relativism were enough to provide the motivation for comparative studies; but later the discipline, beset by its own contradictions, devolved into a web of self-consciousness, turned on itself, became a commentary on its own previous commentaries, as have other specialties. History has simply failed, like other disciplines, to explain, let alone anticipate, the ongoing cataclysms. As for the hard sciences, long ago they reached a stage of mysticism—the only form in which higher scientific findings can be presented to the public.

Is it putting too heavy a burden on critics to expect them to undertake the reimagination of all the academic disciplines? But what is the alternative and who else is going to do it? Novelists are the best historians, and this is more true today than ever; no historian shows the comprehensive, big-picture, total understanding of, say, a Salman Rushdie or J. M. Coetzee or V. S. Naipaul—or a Doris Lessing, when it comes to understanding the history of women's consciousness. Poets reveal human nature better than any psychologist practicing in a narrow niche.

If the critic shuns disciplinary boundaries—acts as economist, psychologist, historian, even physicist if she has the mind and capability for it—then she will train herself as an imaginative writer whose work will have durable value for the reader of the twenty-first century; remember, I am postulating *the critic* as the quintessential writer of the future, her foundational training occurring in expansive criticism over an extended duration of self-apprenticeship. Literature can only be immeasurably enriched by taking up the very mantle of responsible, generalizable, accessible, resonant criticism that the rest of the disciplines have vacated under the auspices of hyper-professionalism.

3. Overcome Specialization.

One of the main reasons for the cultural irrelevance of literary writing today—possibly the greatest reason—is that writers are too specialized and as a result their output seems insular and self-contained, unable to explode out of its bounds.

Once a cultural enterprise enters the academy, it inevitably results in over-specialization. Whereas in the past there used to be poets who were also writers of prose narrative as well as critics and reviewers, and this was true for all branches of literary endeavor, nowadays not only do we have poets who do nothing but poetry, but poets who specialize only in a very narrow range of poetics: a Bengali poet may only write about her personal experiences of assimilation/emigration from a strictly domestic angle in a very specific mentor-derived style, and that is all she will do for the entirety of her academic career; she will not write criticism of other poets, South Asian literature, Bengali literature not in translation, South Asian politics, American politics, American foreign policy, the aesthetics of confessionalism, or her situation in the academy, let alone foray into different styles of writing. If she writes short lyrical poems, that is the only style she will likely ever pursue. The same self-imposed parameters apply to fiction writers, such as Junot Diaz or Amy Tan, who never do anything but exploit their allocated multicultural niches.

The result is immense impoverishment of broad cultural appeal; when a writer restricts herself in such a manner, the subtext becomes thinner, the poem or short story or novel becomes only about itself. In a sense, all creative writing today is living out New Criticism's attitude toward writing, focusing on itself as sealed-off workmanship, but it is New Criticism without its sophisticated and occasionally formidable analytical strategies, since *self-expression* always intervenes as the ultimate criterion of authenticity and reality. There always seems to be a ghostly I. A. Richards or John Crowe Ransom peering over the shoulders of the workshop participant as she formulates a self-contained artifact, hoping to be able to withstand close textual scrutiny, hoping to arrive at a *unity* despite tension. I am describing a contemporary equalization among current workshop writing, the new self-enclosed realism amidst what were thought to be extinct New Criticism standards.

What is the role of the critic in breaking down this constricting specialization? My assumption is that *the critic-in-training is the quintessential writer of the future*. She should take advantage of the new online public sphere opening up to potential infinitude by refusing to focus on a particular genre or region, or to ally herself with a particular writing clique. Critics today are generally offshoots of niches within writing, a situation that must change.

The critic of the future should address all forms of literature—and really, all forms of culture—by seeking out venues high and low, speaking in language sophisticated and vulgar, addressing the common reader and the specialized scholar, sometimes both at once. Practicing in this manner, the critic not only educates herself to be eclectic, transcendent, and visionary, but helps educate her reader to contextualize texts outside their explicit impulses and to see the author as something other than a performer within celebrity culture. In a sense, the author's unity of self, his individuality, is being challenged.

Again, this bears superficial resemblance to post-structuralism's idea of the author being a reflection of his times, but my idea is radically different. The reputation of specific authors may suffer, but the authority of authors as a whole should only grow. This is a deeply humanistic impulse, attacking New Criticism's ultimate bugaboos—W. K. Wimsatt and Monroe Beardsley's barring of the Intentional Fallacy (probing the author's intentions) and the Affective Fallacy (investigating readers' emotional reactions)—and restoring them to their position of centrality. Wimsatt and Beardsley's so-called fallacies built on Cleanth Brooks's "heresy of paraphrase" (which meant excluding the social context from criticism) and T. S. Eliot's "impersonal theory of poetry" (another claim for the irrelevance of the author's biography). Specialization is a cover that allows both alleged fallacies to persist; the critic must blow off this cover.

4. Connect to Other Cultural Fields.

Reading is impoverished today—book culture is impoverished—because it is created and imagined as an activity isolated from other cultural fields like painting, sculpture, film, music, architecture, and so on. How is it possible to evaluate any novel without referring to major developments in the visual and fine arts in a given decade or era? Does Robbe-Grillet make sense without the French New Wave? Or vice versa, actually. What about Donald Barthelme and the New York art scene of the 1960s? Consider the immense flux in twentieth-century art movements, filmmaking, popular music, and modernist and postmodernist architecture, and ask yourself what kind of critic refuses to make obvious and necessary connections.

Again, the post-structuralists have undertaken some of this crucial cultural work of encouraging connectivity, but their problem is obscurity, indifference toward appealing to a general readership, narrow specialization, and a political interest in scoring scholastic points rather than shedding light on particular works of art. The ideal critic I am proposing will make it a habit not to explore connections between fields of culture for their own sake, but to radically expand the range of what it is possible for the critic to understand and convey. I consciously avoid the term *literary* critic in this articulation. Again, a radically open-ended and welcoming invitation to the reader to make sense of the issues at stake should be the central goal.

Reading can move forward only to the extent that other art forms move forward; to the extent that different art forms are segregated and ghettoized, all of them suffer, all of them eventually become sterile and decadent and unable to influence utopian ideals, ceding power to whatever institutional forces embody anti-art. Reading cannot be imagined as an activity in competition with other artistic activity, and the same is true of all other art forms.

It is surprising that with the rise of new media—knowing the possibilities for collaboration, interaction, and open-endedness they present—existing cultural boundaries have not dissolved to a larger and more noticeable extent. One reason is the blindness of media conglomerates whose interest it is to maintain the divisions within the arts, and to take advantage of ever narrower niches. The publishing conglomerates' stated economic rationale for niche marketing is probably overshadowed by the ideological succor provided by spinning off the arts into exclusive, nonconversant niches. We should also consider the elitism of artists of various kinds, including writers, in arguing the superiority of their chosen art form over all others. The critic should ideally mediate among the arts, and, in so doing, bring excitement to all of them; yet this does not entail giving up the critic's essential function of evaluating and judging within a broad frame of reference.

5. Be Global.

National literary divisions and classifications are the least fertile territory for the critic of the future. It is my contention that reading will be revived everywhere in general, or nowhere at all; at the present moment, immense vital energies can be felt emanating from places like India and China, and these should only gather force to an exponential degree in the foreseeable future as a broad global middle class comes into being.

Today American criticism is globally worthless because it is so deeply parochial. The power of coordinated institutional taste mechanisms such as the leading review organs, the distribution of awards and grants and teaching positions, and the endless hype of the publicity machines of the media conglomerates, offers critics a choice between liking or disliking a handful of "major" authors. Needless to say, the class dimension in such ideals of taste formation is evident, and this class solidarity persists across the global landscape. In effect, there does exist a global club which endorses the literary—and cultural—product at an elite level, but which excludes the bulk of the real vitality of the human endeavor, particularly in an age of momentous social transformation. American writing will not ascend to its full potential unless American critics—and it should be clear by now that by this I really mean writers—adopt a cosmopolitan, anti-nationalist, globalizing, universal posture.

How can such a change come about, given the exigencies of class and education and locality? I suggest that such a transformation is easier today than ever, not only because of the pervasiveness of new media influences (all the world really is closer to being one than ever before) but because of the writer's interest in her own survival. The critic, if she thinks of herself as American or British or Indian, is doomed; she will be unable to say much of use, since reality today is global (and becoming increasingly so, despite the efforts of American reactionaries in recent times to stop its progress) and therefore criticism and writing must also be global.

In practical terms, this means that the critic writes not for an ideal reader in a Texas or Pennsylvania town, or even for a broad national audience, but rather for a potentially global audience of one or zero or everyone. Who one writes for changes everything; critics today need to ask the question "for whom do we write?" with great urgency, as do the creators of every kind of art. Who is the audience, and what can we say to it to break down formal and abstract divisions? At present, critics write to the narrowest possible audiences, and targeted reach is a measure of success. The ideal critic must aspire to precisely the opposite motivation.

There is no such thing as strictly national culture anymore; there is no such thing as uniquely national writing or criticism; the writer is either a global person or he is, so far as posterity is concerned, a non-person. And if the critic feels the case is otherwise, she should make a compelling argument why she does. But she cannot avoid confronting this issue.

6. Adopt a Sharp Point of View.

The barriers between the journalistic and scholarly enterprises are particularly onerous when it comes to criticism. Criticism needs a new style, recognizably polemic, argumentative, even crass and vulgar when it needs to be; it needs to not only respond to the aggressiveness of much of popular culture, but to adopt and co-opt that style and transcend it. At stake is more than just reaching out to an audience for criticism—and for readership—that doesn't yet exist; at stake is the very matter of criticism's function, of why the critic is doing her job in the first place.

I would go so far as to claim that arguing from a strong point of view, proving and disproving premises, hammering away at opponents, abusing one's enemies when necessary, overpraising and indulging and hitting hard and delving into personalities—all of it should be on the table if criticism is to be revived as a vital cultural enterprise. The cult of objectivity infects the newspaper business, but scholarship suffers from it too, to its great detriment. The very basis of New Criticism was objectivity, and this has been true of all the critical movements that have followed in reaction to it.

The cult of objectivity puts the critic in a bind right from the start of the project. True impartiality is an impossible ideal, as all critics know well, and this hypocrisy should be laid to rest. The critic must be willing to explore and expose her own biases, her prejudices, her subjective disabilities and strengths, her irrationalities, and her passions and hatreds, so that the reader is challenged to respond or retreat, as the case may be. The reader cannot be engaged if the critic maintains her faux Olympian stance. One result of letting go of false objectivity is that the critic becomes more human; she admits her weaknesses; she cannot be in equal control of all the cultural fields, or even particular branches of literature, and where she is weak, her passion allows her to be honest. Honesty and integrity are integrally linked with passion, not objectivity.

The critic of the future has the chance to be the central cultural figure, because all fields of discourse have been imperialized by polite objectivists. Therefore it is difficult to find truthful commentary on any subject. Something as rudimentary as the blossoming of multicultural literature in all its forms, a mission that has been well underway for almost forty years in the Anglo-Saxon countries, has yet to receive honest critical treatment in accessible forums. Political correctness is part of the problem, but the polite mannerliness of criticism, quite aside from political correctness, is also to blame. How should we evaluate a memoir of addiction or grief? Here again, the critic would have to speak from a strong point of view, otherwise the cloak of authenticity (the raison d'être for much of today's literary writing) cannot be penetrated.

There is much dishonesty in the literary venture today; the critic must rise to the challenge of exposing it and arguing for a more utopian literature by shedding her impartial, pragmatist, fair-minded, genteel persona, and opting for a style of writing that lets her character shine through. Then only can the debate about the merits of forms of literary creation truly commence. Examples from the last century are rare, but would have to include Virginia Woolf, H. L. Mencken, Cyril Connolly, and George Orwell. As the culture becomes higher-decibeled, the critic's voice must also become loud enough to be heard above all the noise and distraction. This doesn't mean shouting or screaming one's positions, but letting the force of one's convictions emerge unfettered. Of course, this also means having convictions in the first place, but if the writer has (re)positioned herself as a critic first and foremost, then there should be plenty of convictions to elaborate.

7. Argue from Personality.

Theory has lately taken a turn toward the confessional. It is most amusing to read the convolutions of graceless prose writers, utterly in thrall to their own self-importance as arbiters of goodness and benevolence, as they strive to inject their bland personas into the usual machinations of theory, so that instead of any sense of the author's autobiography coming through, what the disenchanted reader encounters is the ugly spectacle of theorists posturing as latter-day confessionalists, desperately striving to bring some warmth to their abstract conjectures but managing only to generate autobiographical sketches tacked on to the usual ramblings of theory. The theorist Marjorie Garber exemplifies this leisurely, hands-off approach. Though she speaks in the first person, she fails to invest the point of view with any humor, passion, or dynamism. The sense of disconnect between the academician and the work of art remains palpable; irony penetrates the whole enterprise so that blame or responsibility ultimately cannot be assigned to any party; in the end all we have is a holier-than-thou attitude, the academic deigning to share some private experiences in order to make himself more marketable to peers and adjudicators. Leave it to theorists to create a yearning for standard confessionalism, even if all they fess up to is the predictable repertoire of personal dysfunction.

What I am calling for is a radical subjectivization of criticism, so that the critic's personality can be front and center; it doesn't always have to be, but there should be more than plenty of room for it. What this will require is the expansion of the reduced boundaries of confessionalism from the present arena of private dysfunction to the critic's relationship with society, including her relationships with publishers, editors, and fellow writers, her relationship to work and to literary status or lack thereof, her education and class, her politics as they affect her personal life, her quirks and idiosyncrasies, her acts of violation, solicitude, trespassing, and intrusion, whatever makes her respond personally to the work or author or genre in question.

She can do all this while maintaining her sense of privacy, a paradox which is going to become increasingly central for writing of all types in an age of confessionalist new media. She can do all this and remain an unknown entity, should she choose to. Autobiography can be entirely or partially fictionalized, but that should be of no concern to the reader. What is important is the intersection of the character of the critic, with its irrationalities and foibles, and a work of art that assumes closure, wholeness, perfection. In other words, the writer-critic's life becomes an ongoing, perpetually unfinished, tentative work of fiction encountering equally delusional works of fiction.

That is the nature of the future struggle between critic and writing, and it is also the nature of the struggle between critic and reader, because the reader's interpretation of works of art is crucially bound up with certain verities about the stability of his own personality and that of the author in question. To the extent that authorship is problematized—not from the "death of the author" perspective, as with Barthes and Foucault, but from the point of view of his material relationships within the institutional textures of publishing—the autobiographical mode of narration can have much benefit.

8. Dispute the Possibility of Art.

I believe that this is one of the most important functions of the critic of the future—not to proselytize on behalf of particular works of art, but to quarrel with the very possibility that any art is possible in the age of new media, whose early stages suggest much more radical changes to come. Continuing to try to prove the existence and importance of art, high or low or in-between, is a losing proposition. It creates the opposite of the intended effect. The only way that art can become central again is if it is attacked repeatedly and from every front, from every angle possible, by critics agnostic about its existence, or even militantly atheist toward it. Instead of advocating for art, the critic of the future should passionately foretell its demise, marshal every resource at his disposal to bring it down, to bring the whole miserable enterprise to an end. This confrontational posture is the only service a critic can provide to art at this late juncture; everything else is mere dishonesty that doesn't compel strong artists into being.

How can there be art when hierarchies are flattened as never before, when democracy is stripped of idealism, when the canon has been brought into disrepute, when there is no time for leisure and reflection, when war has long been elevated to the highest aesthetic, when there is no ideology, no utopia, no conflict, no desire worth speaking of? What function can poetry possibly serve when all the poetic dreams have been appropriated by the media, converted into debased forms of visual manipulation and aggressive denial? What role can fiction possibly have in a mass society whose rules and conventions have, for at least a century, been subjected to thorough humiliation, from the modernism of Joyce and Woolf to the postmodernism of Borges and Calvino, so that only a shell is left, mere trappings and rituals, not the spiritual core?

What role can any of the literary arts have when the cultural elite itself frowns on the possibility of literature, when every great work of the past has already been shown to be corrupt from the many politically fashionable angles of today's orthodoxy? So can we say that deconstructionists managed to destroy literature after all? Aside from the fact that this was very much their goal—at least literature conceived naively as the product of great minds resonating with great cultures—this is only a small part of the answer. Twentieth-century mass society militated against art, even as artistic effort reached a pitch of feverish desperation, as it tried to grasp political nightmares and collective self-suicide in its almighty vision.

The critic must absolutely accept and bend to the political nightmares of the twenty-first century (which are on a different order than what has gone on before, since ideology is not a part of the clash, only personal demons extrapolated to the global scale), and accept that there is no possibility of any art, making this her first and last assumption. And from there, she should determine what's left, what's worth exploring for its failures, in a landscape where empty materialisms are fighting it out. The critic must understand that henceforth all successful art will be premised on its own failures. That's the only territory worth rooting around in. Art will conquer all—when it has been completely conquered.

9. Make the Tradition New.

Theorists dismiss the canon as the reflection of specific cultural prejudices that can make no claim to universality. They propound an alternative canon—why should that not be subject to the same criticism of local prejudice?—written by women, minorities, the previously silenced, regardless of comparative literary worth. The creative writers do not understand the canon and don't care about it because all their time is devoted to imitating models of contemporary writing in the pursuit of immediate publication and job security; the very premise of "creative writing" is to divorce creative writing from its contextualization in the canon, and instead to encourage the apprentice to write from personal experience. The mainstream reviewers don't have the intellectual aptitude to grasp the canon.

Which leaves a big hole for the critic to fill, and she must take advantage of this moment where the genres of writing have dissolved to the point where the canon can be made anew. What this means is that there is far greater potential for writing to be revived by means of the existing and the ancient—even the musty—rather than through alleged avant-garde work, experimental break-throughs churned out at the speed of blogs and multimedia. The baroque, grotesque, or impenetrable medieval or ancient work of literature has suddenly become profoundly modern, ahead of our times—and this should be obvious to any critic able to see the current moment of dissolution for what it is.

What about the tradition of the picaresque novel from the sixteenth, seventeenth, and eighteenth centuries, for example? It is avant-garde to the hilt, utterly in tune with contemporary disorientation and disillusionment, which are always cloaked in the mantle of firm belief. What about Middle English poetry? Renaissance drama? Greek prose narrative? Roman satire? Japanese epic? German high romanticism? All of it can be seen, suddenly, as utterly new and charming and fresh, and it is because we have come to the end of the cycle of many genres as they have evolved over the centuries. It is time to replenish them.

This is not a conservative agenda of arguing that a particular canon is somehow supernatural in origin or superior to other canons; Harold Bloom's exercise in *The Western Canon* was one of the more wasteful examples of the genre. The canon is always in flux; nonetheless there is a canon. It needs to be fought with, cut down to size, treated with disrespect most of the time, but it is a curiosity that yields infinite new insights—otherwise the canon wouldn't be the canon. The canon, for the true critic, is transnational, history-breaking, non-obligatory, but despite all this, it can be the greatest force for the revitalization of art.

Defoe, for instance, was operating under very different presumptions about the role of the author in society, had a very different attitude toward "realism" than the one we now take for granted, and treated his readers in a very different manner than current faux-democratic premises allow. The critic is always in search of new models of professionalization of the writing venture—or we might say anti-professionalization. Each era yields its secrets in that direction. Probably the most fruitful activity that any critic can undertake is to dig into the canon in this disassociated manner and come up with new treasure. It turns the very idea of relativism on its head, since in the end the critic discovers that things somehow always remain the same and yet assume different shapes. This is a key way in which the crisis of literature—which is at bottom a crisis of political confidence—can be displaced to different territory.

10. Downplay Politicization.

In some ways this will sound like the most unexpected proposition of all, the most radical, given the tenor of all that has preceded it. But think about it and it makes sense. How is it possible for the critic to play up any political angle when there is no political ideology worth speaking of? Politics is at a similarly exhausted stage as literature, and, in both instances, a consumerist cornucopia disguises the ultimate lack of choice, the lack of quality in either realm. To advocate a particular politics at this juncture would be the greatest dereliction of the critic's duty.

The aim should be to put politics aside, to return literature and art to the center, the exact opposite of what the theorists have done, and of what the creative writers have done. In the case of the former, what has all the subtextual Marxism, the watered-down radicalism, actually accomplished? The net result of theory has actually been a depoliticization of the academy, to the extent that language has been fetishized and politically correct discourse prevails everywhere. The academy would have had a far greater political impact had it not fallen into the trap of taking its own trendy political ideas so seriously and instead concentrated on the foundations of education.

And that is exactly what the critic should aim for. The greatest act of politicization for these times is to refuse participation in any of the debased political ideologies, all of which are various forms of cover for consumerist capitalism of the most vulgar kind. In my own case, I fervently believe in a cosmopolitan politics of transnational civil liberties, anti-religious and anti-nationalist, almost anarchic at times, based on absolutely open movement of people and ideas, and yet I want to reconcile this politics somehow with fair distribution of income and collective responsibility for welfare. But I don't see how criticism can become the vehicle for advancing my politics.

Is it natural for me to select books and authors for discussion who accord with my views rather than those who don't? Perhaps, although if I have certain problems with, say, Salman Rushdie's growing American neoconservative bent, compared to his earlier straightforward British socialism, I don't see how that in any way should affect my estimation of his later novels. The work of art, in other words, needs to be freed again from the political shackles that have bound it over the last forty years in particular. The world, not art, needs to be politicized; the corollary of aestheticizing politics (fascism) is politicizing aesthetics (deconstruction). This is not a quietist posture, actually, but the most radical one for contemporary times. This is also certainly not New Criticism's posture of aestheticism, divorcing the work of art from political and social reality, as the preceding propositions should have made amply clear.

A related trap is creative writing's conservative, realism-oriented, personalized, confessionalist aesthetic, which on the surface bears the trappings of the anti-political attitude I am advocating; but there is actually no similarity. The creative writer refuses to accept her brand of politics as such; she thinks of herself as apolitical, enamored of objectivity—which in the case of writing masquerades as realism.

Literary artists like to think of themselves as liberal; yet mass taste demands conformity to the status quo. As a result, there is a perpetual schizophrenic split between the writer's needs and the reader's needs, and blandness and mediocrity come to pervade writing and criticism because it is impossible to reconcile the two conflicting urges. If the critic can address the problem of politics with the subtlety I propose, she can end up redefining the problem of authenticity for our times—just as in directly interjecting her personality into criticism, she can help redefine the problem of confession and privacy.

The redefinition of the critic's function in society is a redefinition of writing's function in society. To rethink criticism is to rethink writing. The agenda presented above is no doubt too idealistic—and some would say imposes too heavy a burden of erudition and responsibility on the critic—but since when were manifestos written without a healthy dose of utopianism? I would actually argue that the scale of the notions presented here is rather modest.

The critic cannot emerge into her full-blown mature shape after a short period of study or brief apprenticeship; rather, she will have to yoke herself to a lifelong project of increasingly deeper and broader investigations of the whole cultural field. I am propounding, for one thing, the extinction of the entity known as the literary critic, for she will not limit herself to literature alone. She will range in speculation across all branches of knowledge, from the sciences to the humanities, making books and their authors and her own authority question marks for readers, signposts illuminating the enormous scale of knowledge that all of us will miss in our lifetimes because there simply isn't time enough.

The critic as I conceive her militates against mortality—all writing should have this ultimate goal in mind, or it isn't true writing—by setting up impossible standards for readers to uphold. Modern reader-reception theory is rather a tame affair, leaving the reader the option of responding to the text at his given level of understanding; this is valid to a point, but readers are forever changing into their ideal selves, just as writers are, and only the critic can mediate in this interaction to the benefit of both.

The present moment is truly a crossroads, as not only literature but all art lies in ruins, annihilated by the seductive temptations of mass media, rejected by elites and ordinary readers alike, at odds with the various styles of faux democracy being propagated from the bully pulpits of the media masterminds. At the same time, it is precisely at the moment of absolute devastation that the greatest rejuvenations can occur, and the unprecedentedly global nature of emerging political developments holds the greatest hope for a truly cosmopolitan, metanationalist art of the future, one that will fundamentally alter the self-perceptions of cultural agents.

Theory in the academy, just like creative writing in its institutionalized form, will persist for the foreseeable future; but criticism should have nothing to do with either of them. It should be an independent activity, rooted in the firmest of beliefs—or disbeliefs—toward the author-critic, whose only allegiance should be to her own sense of reality. Reality itself will be replenished if anything close to the model I am advocating takes hold in the new knowledge-ideas-socialization public sphere, bending it in the direction current authorities in the academy and media fear.

In my vision for criticism, imaginative writing is no longer exploited to score political or sociological points, and the work of art is judged above all else for its artistic qualities. My assumption of an encyclopedic, expansive, egalitarian criticism raises these questions with great urgency: What are the new descriptive norms? What is the new public sphere? If liberalism's shared mores no longer prevail, what constitutes "humanism"? The critic's very definition of these questions—as was true in a different context in the constitution of the public sphere in England, France, and Germany in the early eighteenth century—should help bring about a new subjectivity. The extension of the global public sphere is a fundamental prerequisite for the kind of criticism I am proposing. I would like to see culture elevated over politics as the indispensable arena of playful risk-taking; my feelings on the embrace of risk in the new global arena are more akin to Ulrich Beck's openness than Habermas's caution. I fully accept the emergence of the post-industrial subject in the West, and would like to see criticism push toward universal tolerance based on the extension of that identity in the rest of the world. Eliot's Tory New Criticism was founded on the conservative values of hierarchy, order, and maturity, and it accorded very well with the inception of creative-writing workshop orthodoxy in the 1930s; post-structuralism went on to fight New Criticism values that were misplaced to begin with. In other words, there was a titanic clash between the two leading forces in criticism, unfortunately taking place on the wrong foundations. The ground looks clearer now.

Symposium: What is the Present State of American Poetry?

This seems to be a particularly angst-ridden moment for the followers of American poetry. Is it vigorously alive, extending its tentacles into new corners of consciousness, or is it a moribund corpse, having long been administered last rites? The debate is particularly acute now, as new avenues of poetry publication proliferate like never before and there are more "poets" writing and publishing poetry today, even as critics claim that the MFA system has led to uniform mediocrity and tentativeness. So which is it, and is there a way to put this conflict in some bigger historical context?

I asked the poets the following questions: Is American poetry at a dead end? Have American poets kept or betrayed the great legacy of modernism? What worries you about the present moment in poetry? On the other hand, where do you see signs of life? Where is the most promising work coming from? What is your advice to a young poet trying to make sense of the current poetry scene?

National Book Award-winning poet, translator, and critic Clayton Eshleman is the author of more than thirty books, including *Grindstone of Rapport* (Black Widow Press) and *Juniper Fuse: Upper Paleolithic Imagination & the Construction of the Underworld* (Wesleyan University Press).

Elder poets such as Gary Snyder, Adrienne Rich, Jerome Rothenberg, Robert Kelly, and the late Gustaf Sobin, for example, have, over the past two decades, in their own fashion, developed and extended the work of Pound, Williams, Stein, Rukeyser, and Olson. The elder poets I mention above have continued to affirm poetry as a form in which the realities of the spirit can be tested by critical intelligence, a form in which the blackness in the heart of man can be confronted and articulated.

The hundreds of undergraduate and graduate university degree programs offering majors in writing poetry and fiction worry me. This system is producing thousands of talented but unoriginal writers, many of whom would not be writing at all if it were not for jobs. Once upon a time, there was a "left bank" and a "right bank" in our poetry: the innovative vs. the traditional. Today the writing scene resembles a blizzard on an archipelago of sites. Not only has the laudable democratization of poetry been compromised by being brick-layered into the academy but with few exceptions there is a lack of strong "signature" and a tacit affirmation of the bourgeois status quo, the politics of no politics.

There are a number of poets who are wonderful exceptions to the situation I briefly just described. Rachel Blau DuPlessis, Ron Padgett, Anne Waldman, Nathaniel Mackey, Michael Palmer, John Olson, Andrew Joron, Will Alexander, Christine Hume, Kevin Davies, Lara Glenum, Linh Dinh, and Kristin Prevallet, to name only a few, are all publishing poetry that bears the stamp of originality as well as the influence of earlier major figures.

My advice to a young poet would be to leave this country and see how other people live. Translate, for the "assimilative space" opened up through the translation of complex texts carries a greater learning potential than reading poetry written in one's native language. Read books that no one else is reading so that you can bring into poetry information that has remained outside of poetry.

Keep a reading notebook and start writing reviews of the books that you adore or detest, stating clearly why. Take on poetry that is beyond you. Serious poetry commentary is a kind of "endangered species." The major critics of the past several decades have all been non-poet advancers of conventional verse.

Annie Finch is a poet, translator, librettist, verse playwright, editor, and critic. Her books include *Spells: New and Selected Poems* and *The Body of Poetry: Essays on Women, Form, and the Poetic Self.* She directs the Stonecoast MFA program in Creative Writing.

American poetry is at a dead end. And that's a good thing! American poets have betrayed the legacy of modernism completely, and in the most insidious way: by getting stuck in it. The strains of Williams, Eliot, Stevens, and Stein between them still hold most of American poetry in deadlock. Modernism was such a powerful turning that its centrifugal force flung poems far away from each other and from the central uniting energy of the art. So we have schools of poetry still splattering poems up against their separate walls of image/anecdote, intellectual pedantry, cultural refinement, and language experiment. The disembowelment of the art was, of course, facilitated by the twentieth-century technologies of the typewriter and the computer screen, which kept poetry away from its own center by severing it from its writers' and readers' mouths, ears, and bodies.

It worries me that so little published mainstream poetry is intended to be heard by its readers. As a result, people who encounter a poem on the page tend to think it exists on the page—they don't hear its patterns resonating aloud inside them. Since repeating language patterns are the core distinguishing feature that demarcates poetry as a genre from any other form of language, there's a lot at stake.

I do see signs of life. Poetic form and meter are increasingly hip, and poets with ears trained in performance poetry are using their skills to learn meter; we see more and more of this at Stonecoast, the MFA program I direct. Poetry is increasingly apparent on the radio, in ads, and other places that non-poets hang out. This is a healthy sign for the art, since general readers/hearers keep us honest; they remind us that we have a needed role to play in the culture. And long-overdue appreciation is finally growing for the three modernist poets with the best poetic ears: Crane, Hughes, and Millay.

I just finished teaching dactylic, anapestic, iambic, and trochaic meter to a diverse group of poets at Stonecoast. As a class, their poetic ears were sharper and quicker than those of any group of poets I've ever taught. They loved learning these basics of their craft, and their work blew me away. There are plenty of young poets out there who are serious about reconnecting poetry with its roots, its body, the earth's body, its readers' bodies—not to mention souls. We really have no choice—this is the job of poets at this moment. The planet demands it.

Poetic fashions change surprisingly fast, so don't spend too much energy on them. Read everything aloud to yourself, get to know your poetic ear, and trust your own judgment. You will recognize the muse's presence, not in thoughts or images, but when a voice whispers inside you and your body knows it is true. Carry a pad of paper with you everywhere and sleep with it by your bed. Learn all you can, read all you can, grow all you can, and always remember the muse comes first. Poetry is a sacred service, and your country needs you. So only do what feels right. Don't waste poetic words. Revise.

Ron Silliman is the author, co-author, or editor of more than thirty volumes of poetry and criticism, including *The New Sentence*, *The Age of Huts (compleat)*, and *The Alphabet*.

Fifty years ago, there were well under a thousand poets writing and publishing in English. Today, there are easily over twenty thousand. A dead end? Hardly. But what is changing—and unsettling to those who look at poetry without looking at history—is the relation of the poet (and poem) to audience. Writers who want to have just a few poets, each with a mass audience, are doomed to disappointment. But we have not yet articulated in any settled manner what a "successful poetry career" will look like if there are twenty times the number of poets, but perhaps only two or three times the number of readers we had fifty years ago. Every single poet is having to figure this out for him or herself. It's worth keeping in mind that we're in this together.

Have American poets betrayed the great legacy of modernism? One might make this argument for those poets who write as if modernism itself never existed. But with friends like Ezra Pound and/or T.S. Eliot, modernism hardly needed enemies. I've often thought that the real question here is what would happen if we went back and actually attempted to answer the great questions of form and function that literary modernism asks. In that sense, I tend to think the best current writing isn't postmodern, but rather neomodern. The work of Linh Dinh, Prageeta Sharma, Tao Lin, Tan Lin, Eileen Tabios, Hung Q. Tu, Mytili Jagannathan, Tsering Wangmo Dhompa, Brian Kim Stefans, Pamela Lu, Bhanu Kapil, and other younger writers who excite me all strike me this way.

What worries me most is the survival of poetry in a world in which the depredations of capital go literally unchecked. Having twenty thousand or twenty million poets won't help one bit if the biosphere is screwed. In the past thirty-five years, we have seen the top one percent of the wealthiest people in the United States increase their control of the economy from under ten percent to nearly thirty percent. That yields a very unstable society. In the 1930s, the last time we saw that concentration of wealth, you had the far left as well as the far right contesting the status quo. I'm afraid we've ceded the field to the far right this time around, which means that George W. Bush may only be the worst president we have had to date. What would Sarah Palin or some other Fox surrogates do in power? The words Yugoslavia, Spain, Romania, Germany all come to mind.

There are hundreds of good young poets, many of them coming from communities previously unrepresented in the U.S. cultural mix. Is it an accident that the list I gave two paragraphs back consisted entirely of poets with at least some Asian heritage? As always, the most promising work arrives when new participants ask questions in new ways. Or hear the old questions with new ears. Just as it was not an accident that Gertrude Stein was a Jewish Lesbian at a time when that phrase did not trip lightly off the tongue, or that William Carlos Williams was half-Puerto Rican, so it is not an accident that American poetry today—and British, Canadian, Australian—is enriched precisely as its deepens its understanding of who writes to include the kinds of people not previously acknowledged. And as global communications expand the field, we're going to have to recognize that the English-language literary landscape includes broad parts of South Asia, Nigeria, South Africa, and elsewhere. If we can just keep from destroying the planet, we may be on the cusp of the first global renaissance. But that is a very big If.

My advice to a young poet would be to know your songs well before you start singing, to paraphrase Bob Dylan. You need to both understand the full field and history of writing and to recognize that we are in the very first moments of whatever the next age in history will be, and that the poetry of the future cannot simply be the past dragged on by habit. This is necessarily a both/and requirement. One without the other will only lead to work that is arid and pointless. But the two together yield almost limitless possibilities. And then there is that third requirement, which is that we have to rescue the planet if we are to have futures of any kind whatsoever.

Danielle Pafunda is the author of *Iatrogenic: Their Testimonies* (Noemi Press), *My Zorba* (Bloof Books), *Pretty Young Thing* (Soft Skull Press), and *Manhater* (Dusie Press).

This is where, if I say yes, American poetry jumps up and grabs me by the throat, right? I am not falling for that one. American poetry is a live wire. In fact, it is a tangle of live wires.

1. American poetry contains multitudes.

What we have here, lucky ducks, is an embarrassment of riches! What's your pleasure? Postmodern sonnet? Erotic elegiac? Schoolgirl gothic? Conceptual choose-your-own-adventure? Brokenhearted? Ball-breaker? Belletricky? There are literally thousands of American poets. The magazine *American Poets* goes out to approximately nine thousand subscribers. There are poetry enthusiasts reading up *right this very second*. I suppose it is possible that all these people could be gathered together at a dead end, but then wouldn't that make the dead end a destination? Come to the dead end of the world! We have milk and cookies and bonfires! Thar be monsters!

2. American poets = millipedes.

I went to college in the middle of the woods, and we had one dormitory, formerly an eldercare facility, which was thoroughly infested by some sort of transparent millipede. They were spooky ghostly things, up to six inches in length. Hard to believe they weren't the riverside nightmares of the dying. Hard to believe they wouldn't crawl in your ear and plant something. Worse than discovering one in your room was chasing one around your room. They could scurry so quickly that they seemed to be running in several directions at once, splitting apart and reassembling. If you were unfortunate enough to live in one of the rooms with a drain in the floor (morgue? infirmary?), the bug might scuttle down out of reach. You would put a textbook over the drain and hope the little creep would move on to haunt someone else.

My point is, whatever you do, these millipedes are going to scurry all over your room at night, and you might, now that you know better, quit chasing them down the drain and find out if they have any secrets worth hearing.

3. American poetry: person, place, thing, or way?

I have been teaching poetry (the craft, the literature) for a decade now, and it often turns out that students want to know what poetry *is*. Not what it is building down there, or who has the most, or which is the greatest, but actually what it consists of. One of the things I think poetry *is*, I say, is a set of strategies. These strategies make art happen in the plastic of language. They deliver ideas that aren't easily articulated in prose. They administer emotional cocktails. They help you hurt your reader in just the way he or she is looking for. They complicate our systems of representation so that when we speak our speech is as fucked up as our lived experience deserves.

4. But just in case . . .

If it turns out that I'm wrong, and American poetry is all *gasp-gasp-rattle, the money is in the mattress, don't let Aunt Georgia get her hands on Nana's brooch*, then let me say this: poets have always been grave robbers. We will just dig it right back up, slap some Frankenstein bolts on its skull, and hook it up to the juice.

The legacy of modernism: If we mean *Great*, as in the lone transcendent mind, escaping body and berth, recasting history in its own image, lurching (leching!) through the centuries, marking every muliebral fragment with its initials, contemplating eugenics, lolling in Freudian privilege, then boo! hiss! I certainly hope we're betraying it.

If we're talking about the great legacy of modernist freakout—horror in the face of global warfare, the dissolution of the marriage between progress and improvement, the emperor's-new-clothes revelation that the self is an ever-shifting and incoherent cuckoo bird, masculine hysteria, cyborgery, civil rights, and all the seeds of the postmodern condition—then I cheerily submit that we're keeping that legacy alive and kicking. Even those of us who embrace the spectacle and our slip-sliding within it struggle against the instability. Those may be my favorite American poets. Those who long for and reject stability simultaneously. Those who are attracted to and repulsed by those institutions that confirm, and those that deconstruct "the real."

I'm pretty thrilled by poetry in the present moment, but here are two things I cannot abide:

1. Churlishness.

2. The seventy percent men: thirty percent women publishing ratio, and the equally/even more disturbing ratios for race, class, disability, LGBTQ, and any other marked category we can imagine.

One of my favorite things about poetry is that I cannot predict where the most exciting reads will come from. Sometimes it is a one-off from a student taking my class on a whim, other times it is something brilliant *finally* getting translated. Hiromi Ito's *Killing Kanoko* where had you been all my life? I would say, though, on the whole, the *most* promising work seems to be coming out of those people who can't sit still. The poets who stay up late and go to their day jobs early, the poets raising manic toddlers, the poets who've got novels in the works, presses of their own, journals, side-businesses, a zillion heartbroken friends to shoulder, partners, gardens, causes, fixations, obsessions, visions of the future which demand tending today, *work, work, it's all work,* Andy Warhol channeled by The Velvet Underground zeitgeist.

Instead of trying to master the field (gak! and yawn):

1. You find poetry you like the same way you find music you like. It's simultaneously intensely personal and surprisingly communal.

2. If you cannot find what you are longing to read, then you have stumbled upon an excellent opportunity! Now you may write what you are longing to read, or start a journal and publish it! Start a press! Publish your friends! Publish yourself!

3. Did someone tell you there were too many presses, too many journals? If you were in a garage band, how would you respond? Very good. Do that.

4. Try. Try very hard not to get dispirited by the grim proclamations and the tales of woe from those who feel poetry's handlers betrayed them. When the future gets here, it will be different than we imagine it, and there is a fine chance, I have a dark angel Polyanna suspicion that it might actually be good.

Rebecca Seiferle's poetry collections include *The Ripped-Out Seam, The Music We Dance To, Wild Tongue,* and *Bitters.* She is the founding editor of *Drunken Boat.*

It may be that some poets have arrived at a dead end; for one way to be successful as a poet in American culture has been to carve out a niche, a particular "voice" or style that is recognizable as a brand name, and to cultivate that niche for decades. There are perhaps styles of poetry that are at a dead end; I went to an MFA graduate school where Allen Grossman arrived as visiting faculty and announced during his lecture that the work he'd read from the program was "written as if Modernism hadn't happened." There is always a kind of "new" poetry that seems to create a sort of anonymous voice, as if the poems written by its various practitioners could be read as if written by all, a kind of pastiche of vernacular and high diction and appropriation. But that has always been the case; there have always been styles and practitioners who have reached dead ends, and sometimes the dead ends are only obstacles through which something breaks through. Whitman for instance was a hack journalist before whatever happened to him happened and the doors flung open.

What worries me the most about the present moment in poetry is the degree to which it's been taken over by the business of being a poet and subverted by the corrupt language of our culture. The attitudes and jargon of our consumer culture are perfidious, and poetry is not unaffected; hence, the cultivation of a "voice" as if it were a brand name, the isolation of the poetry-ego viewing others' experiences as material for one's sincere posturing, the round of networking and readings and mutual publications not unlike any social network with business connections.

Poetry when it lives takes language back to its roots, makes us consider the oppression that is often embedded in the etymology of the word and its practice upon the tongue; often exacting and difficult, poetry requires an encounter which puts the poet's intention and ego and persona as much at risk as anything else.

This is precisely why poetry matters; though it may go unnoticed as a whisper in the noise, poetry has the power to speak and be heard at some other level where American conversation seldom reaches. The fear of feeling is how Rukeyser explained America's reluctance for poetry. But that capacity for feeling, for the word to reach another from another, to feel one's self flowering open in the presence of a space that allows and accepts feeling and empowers the un-named experience, is precisely why it is impossible to say poetry is at a dead end.

My advice for young poets trying to find their way in the current poetry scene is to resist, resist fashion, resist careerism, resist cultivating poetry as if it were a brand; cling to the "uselessness" of poetry, its marginality, its difficulty, its complex joys, because poetry's use is a human use, to create a space for expe-rience and feeling that might otherwise never find an open door, an open room, an open border, or arms open to the rain.

Elaine Equi is the author of *Ripple Effect: New & Selected Poems* (Coffee House Press), a finalist for the Griffin Prize.

This seems like a funny question to ask when probably more people than ever before write poetry. As someone who teaches in two Creative Writing MFA programs (at The New School and City College of New York), I can attest to its popularity. Clearly something about poetry is still quite compelling.

From the 1970s on, a lot of experimental writing questioned the convention of having a central speaker (one voice talking) in a poem. Simplicity, sincerity, and singularity were out. Multiplicity was in. As a result, all kinds of collages and mash-ups became popular. It was interesting for a while, but ultimately (at least for me) not very satisfying. For some reason, no one seems to think their thoughts are their own anymore—or they just don't want to own up to them.

One challenge for contemporary poets would be to discover a new kind of voice that could encompass or easily move between both the private and the public sphere, the individual and the group mind. I'm not sure exactly how it could be done. Whitman is one example, but I'm thinking of something less transcendent.

Also, because of the influence of technology, people today are very excited by notions of networking and dialogue. So potentially this period could lead to a real renaissance of collaborative writing and cross-genre work. All in all, I'm pretty confident about the resilience and adaptability of American poetry in the twenty-first century. It's movies and TV I'm worried about.

Campbell McGrath is the author of nine full-length collections of poetry, including *Shannon: A Poem of the Lewis and Clark Expedition*, and is the recipient of a MacArthur grant.

If Modernism has left a legacy, a final bequest, at least it proves that the beast is dead at last, and we can lay down our pitchforks, and sleep in peace. Or, we would be able to sleep, except that Modernism's legacy is in fact the ethos of fragmentation that bedevils contemporary American poetry like a nest of vampiric bedbugs. Could we send that legacy back? Or at least have it fumigated before nightfall?

American poetry, on the contrary, is neither dead nor at a dead end. There may not be any great revolutionary movement afoot, but there is much ardent hewing of lumber in the forests of Poetry Land. Many of those trees end up as sawdust, sure, but there's some good carpentry and furniture-making as well—there are plenty of roads through the yellow wood. I'd assert that liveliness reigns in Poetry Land. I attended my very first AWP Convention recently, and was amazed at the energy on display in the vast warehouse full of poetry journals and webzines and other innovative publishers that jammed the convention center in Denver. Of course, much of that publishing takes place online nowadays, but those of us raised on books are just going to have to get used to the virtual transition taking place. When it comes to the economics of online publishing, poets are way ahead of the curve, having not been paid for our writing these last several centuries. To all those prose writers and journalists bemoaning their lost paychecks I say, welcome to Poetry Land, Comrades!

Finally, I'll risk restating the obvious by venturing that there's only one useful piece of advice for any young writer: write. Pay no attention to the state of American poetry, the death of the book, the legacy of Modernism, the bedbugs in your cheap apartment: ignore as much as you possibly can get away with and write. Resist the careerist temptations of PoBiz. Stay home and write a poem. There is no particular place to get to in Poetry Land, anyway. The point of the journey is the journey itself, the process of writing poetry, which hopefully you consider enriching and indispensable. If not, spare yourself a lot of grief. Go back to that fork in the yellow woods, watch out for ATVs driven by gun-toting meth heads, and pick another road.

Carmen Giménez Smith is the author of *Odalisque in Pieces, Bring Down the Little Birds,* and *Trees Outside the Academy.* She is the publisher of Noemi Press and the editor of *Puerto del Sol.*

For some reason modernism figures as a cultural lynchpin, and, depending on who you talk to, is the dawn of a new day or the arrival of the antichrist. But if you pull modernism out of the intense scrutinizing lens of history and scholarship, you see earnest artists shaped by context—the houses they're living in, the foods they're eating, the amount of light they had in a day. The historical moment these artists lived in is bookended by two of the greatest wars this world has ever seen. It's very likely that some of these poets aspired to greatness, had lofty aesthetic aspirations (to change the course of history, for example), but they were constrained by their conditions, unaware that conditions existed. We live today in a microcosmic world in which a gesture is recorded, analyzed, and historicized in a matter of days. Nothing is allowed to fester or bloom before it gets vanquished by the masses. We simply don't know that in a hundred years Billy Collins and Flarf won't be considered under the same terms.

Chad Prevost is the author of a collection of short prose, *A Walking Cliche Coins a Phrase*, and a poetry book, *Snapshots of the Perishing World*. He founded C&R Press with Ryan G. Van Cleave.

If we're looking at the growth of MFA programs, or how incredibly serious many people are about the "po biz," or how many thousands of small magazines are publishing poetry, then I suppose not.

America is a really big place, and there is an awful lot going on for poetry these days even in these difficult economic days. So, while we may have recently seen the terminations or cutbacks of some major poetry programs, such as the Dodge Poetry Festival in New Jersey, there are still people out there "following their bliss," and working hard at their craft and working hard at getting the word out there.

I don't know that all that much has really changed in America related to poetry in many decades. There were never really that many readers in the first place. Few to none—other than perhaps Billy Collins and Maya Angelou—are making (or have ever made) a living from sales of their books peppered in with a few readings. Everyone needs a day job. And this is also widely true for musicians, painters, and fiction writers, although their audiences are generally larger than for those who primarily write poetry.

Just think of the amount of attention with which T.S. Eliot and Wallace Stevens and W.B. Yeats get taught in academic contemporary poetry settings. Were Modernists betraying Romantics? Victorians? If I define Modernism as High Modernism, and distinguish it between the mid-twentieth-century definitions of the "cooked and the raw," or between "elitism" as opposed to "populism," then, perhaps yes, American poetry today has "betrayed" the highly educated, elite impulses of the High Modernists (in many ways, the fundamental pull of all "postmodern" thought is a reaction against the modern). But it's also a way of reading history. There has been an ongoing tension between the impulses of the highly refined and the layman's voice throughout the past several centuries of poetry. But if we're being more inclusive in our definition of Modernism, and basically taking in every major figure from the general era, like, say, Frost, or Marianne Moore, or William Carlos Williams and mixing them up with Auden, and a dash of "objectivists" David Jones, Basil Bunting, David Ignatow, and Louis Zukofsky, sprinkled in with "new historicists" Robert Penn Warren, Theodore Roethke, Elizabeth Bishop, as well as others like Richard Wilbur, Randall Jarrell, and John Berryman, then it's difficult to say who's betrayed whom and how.

What worries me is that we are becoming an increasingly less literate culture. It's about our education system, sure (I see it every day in the composition writing of my freshmen), and that there are so many distractions and other forms of media and entertainment. The countless other distractions are not so much a good or a bad thing. It just is. It disappoints me that there are so few places where one can read authentically critical reviews of poetry. Perhaps it's because the literary world is so small that we all feel like we need to write and publish little more than affirmations? Reviews have been reduced to marketing devices, which are basically either laudatory or descriptive. When I have come across the places that do authentic critical evaluations, both my intellect and my inspiration—the head and the heart—are stimulated. Gerry LaFemina and Dennis Hinrichsen nobly ventured into this domain with *Review Revue*, but it has only limped along the last few years, and had a very small subscription base in spite of how excellently it was put together. *Contemporary Poetry Review* online was publishing some fine stuff for a while.

Wayne Miller is the author of *The City, Our City, The Book of Props,* and *Only the Senses Sleep*. He edits *Pleiades: A Journal of New Writing*.

At any point in poetic history, one finds hand-wringing about the state of the art. These days, Tony Hoagland is concerned about the "skittery poem of our moment," Ron Silliman complains about the pervasiveness of the "School of Quietude," Franz Wright worries about the chatty sociability—the lack of focused quietness—found in the "MFA generations," Dorothea Lasky is bothered by too many poets writing "projects," John Barr complains about the lack of safari-going among today's poets, Ange Mlinko decries the legacy of Lowell's "tyranny of psychological verismo," Michael Theune frets that "middle-ground poets" don't have clear evaluative criteria, Anis Shivani worries about the "mechanical" nature of our poetry, and numerous poets have asserted in response to Ashbery that "the emperor has no clothes."

I say "these days" because we could also be in some other historical moment when, say, William Carlos Williams is complaining about T. S. Eliot's "conforming to the excellencies of classroom English," or M. L. Rosenthal is bothered by the "shameful" nature of Confessional poetry, or France is scandalized by Baudelaire's "incomprehensible" and "putrid" work, or Ezra Pound is attacking the influence of Walt Whitman, whose *Leaves of Grass* "is impossible to read [...] without swearing at the author almost continuously," or the Acmeist poets are decrying the lack of craft in the work of the Russian Symbolists, or Dunstan Thompson is complaining of "the smugness, the sterility, the death-in-life which disgrace the literary journals of America" in that poetic nadir of 1940—the same year Auden published *Another Time*, E. E. Cummings published *50 Poems*, Kenneth Fearing published his *Collected Poems*, and Kenneth Rexroth and Robert Hayden made their literary debuts.

The legacy of Modernism is alive and well—though, frankly, it's so broad as to be pretty much unbetrayable. After all, the Language poets and Philip Levine both envision their work as building on William Carlos Williams. Robert Bly thought "Deep Image" poetry was a return to true Imagism, yet Ron Silliman lumps Bly and James Wright with many of the "academic" and Confessional poets Bly excoriated in *The Fifties*.

All poetry lives somewhere on a spectrum between Classicism and Romanticism. If high Modernists such as Eliot, Pound, and Moore tilt toward the Classical side, and the Confessional and Beat poets inhabit the Romantic, then we've more or less marked the boundaries of the Modernist legacy. But that gives us quite an aesthetic and intellectual range to play around in.

Many American poets frustrated by 1980s post-Confessionalism—which leaned largely on personal narrative and ad misericordiam for its effects—have turned back to the high Modernists, Objectivists, and New York School to balance out a poetic that was, in the end, too baldly Romantic. Sometimes this turn has produced new work that's mechanical, emotionally flat, or unparsable—but that doesn't negate the fact that this rebalancing is mostly a good move, one that's hardly a betrayal of Modernism. Indeed, it's a backward turn similar to Eliot's when he exalted the Metaphysical poets over the Victorians and Romantics.

There are a number of things that worry me about poetry today:

1. Ignorance of poetic—and literary—history. I was once on a panel with a well-published poet who said she had little use for the Modernists because her work was about collage. It's just this sort of foreshortened view that leaves poets thinking either (a) that all poetry must be built around reportage of personal epiphany, or (b) that Dadaism is new.

2. I worry when I hear writers say they're not interested in reading—or writing—"great poems." I still subscribe to the quaint idea that poets write in the hope of producing a few great works—works that, assuming society doesn't collapse in one of its many possible conflagrations, people will continue to read a hundred years from now because those works will continue to be valuable. Call me an optimist.

3. I fear that America's most visible and influential critical apparatuses have yet to notice how much American poetry has decentralized. Our next important poet could just as easily be living in Cleveland, Houston, Chico, Tucson, or Lincoln as (s)he could in New York or Boston. How long will it take the *New York Times Book Review* to pay attention?

4. Childishness. I understand that poems written in the whiny idiom of a fifteen-year-old about Barbies and action figures and teenagery romance are, at their best, intended to approach seriousness through the back door. But, come on: we're adults. We don't need to apologize for having adult concerns. And if we haven't stumbled upon them by the time we're in our mid to late twenties, we should go looking for them. Call me stodgy.

Claudia Keelan is the author of many books of poetry including *Refinery, The Secularist, Utopic,* and *Missing Her,* and a book of translations called *Truth of My Songs: Poems of the Trobairitz.* She edits the journal *Interim* and teaches at the University of Nevada.

I live on a street that is a dead end, and it used to worry me, until I opened my eyes and saw the sign out my window for the symbol it is. In time, there is no such thing as a dead end, and if there are tendencies in our current poetries that betray the legacies of modernism, they are those which refer back to symbolism and the fetishizing of the poem-object. Mostly, though, I am not at all worried about our present moment in poetry. The work I see as editor of *Interim*, and the work written by my most gifted and generous students, is an extension, a provisioning, of the arm of modernism which legitimizes the genuineness of experiment, dares sincerity, and provides those who come after with examples of poets whose lives and work spoke truth to power.

The modern exists in every century and to find it I reach back to the pre-Socratic writers, to the Troubadours, to Blake, to Whitman, to Pound, to Williams, to Stein, and continue forward to Oppen, Niedecker, and to the many poets writing now who continue and redirect the liberality of modernism into our present concerns. The human form divine, the Body Electric, and the compositional methods that urge our poetries to the new(est) available reality—these are the preoccupations of my modernism. Brenda Hillman's *Practical Water* has recently been my company, as has Ronaldo Wilson's *Poems of the Black Object*, and the poems of Adam Strauss, a former student of mine who has not yet published a book. Any work that makes a sound serving the whole, that's where we must go—it's not worth anybody's time to read anything that doesn't serve so, and yet, one must read widely, read almost everything, in order to recognize the sound of which I speak. "The whole" isn't a synonym for "the human," though the human is part of it. If one can eke out a place in the plenty that is the poem without need for any other ownership except for the pleasure of being there, one doesn't need to worry or make sense.

Shelley Puhak's first collection, *Stalin in Aruba*, won the Towson University Prize for Literature, while her second collection, *Guinevere in Baltimore*, was selected by Charles Simic for the Anthony Hecht Prize.

Dead end? No. But we're not yet at a crossroad either. Perhaps we're still circling around a great suburban roundabout, deciding which exit to take. A precise answer about the legacy of modernism would depend upon whether we agree what that legacy entails. Precision and "direct treatment of the "thing"? The musical phrase vs. the metronome? Dislocation and fragmentation? Order and unity? Something else entirely? I feel more comfortable saying we aren't following in the modernists' footsteps by working on our own legacy, in the sense that my generation hasn't yet produced forms or styles that radically break with our predecessors, that we have no clear manifesto, that we aren't sure what we are currently trying to correct or perfect or rebel against.

If I'm in a pessimistic mood, there's lots to worry about, but it's already been better articulated by critics like Dana Gioia, Marjorie Perloff, and Hank Lazer. I agree with their collective concern that many American poets are churning out technically-polished poetry that is safe and superficial, that misses the opportunity to shape the world, not just chronicle a reaction to it. Mostly, though, I worry about my own increasing dependence on technology: I'm hunched over my laptop, addicted to Facebook and my iPhone, and connected 24/7 via email. I worry about the lack of uninterrupted time and space for both poets and readers.

I'm thinking specifically of recent articles like "Is Google Making Us Stupid?" (by Nicholas Carr in the *Atlantic*, July/August 2008) and the emerging neuroscience behind the debate these have spurred—evidence that surfing the web strengthens new neural pathways and weakens others, that our brains, ever malleable, are evolving. If the science holds up, what are the implications for our collective abilities to concentrate and contemplate, to read closely and critically? I wonder how these changes in perception, positive and negative, will fundamentally alter the way we compose and read poetry.

If the poetry scene has become more fragmented, it has also become more decentralized and democratic. The great thing is that, as a reader, I have more access than ever before, to a wide range of voices and styles. The work that excites me the most is not coming out of Knopf or Norton or the academic powerhouses; it is coming from small independent presses like Graywolf and Soft Skull and Marsh Hawk, just to name a few.

Symposium: Short Stories vs. Novels— Which is the More Rewarding Form and Why?

Whether already well-known or just getting established, these are some of our best short story practitioners—and in many cases dual practitioners of the novel as well, which makes for interesting comparisons of the two art forms. Writers of different styles, from domestic realism to gritty postmodernism, share a diversity of opinions.

The questions I asked each of the writers were these: What do you like about writing short stories, and if you also write novels, how do you compare the writing? What are some of your most important models for short story writing, and have these influences changed over time? Does the short story make fewer demands on a writer than does a novel? Who are some of the most important short story writers today? Do you read short stories from other languages, and, if so, do you notice a difference from the American aesthetic? How do you chart your own development as a short story writer? What can be done to strengthen the art of the short story in America?

Don Lee is the author of a story collection, *Yellow*, as well as the novels *Country of Origin*, *Wrack and Ruin*, and *The Collective*. He teaches in the graduate creative writing program at Temple University.

Writing novels—especially the first drafts of them—is a mindfuck. It's a long, long haul, a marathon, a slog that's interspersed with (very) occasional bursts of inspiration. Mostly, though, it's misery. You're just trying to hang on, just trying to grind it out to the finish, and the entire way, you worry. You worry that you'll get lost, way off-track, and have to start over. You worry that you won't have the stamina and you'll bonk, and everything will fizzle into incoherence. You worry the pages you've amassed are shit. You worry you will have to quit—who were you kidding, you never had the balls for this. You worry that it will never be over. Yet you make yourself push on, desperately clutching to the hope that all this work will lead somewhere.

Writing stories, in comparison, is a leisurely delight, a walk in the park. Even if you don't know where you're going with a story, you know the project will be finite, there will be an end. Not to say writing a story is easy (and, in fact, it requires more intense concentration, more care and artistry), but it feels entirely doable, manageable, because it will not take two or three or four years of your life. It will take, instead, months, or perhaps, if one's lucky, weeks. You have time. You can spend three hours on a single sentence, trying to get it just right, perfect—a wonderful luxury, the kind of dawdling that's usually impossible with a novel.

Another difference. In a story, you feel freer to experiment—with language, with structure. Moreover, you're welcome to indulge in some very unsavory subjects and characters. The latter is more of a risk with novels. It might alienate readers, and the general attitude among American publishers is to discourage the impulse—a shame, I feel. Frank O'Connor, in his seminal volume *The Lonely Voice*, said, "There is in the short story at its most characteristic something we do not often find in the novel—an intense awareness of human loneliness." The short story, he went on, is especially suited for portraying "submerged population groups," "outlawed figures wandering about the fringes of society." In other words, the short story should be especially suited for the population of the U.S., a nation of misfits and loners.

So then, particularly in this quick-hit, attention-deficit era, it's curious that the short story is not more popular, and that publishers are not more supportive of story collections. I blame high schools, teaching the same old stodgy standbys, so most of the public only associates the form with boredom. Yet when new collections do come out, there is interest. They get attention, reviews, even sales. There are readers out there who appreciate them, and the level of craft and invention in stories by young writers has, if anything, only gotten better. Also enlivening is the number of small presses that have cropped up recently, fearlessly investing in the form. Alas, by dint of their size, their reach is limited. It's the mainstream publishers that need to catch up—a familiar and perennial complaint. I say to them, to anyone else who is not yet a convert: Do not be afraid to submerge yourself. Get unsavory. Get dirty.

Richard Burgin's twenty books include the novels *Ghost Quartet* **and** *Rivers Last Longer,* **and his recent story collections include** *Shadow Traffic, The Conference on Beautiful Moments,* **and** *The Identity Club: New and Selected Stories and Songs.* **He has edited the award-winning journal** *Boulevard* **for more than thirty years.**

Isaac Bashevis Singer (with whom I had the good fortune to do a book of conversations) told me that he considered the short story a superior literary form to the novel because in it the writer can more clearly achieve literary perfection. He felt the novel was a story, only a longer, more complicated one, and thus, because of its length, the writer generally makes more aesthetic mistakes, than in a story. Jorge Luis Borges, with whom I also did a book of interviews, felt the same way. I, myself, wouldn't say the story form is superior to the novel, but it is certainly its equal. One also gets the satisfaction of completion more often with the short story. (I've published seven story collections but only two novels.) Finally, it's also true that I've had more success as a short story writer than as a novelist, which also influenced to a degree what I focused on.

There are as many different kinds of great stories as there are great novels so even my short list of the most important stories is pretty diverse and would certainly have to include, in no particular order, Chekhov's "The Lady with the Dog," Poe's "The Fall of the House of Usher," Dostoevsky's "The Dream of a Ridiculous Man," Tolstoy's "Master and Man," Kafka's "In the Penal Colony," Joyce's "The Dead," Faulkner's "That Evening Sun," Hemingway's "A Clean, Well-Lighted Place," Crane's "The Blue Hotel," Carver's "Cathedral," Beckett's "The Expelled," Singer's "The Bus," O'Connor's "A Good Man Is Hard to Find," and Borges's "The Aleph." That's, of course, just a skeletal list. If this were a symposium on the long story or novella (my favorite form) I'd certainly include "The Death of Ivan Ilyich," "Notes from Underground," "The Metamorphosis," and Thomas Bernhard's neglected masterpiece, "Concrete." Over time, I think this list would continue to expand, not contract. The old classics, I find, are more relevant than ever.

The short story is just as demanding a form as the novel, though the demands are different. A novelist has to develop a sustained story with (generally speaking) more characters and complications than in a short story. A short story writer, on the other hand, has the challenge of thinking and writing in a very condensed way (not as easy as it may sound, especially in our era of endless verbiage, as if the whole world were a talk show). It is equally difficult to be excellent at either. In my case, I began as a novelist and found (and still find) it difficult to write in the condensed form of short stories. Even at present, my stories sometimes still have a novelistic feel to them—that is, my characters often evolve, a longer period of time goes by than is typical in a story, and I sometimes tell my short stories from multiple points of view, all techniques associated with the novel.

The names William Trevor and Alice Munro leap to mind as the most important models, as do Joyce Carol Oates and Stephen Dixon, but rather than list the usual suspects, I'd like to mention some of our most important story writers who are underpublicized whether because of youth or simply because of literary injustice. I'm thinking of Paul Ruffin, Eric Miles Williamson, Marc Watkins, George Williams, Nathan Leslie, Anis Shivani, Colin Fleming, Elizabeth Orndorff, Glenn Blake, Giles Harvey, and Jean McGarry, among many others.

Most of my favorite writers don't live in the United States and don't write in English. Generally speaking, European and Latin American writers are more at ease with ideas like Dostoevsky, Borges, Sartre, etc. than their American counterparts, and at the same time have more extravagant metaphorical imaginations like Kafka or Borges. Americans tend to concentrate and be very good at rendering raw, direct experience.

I began by writing first-person stories, though my monologues only rarely drew directly from my personal experience. For example, my monologists were sometimes women. I then began experimenting with multiple narrators and multiple points of view. Now, I feel that any technique a novelist uses can be equally valid for a short story writer, and I let the story "choose" its method of narration as naturally and spontaneously as possible.

The United States probably has more literary magazines and small presses than the rest of the world combined, so we can't really fault the little magazines and presses. The only thing that could really make a difference is if "major" media outlets and publishing companies opened their doors (through shame perhaps? I doubt it) to publishing more short stories. The short story, like jazz and basketball, is one of the few things Americans, or some of them, anyway, have mastered. We ought to be celebrating that more often.

Dawn Raffel is the author of a novel, *Carrying the Body*, and the story collections *Further Adventures in the Restless Universe* and *In the Year of Long Division*.

I have written two collections of stories and one novel. What I love about stories is that you can begin with an image, a feeling, or a phrase and see where it leads you. It's a journey without a map. With a novel, although you will encounter surprises along the way, you need a clearer sense of structure and story from the outset.

I read stories voraciously, often with admiration, but I try to avoid models.

The story makes different demands on the writer. The story is a sprint in which every step and every breath and every flicker of an eyelash matters; a novel is a marathon, a test of stamina, faith, and will.

Some of the most important short story writers today are the most important short story writers of yesterday. Flannery O'Connor, Katherine Mansfield, Grace Paley, and Tillie Olsen (yeah, I'm picking just the women right now) are gone but their work isn't. If I get started on "today's writers" I'm going to inadvertently omit people, but I'm going to cite Christine Schutt, Gary Lutz, Ben Marcus, Antonya Nelson, Stuart Dybek, Amy Hempel, Jim Shepard, Diane Williams, Terese Svoboda, Brian Evenson, Michael Kimball, and Yannick Murphy—writers whose work could be mistaken for no one else's. I am excited about a generation of newer writers, including Justin Taylor, Robert Lopez, Laura van den Berg, Kim Chinquee; there's a whole army of brave souls coming down the pike who are going to break all the rules and our hearts along with them.

Short stories originally written in other languages feel less workshopped than a lot of what's published by mainstream American publishers.

I'd like to take a machete to the notion that writing stories is practice for "the real thing"—the novel. A story is not a miniature novel. They're two different forms.

Belle Boggs's debut story collection, *Mattaponi Queen*, won the Bakeless Prize and was shortlisted for the Frank O'Connor Short Story Award.

Novel writers and aspiring novel writers often talk about Anne Lamott's concept of "shitty first drafts" as a staple of their process, but I don't like working that way—it doesn't inspire me to keep going. I like working slowly and deliberately, getting the voice right as I go, getting the lines right, and so a short story is just a more practical thing for me to work on sometimes. I like the feeling of completion and fullness that comes from drafting a short story, seeing a story to its end in a couple of weeks or months.

I started writing the stories in *Mattaponi Queen* the summer after my first year of public school teaching in Brooklyn. Every day I'd go to the Rose Reading Room in the New York Public Library and write for the whole day. I was highly conscious of the limited time I had that summer, and every hour in that beautiful, quiet room felt like a luxury. I wanted to write something from beginning to end, and I knew that if I started a novel I would only have the beginning once school started in August.

I drafted a few of the stories in the collection that summer, wrote hardly anything during the school year while teaching first grade, then returned to the collection the next summer. I should say that I love working on a novel, the way the characters live in your head, and I think that's why so many of the characters in my stories appear in other stories. Skinny, for example, appears briefly in "Good News for a Hard Time," one of the first stories I wrote, but I wasn't done with him, so I had to give him two more stories.

I don't think you can compare the two in that way, but short stories are wonderful for writers and readers who have time constraints. There's something very enduring and mentally portable about a great short story—although as a reader I love to disappear into a novel, I reread my favorite short stories more often than my favorite novels, and this makes me feel closer to them.

Some short story writers who are important to me as a reader are Lydia Davis, Joy Williams, William Trevor, Joan Silber, Ha Jin, Sherman Alexie, Annie Proulx, Maile Meloy, Mary Yukari Waters, and Bonnie Jo Campbell. I like subtlety, authority, beauty, humor, and surprise, and these writers all deliver. But my absolute favorite, and a writer I think is universally important, is Edward P. Jones. Take a story like "Old Boys, Old Girls" from *All Aunt Hagar's Children*. At the end of twenty-six pages, something you could read in an evening, you have the richness of a novel, the profundity of a great collection of poems, the sense of transport and new understanding of a powerful work of nonfiction. Jones's characters don't feel like characters, they feel like people, and that's really difficult to achieve.

I think writing short stories has helped me understand more about my characters and what I want for them. The new project I'm working on is a novel about a group of musicians who live in Virginia in the late 1920s. It has a lot of characters who are all living in the same environment, so it feels a little like working on my collection, like working on stories. An issue for me with this book is restraining myself from exploring every character. I'm just interested in all of them, so I find myself writing everyone's stories, at least in my head, and then choosing what to leave out.

I'm pretty impressed by the oral storytelling that's being promoted by places like The Moth and The Monti, and by how much people love to hear those true, strange, sometimes funny, sometimes devastating stories. Oral storytelling is where it starts for me, as a Southerner—it's not where my books start but it's how I learned, at a very young age, to love stories. So as a teacher that's where I'm going to begin this fall, with oral storytelling and true stories, with voice.

Greg Taylor, a man from North Carolina who was convicted of a murder he didn't commit, then exonerated and released from prison seventeen years later, is going to tell his story at The Monti this September, and I can tell you the crowd will be spellbound. People who've experienced things like that should be telling stories, we should be listening, and the telling will make its way into art in one way or another.

Lori Ostlund's story collection *The Bigness of the World* received the Flannery O'Connor Award, the California Book Award for First Fiction, and the Edmund White Debut Fiction Award. Her novel *After the Parade* was recently released.

There is still a tendency in publishing to want a novel; thus, we have a lot of writers who are being asked to prove themselves by writing and publishing stories in journals, and once they have done this, they are expected to write a novel. This assumes that someone who writes a story can write a novel, and that simply isn't always the case: some people are fundamentally novelists and others are short story writers, and yes, some can do both quite well. Novels are a more forgiving form in some ways. A short story should be perfectly crafted at the word and sentence level.

I'm working on a novel now, and I find myself wanting to micromanage every sentence in the same way; as a result, I end up unable to go forward. Also, I find it very difficult to create a bigger narrative arc. In the beginning, I wrote each chapter as though it were a short story—with a climax and resolution—which created an emotional roller coaster for the reader. I like the particular demands that stories make and feel more comfortable meeting them. I would never use my preference to argue that short stories make fewer demands on the writer. In fact, given the reality that many readers find short stories more daunting to read, it may be that they make more demands for the writer also.

Over the years, I have loved Carver and Munro as well as numerous other short story writers. I love Paul Bowles, and I do remember feeling that he was asserting a bit too much influence on me at one point. My writing has been heavily influenced by travel, other art forms, and the stories that people tell me, often in odd situations.

I did not do an MFA, and for me this has been a good route. I grew up in a town of four hundred people, so when I left, I needed to be out in the world, learning about it. Academia was comfortable for me, but it too can be provincial. I wrote off and on during my twenties. My first story appeared in print when I was in my early thirties, and something about seeing it in print, which allowed me to view it more objectively, made me realize that I had not reached the level that I wanted to be at yet, so I stopped sending work out for several years and focused on writing and reading. This was the most important step in my development. Once a person starts publishing, it's very easy to take that outside acknowledgment as an indication that one is good enough, but I was a much different writer at thirty than at forty, and I'm glad I gave myself that time.

One of the books that had a tremendous impact on me was Adam Haslett's *You Are Not a Stranger Here*. I like writers who are not overly prolific. Within the United States, the aesthetic varies widely and is often defined by culture or region. When my book came out, reviewers noted the darkness of the stories, including the dark humor, attributing it to my Minnesota roots. One characteristic of contemporary American writing that is a reflection of our current culture is the push for writers to create characters that readers can "connect" to—that is someone that the reader likes or could be friends with (which is similar to the criteria that gets applied to politicians also).

I would like to see less attention paid to trying to predict new trends or jump on the bandwagon of existing trends. I also worry about the emphasis placed on discovering the next young writer. When a writer is discovered early in his career and praised too much, the writer might stop working at improving his craft with the same degree of commitment.

There has been a movement toward flash fiction and short shorts, which are not my favorite forms. Short shorts can be created more quickly and will often find a journal home more easily because they demand less space. I notice a trend among writers to produce work more quickly, which suggests that less time is being spent on craft. I see more published work with sentences that seem rushed or designed for no other purpose than to carry the plot, which is unfortunate because the pleasure in reading happens first at the sentence level. Writing is increasingly viewed as something transitory, in part because of technology, so it follows that not as much attention will be paid to crafting it. This is a self-fulfilling cycle: a story that is less carefully crafted will, in turn, not be remembered for long. I think that we need to slow down and do what is best for our work rather than rush to meet the demands of the publishing world.

Gina Ochsner is the author of the story collection *The Necessary Grace to Fall*, which won the Flannery O'Connor Award, another story collection called *People I Wanted to Be*, which won the Oregon Award, and the novel *The Russian Dreambook of Color and Flight.*

Writing short stories and writing a novel I discovered was and was not at all alike. In both forms a strong sense of narrative propels the larger story forward. But because I had been writing stories first and only, I had become accustomed to thinking in small, tight modular "boxes," in which scenes were like boxes or rooms in a small house and expository or summarized segments acted like little corridors or hallways linking rooms together. It was very difficult for me to force my gaze up and out and think of story pitched across a larger canvas. "Think long, think big," my writer friends encouraged. "You first," I'd counter. A novel, I also discovered, demanded from me a looser grip on the reigns, and I found this very unsettling. What would these people do and what would they say if I allowed them this kind of freedom of movement and thought? Well, it's the best question I could have been asking, I think, because the novel *is* a more expansive form, insisting upon larger, longer dramatic movements, and, happily, the form itself is capacious and roomy enough to accommodate.

Having said that, I still think the short story as a form is such fun. It's a completely malleable form, open for endless experimentation. When I'm reading a terrific short story, say something by Millhauser or Munro or maybe Gombrowicz, I'll think to myself: Wow! This writer is having fun. And wow—look how mischievously he or she has infused and amplified energy in the piece via voice, or language, or narratorial design.

I'm actively hunting up anything written by someone who is not like me: a North American who writes only in English. I'm afflicted with a niggling sense that the only way I'll learn how to craft distinctive architectures and voices is to study work outside the traditional canon of "Anglo" writing.

Anne Sanow's story collection *Triple Time* won the Drue Heinz Literature Prize and the PEN New England/L. L. Winship Award for fiction.

I've noticed, in writing my novel, that I still think in terms of story arcs. In a good short story there is always more than one arc comprising the narrative; in the novel, there are simply more of them. I'm making associations and links in similar ways, but on a broader canvas. And when I take a break from the novel to push around at a story-in-progress, I notice that I'm writing longer.

I came of reading age during the glib and minimalist 1980s, and I was hooked by the way writers like Amy Hempel, Mary Robison, Raymond Carver, and Susan Minot could pare back language to some point of pungency. It wasn't the right approach for me; I often sounded coy or pretentious, and sometimes probably just dim. I wasn't inhabiting my stories. What I did learn was how to listen to prose: the pared-back language meant that I absorbed every beat, every syllable, every way one sentence was part of carving paragraphs and sections. To this day, I carry around a mental list of single words, perfect sentences, and punctuation choices made by writers I admire—seemingly small choices that electrify an entire story.

After floundering unsuccessfully in the minimalist style, I became exasperated with my inability to convey as much story as I wanted to and by the distance I felt from what I was writing. I started paying closer attention to writers who went long: Alice Munro, Andrea Barrett, John Cheever, Katherine Anne Porter. My own stories expanded. I was trying to figure out how to craft short stories that could be novelistic in scope. And then three writers made an enormous difference to the way I was working: Mary Swan (whose wonderful, sixty-plus-page story "The Deep" won the O. Henry award in 2001); Marshall Klimasewiski (his long stories are collected in *Tyrants*, published in 2008); and Carol Azadeh, an Irish writer whose one book, *The Marriage at Antibes* (1999), is five very long stories that are brilliant. These were writers who were not only going long but incorporating history; experimenting with language and form within longer works, as I'd usually seen in shorter fiction; stinting neither on smarts nor emotion.

It's true that with a short story one need not keep as many elements in play, and it can be easier to see towards the end. But if you want a lot of texture, a fuller fictional world, and a longer reach, then there's a great deal for the writer to mull over. And here's where the lessons I take from minimalism come in: in a short story, even a long one, you've still got to practice an economy of a kind that you don't in a novel. So that makes demands on the writer, certainly.

Alice Munro and William Trevor are as inspiring as ever. I hope that Lorrie Moore returns to the form—we need the brutally sharp wit she had on display in *Birds of America*. Anthony Doerr. Yiyun Li. Chris Adrian, whose use of the fantastic (angels, allegory) in his short stories is something I'd normally eschew but can't in his case. Salvatore Scibona's stories (especially the one in *A Public Space*, "The Woman Who Lived in the House") have a way of being both formal and experimental that is thrilling. Bonnie Jo Campbell's *American Salvage* left me with my jaw dropped. The stories in Dylan Landis's linked collection

Normal People Don't Live Like This connect in ways I didn't anticipate. Another first collection I loved recently is Lori Ostlund's *The Bigness of the World.* Lydia Peelle and Paul Yoon are writing beautiful, serious, lyrical stories And three people who don't yet have books out but publish regularly in literary magazines: Charles McLeod, David Schuman, and Sophie McManus.

In writing my collection, which was set in Saudi Arabia, I wanted to be informed about literary traditions in Arabic and read what I could find in translation. These stories recalled for me stories I'd read translated from Chinese or Russian: a good deal of symbolism and parable, standing in for what cannot be written for fear of persecution. Then again, there's a world of difference between reading short fiction published by Saudi authors, and, say, Lebanese authors, where the culture is a more open one. Now there's more Arabic writing available in translation, and writers are taking more risks by working in a realist mode. I've also read stories in the original German by Peter Stamm, Judith Hermann, and Ingo Schulze, most of which I find fairly blunt and stark. We need more global story writers available in translation; smaller publishers are taking on this task.

Part of the strength of the short story in America is diversity: our perspectives have broadened with writing that is more global in scope, and it's reshaping the very idea of what an "American" story is or should be. It's getting more and more difficult to throw around terms like "realist" or "experimental" or "transgressive" with any precision.

Art and commerce do need to at least be kissing cousins. We could not survive without the independent publishers, indie bookstores, literary bloggers and reviewers, and revolutionary literary magazines like *One Story* which support and promote the short story. And writers who open up conversations such as this, Anis: thank you.

Marisa Silver's books include the novels *No Direction Home, The God of War,* and *Mary Coin,* and the story collections *Babe in Paradise* and *Alone With You.*

Ah, the plight of the short story. It's alive! It's dead! It's alive again! It's like the old grandmother who is pronounced a goner on her pallet only to sit up and yell at her family one more time. Honestly, has the short story ever died? I don't think so. Does it have a smaller audience of readers than the novel? Sure. But why do we compare them? The comparison is as useless as comparing watercolor paintings to oils, or a concerto to a symphony. A short story is not a "mini-novel." It's a discrete form that requires the writer to work in different ways than if he or she were writing a novel and requires of the reader a different sort of attention and a different set of expectations.

What I like about reading short stories is their thrilling sleight of hand. When a story works, an entire universe of characters and emotion and thematic resonance explodes in the space of twenty or so pages. What I like about writing short stories is the attention to compression required in order to pull this off, and how the negative space of the story—what I choose not to write—becomes as much a part of the story as the words that I put on the page. Writing a story requires me to distill issues like character and structure and time to their very essence. I have to figure out, in very few moves, how a character can become so alive to a reader that he or she vibrates on the page. I have to select the two or three bits of action and behavior that are ripe with association so that the reader not only grasps the situation of the characters in the particular moment in time, but that they also grasp how the particular moment of the story reaches across time and beyond character to illuminate something larger about the problem of being alive. I think about what is suggested but not said, how a past can be conjured in a sentence rather than a chapter, how a line of dialogue or a gesture can contain a multitude of meaning. And I have to do all of this without trying to do any of it, because if I try too hard to load up a story with meaning, it will fall flat, burdened with the weight of too much intention.

To me, stories have the possibility of exploring states of being rather than large arcs of multilayered action. When I write a story, I feel like I am taking a particular moment in space and time in the life of a character, bringing a big hammer down and smashing that moment to bits and then looking at every single shard that I can collect off the floor. I don't try to fit them together correctly. I try to find out how the new jagged edges might bump up against one another, how they might scratch, how the unlikely juxtaposition of pieces might allow me to see more deeply and accurately what that person is experiencing at the moment of the story's telling. Most important for me, I want to come to the end of a story with the beginning of understanding. I want the story to end and I want my mind to vault beyond its plastic limits into the unanswered mysteries the story reveals.

The short story pantheon is filled with many Gods—Joyce, Munro, Chekhov, Deborah Eisenberg, Peter Taylor—the list is long and varied and inspiring. But the stories I turn to again and again are those of William Trevor. In his hands, the smallest story, the most provincial of characters, the tiniest emotional gestures are deftly orchestrated so that entire worlds of emotional truths are exposed. And he does that most cunningly—he presents stories that seem to be about one thing but that, by their end, are about something different, something deeper, something more disturbingly truthful about human nature. His stories widen the gap between what we think we know and what is yet to be understood, a gap that embodies the whole reason to read in the first place.

Aamer Hussein's books include the story collections *This Other Salt, Turquoise*, and *Insomnia*, and the novella *Another Gulmohar Tree*.

I was recently writing a short piece after spending the better part of three years on longer fictions; it took me only a couple of days to write two drafts to a word limit of twenty-five hundred. I felt I could breathe. With longer works I'm aware of the architecture of the whole book and don't feel able to work on each chapter as if it were a self-contained piece; I roam from room to room instead of focusing on the decor and construction of one. Novels also allow for slack and clumsy passages. What I like best about short fiction is the paradoxical flexibility the form allows; the overlap between other genres such as memoir, poem, travelogue, or even, at times, ironic lit crit.

I began under the influence of the Chinese writer Lu Xun, the Japanese Jun'ichirō Tanizaki, the Norwegian Cora Sandel, and Marguerite Yourcenar. I was rereading Lu Xun in a new translation recently and still admired him hugely, but feel I'm some distance away from him now, especially from his polemical side, though his influence lingers in my frequent use of the tricks and tropes of memoir or pseudo-memoir. I feel I'm now largely uninfluenced as everything I learned has been though a process of osmosis. I love Ryūnosuke Akutagawa, Isak Dinesen, Eudora Welty, Tennessee Williams, Muhammad Basheer, Qurratulain Hyder, Intizar Hussain, Saiichi Maruya; oh, the list goes on.

I think the short story makes many demands on the reader. A good short story requires that you read every word carefully and usually that you reread the story. A collection of stories has, at its best, more range and depth than a novel. As a practitioner I still feel that short fiction comes most easily to me, though I've found some of my fictions becoming longer, hence the recent shift of direction. However, both my recent books were originally short stories.

Recently, I've enjoyed Lydia Davis's work more than that of any other short story writer in English. I think Lorrie Moore is important as a dedicated practitioner. In England, the genre is in decline, probably because publishers won't take a risk, and many writers are dismissive of the form.

I read stories in the original Urdu, Hindi, Italian, French, and Spanish, and in translation from Arabic and other languages. I don't feel that North

America has a monopoly on prowess in the form though it has definitely and consistently produced wonderful practitioners; my own influences have been largely non-Anglo-Saxon, so judging the formal differences is very tricky for me, but perhaps other traditions rely much less on the fleeting moment. In the nineteenth century, short fiction by, say, Kleist in German, Pushkin in Russian, or Villiers de L'Isle-Adam in French told an entire story, and I think that in Spanish, Italian, and the Romance languages this tradition persisted through much of the twentieth century. Reading mid- to late-twentieth-century Urdu fiction was a minor revelation; the ways in which realism and fable, tradition and postmodernism are juxtaposed.

I think my work has become simpler as the years have gone by. And I'm perhaps more able to cast memory in the mold of storytelling. In style and themes, I became, in midstream, less cosmopolitan in my approach and made connections with my Urdu literary heritage. Formally, the approach of a certain heaviness signals that I'm straying away from the sparser terrain of the story into the woods of the novella or novel and I follow my instinct if that seems to be the case. But I'll always go back to my original dedication to the translucent brevity of my chosen form.

In America, read your own masters, from Welty to Tennessee Williams, Donald Barthelme to Katherine Anne Porter, Richard Yates to Jean Stafford: there's a wonderful range. Then move to the Latin Americans—Borges, Julio Cortázar—and the Europeans. About England, I'll remain silent: I think the form is popular only in Creative Writing classes.

Larry Fondation is the author of the novels *Angry Nights* and *Fish, Soap and Bonds*, and the story collections *Common Criminals*, *Unintended Consequences*, and *Martyrs and Holymen*, all set in inner-city Los Angeles. His three most recent books are collaborations with visual artist Kate Ruth.

My fictional project is largely one of compression. I am very influenced by the visual arts, which are generally less "conservative" than literature, perhaps still the most conservative of all the art forms. I try to find what Henri Cartier-Bresson called, in photography, "the decisive moment," the idea being to evoke a broader, more complete story at a given moment in time. I mostly leave backstory to inference. So, the short story is a "natural" form for me.

Contemporary life is fragmented and discontinuous, and our stories follow suit—punctuated by a choppy, irregular rhythm. The short story is the ideal form of fiction for our times, though we have not recognized that notion yet.

Without an apologia for short attention spans, the short form in fiction mirrors the pop song, even of the "indie" variety, in and out in five minutes or less.

Despite the endurance vs. stamina debate, I think the short form is the more demanding. It would be better to have ten years than two to reconcile quantum mechanics and relativity. Or an hour to pick up the cutest boy or girl at the bar rather than five minutes . . . well, perhaps.

Larger-than-life influences and models include Chekhov, of course, and Stephen Crane, Beckett, Borges, Paul Bowles, Nelson Algren, Denis Johnson. Today there are some excellent writers working in the short form: Dennis Cooper, Barry Graham, and Harold Jaffe, who has invented a kind of new form with his "docufictions."

I read a fair amount of European literature and have begun reading contemporary work from Iraq and Korea. The conservatism of both form and content that haunts American storytellers is not so present in other countries. Writers from other nations do not seem so obsessed with "parlor fiction" or so fearful of "public fiction." I am not advocating didactic fiction, but rather, relevant fiction—fiction of the world as opposed to that of the living room. I'm not alone in not wanting to read more stories about the troubled lives of over-privileged people—particularly in these times.

In terms of form, if contemporary American literature were jazz, we wouldn't have gotten as far as bebop. Sure in the 1960s and 1970s we had Donald Barthelme, Ronald Sukenick and all. And while I do not write in a style terribly similar to theirs, I do see myself as a kind of "experimental realist," or "post-realist," who is greatly indebted to them. By contrast, a reading of today's journals would largely suggest that these folks had never written at all.

Though most contemporary American writers would no doubt define themselves as political progressives, we do live in a reactionary, "Tea Party" moment in time, and our literature reflects that—albeit perhaps unconsciously.

Among recent European writers, many seem to hybridize and blend elements of the short story in their longer work, taking advantage of the strengths of the short form—its precision, its sharper edges. The late Max Frisch and Dubravka Ugrešić come to mind as writers who build novels from briefer fragments. Irvine Welsh often does the same. (Among Americans, Mary Robison is an exemplar of such a method). And, recent Nobel laureates Herta Müller and J. M. G. Le Clézio are both excellent and cutting-edge short story writers, as well as accomplished novelists.

All six writers I just mentioned delve deeply into the public as well as private realms of fiction. Their work all has a social and political relevance in the best sense; it illuminates the times we live in. For example, Robison's *One D.O.A., One On The Way* is the best book we have on post-Katrina New Orleans. Form and content do indeed go hand in hand.

As for the current state of the story, there is a glimmer of hope: small presses continue to do a good job, and even some of the larger houses, notably the Harper Perennial imprint, are fueling a possible short story resurgence.[2] And music's DIY ethos could serve as a model. Artists in every creative medium always complain—typically justifiably—about their "industry." But, as writers, the best thing we can do to strengthen the art form is to strengthen our writing, to rise to the challenge of chronicling our complex and troubled era.

Alyson Hagy is the author of the story collections *Madonna on Her Back, Hardware River, Graveyard of the Atlantic*, and *Ghosts of Wyoming*, and three novels, *Keeneland, Snow, Ashes*, and *Boleto*. She teaches at the University of Wyoming.

I think of writing short stories as being comparable to composing chamber music or Old World ballads. Stories may be short, but the best ones are so full, so capable of expressing the best of language, character, and plot, that the experience of reading them feels complete. Stories are songs, and they can move and engage readers even if they don't have the symphonic heft of a novel. It's not the length of stories that fascinates me; it's the density. You can try to put as much in one story as the structure can possibly bear. Or you can try to pare the form down and hone only the tiniest flicker of a narrative, something that is very close to a poem. Working in the short form allows me to play. The longer I work as a writer, the more important it becomes for me to play, to discover, to be surprised.

---

2. In the spring of 2010 I had a phone conversation with then Harper Perennial editor Calvert Morgan on precisely this subject, and would have liked to have included the interview in this book had it not been for limitations of space. It can be found online at: http://www.huffington-post.com/anis-shivani/interview-with-calvert-mo_b_595704.html. Here's some of what Morgan had to say about Harper Perennial's emphasis on short story collections: "We're in a desperate, possibly foolish love affair with the short story. Last year we had a campaign called Summer of the Short Story, and we published six new collections along with a series of new collections of classic shorts we had in our backlist. The blog I mentioned, http://www.fiftytwostories.com, is a way of bringing attention to both our own writers and new writers who submit their work to us. I think some of the young writers I've heard from through the blog will go on to have really great careers. One reason to be interested in the short story is that it's a form many talented authors explore early on—and I always hope they continue to write stories throughout their careers because it's such a rich and challenging form. And I think there's a lot of excitement about the form in the cultural dialogue these days—people debating form versus style, processing influences and exploring new shapes—and I find that exciting."

I've published three novels. Novels require sheer stamina. And, for me, that means hours and days and weeks of uninterrupted time. I'm at the point in my life where I'm willing to try almost anything in prose. But I will spend months trying to talk myself out of starting a new novel because the time investment will be so significant. I almost never try to talk myself out of beginning a new story. There's too much to learn there—even in the failing.

I wasn't able to imagine myself as a writer until I was introduced to the stories of Flannery O'Connor, Eudora Welty, and Katherine Anne Porter. That first seduction was based on sound. The characters in those stories sounded like the people I'd grown up with. I wanted to join that writers' choir. Only later did I begin to think about things like structure, and my models shifted. Ann Beattie. Charles Baxter. George Garrett. Raymond Carver. Alice Munro. I devoured contemporary short fiction in the 1980s and 1990s. The next phase involved going back and looking at earlier American sources—Sherwood Anderson, Ernest Hemingway, Mark Twain, Jean Toomer, Edith Wharton. I also began to read poetry more regularly, and that has probably had as deep an effect on my work as anything else. Anne Carson. W.S. Merwin. Those writers have truly bent the rim to the wheel when it comes to language and form. Recent influences? I read widely and instinctively. Lydia Davis followed by Haruki Murakami followed by Edward P. Jones. How do great writers shape narratives that haunt and surprise us? I mull that question over every day.

I work intensely on both forms. But it can take me all day (or more than that) just to reread what I've drafted in a novel. I can reread a story, tinker and placate and revise, then reread it again all in a single workday. That can be very gratifying, particularly if there's a day job to attend to.

The difference in aesthetic between American short stories and those in other languages fascinates me. Chekhov had his aesthetic. Borges had his. Cortázar. Luisa Valenzuela. Yukio Mishima. Gabriel García Márquez. The impulse to organize culture with stories seems universal. But the aesthetics vary greatly. I am not as well read as I should be. I know very little about the stories of Africa or Central Asia, for instance. I plan to keep plunging in.

I try to press myself forward on two fronts. Is the story urgent enough to take up a reader's time and energy? Is it a tale worth telling? And am I taking some kind of risk—aesthetically or thematically or dramatically? I don't want to tell the same bits over and over. I want to lurch and change as America lurches and changes around me.

The American story seems as healthy to me right now as it's been in my lifetime. Collections may not attract large advances in New York, but the independent publishing scene has never been livelier or more freewheeling. The advances in electronic media seem to have bolstered communities of writers and readers who like short fiction. It's easier to find smart, compelling reviews of short fiction. It's easier to buy the books you want. The blog scene is hopping. I've also had folks stop me on the street to talk about how much they like to listen to story podcasts while they commute or work out or whatever. And it seems possible to me that the increased use of Kindles and iPads and those kinds of devices will link more and more readers to short stories. So I think it's an exciting time. There is no American "house style." There is a lot of innovative work out there. There is also a wealth of good, old-fashioned storytelling. What's more, I'd argue that people may indeed be reading less, but they crave narrative as never before. America is an anxious, shifting, bawling, brawling nation right now. There's plenty of good, important work for writers to do.

Ben Greenman is the author of several books of fiction including *Correspondences, Superbad/Superworse, A Circle is a Balloon and Compass Both: Stories About Human Love,* and *Celebrity Chekhov.*

A short story can fertilize, grow, and peck its way out of the egg (aka my head) in a few days or a week. A novel gestates for a year, minimum (although there are cases when it comes quicker, most people would tell you that's premature). It's not easier, really, but it can feel more creatively compressed and intense: a one-night stand rather than a long courtship. And now that I'm all tangled in metaphors of sex and birth, I'll add a more external consideration: short stories affect readers differently than novels. This is true for individual works, but it's especially true when stories are collected. For me, that's the best part of the process, deciding which stories to place next to each other. It's like collecting a bunch of songs and making an album: you can have variety, change of context, chicanes and chicanery.

More of my models have come aboard over time, though the earliest ones haven't disappeared. There are genre writers, crime fiction especially, who are geniuses at setting up and then discharging a mystery in a short space. There's Borges, of course, who did things with the form that other people couldn't imagine. There's Chekhov, who I'm cowriting a book with. There's Poe and Melville and Mary Robison and Mary Gaitskill and Julian Barnes and Haruki Murakami and so many others. I don't read as many contemporary short stories as I'd like, either by living writers or recently deceased ones, partly because I like to go back in time to mostly forgotten early twentieth-century writers like Grace

Sartwell Mason or L. Parry Truscott. It's amazing to see what they were writing about, and how it is or isn't recognizable when read against current short fiction.

Does a home make fewer demands on an architect than an office building? Does a small canvas make fewer demands on a painter than a large one? It makes different demands: more economy, more responsibility for interpretation offloaded to the reader.

I'm not sure there's a single American aesthetic. Is there? The country is so huge that it's like many countries all rolled into one. There are places (and consequently, groups of writers) where nature is a player. There are places (and writers) that are preoccupied with form. I think that probably these groupings, if really studied, would yield some kind of aesthetic taxonomy: how irony is used or misused, whether realism is a precise blade or a cudgel, if funny names should be permissible.

I have tried to take chances whenever possible. Early on, that meant more experimentation, and stories like "What 100 People, Real and Fake, Believe About Dolores," which is a kind of crime scene related by, as the title indicates, one hundred people, both real and fake. As my career has gone on, taking chances meant more emotional openness and honesty: more incorporation of real-world problems, maybe a little more formality. I have always been somewhat skeptical of plot in short stories, though I'm envious when I see it done well.

As for strengthening the art of the short story, this is an impossibly complex question, because it's tied to so many other things, and so many of those other things are slippery: to attention spans, to technology, to alternate sources of narrative and character, to distribution networks, to processes of critical vetting, to the economics of writing fiction. I think that one of the things we can do is to be brave about how we get short stories in front of people, and flexible about what exactly a short story is. Journals like *Electric Literature* are helping to lead the way out of the cul-de-sac, though who knows what kind of traffic they'll encounter.

Symposium: What is Distinctive About Arab-American Writing Today?

I asked some of the brightest stars in the Arab-American literary firmament what they thought stood out about Arab-American writing today. Every new strain of literature in this country undergoes familiar periods of marginalization and ghettoization (perhaps self-reinforced), before breaking into the mainstream. At some point, readers and critics stop thinking of the hyphenated literature from an exoticizing perspective, and instead treat the writing on its own merits. To what extent has this process already happened with Arab-American writing, or is still happening? Who are the writers making the most original contributions, in fiction, poetry, and other genres? Are there circumstances unique to them, in finding acceptance and legitimacy for their work, or is their path to recognition perhaps even aided—in a strange twist of irony—by the negative attention recently focused on the Middle East?

Sinan Antoon is an Iraqi-American poet, novelist, filmmaker, and translator, the author of two novels, including *I'jaam: An Iraqi Rhapsody*, and two poetry collections.

To self-orientalize or not? A few months after 9/11 I was invited to a conference at Tufts University on "Arab-American Writing Post-9/11." I submitted an abstract for a paper entitled "A Rabid American Writing Today." The organizers corrected the title thinking "Rabid" was a typo! To write and try to publish (let alone work, and live) in the U.S. while Arab or Muslim after 9/11, means choosing one of two paths. The first entails self-orientalization and on it one proceeds to perform one's circumscribed role as the entertaining, but always safe and grateful, Arab in the grand political and cultural circus. There are always openings and many Arab Americans are more than willing to play the role (you know the names).

There might be an improvised moment here or there and some indignation, but the narrative is, more or less, fixed for the Uncle Toms. The other path is that of standing outside the coliseum and distracting and disturbing the citizen-spectators on their way in or out. Screaming, at times, if necessary, to point to other directions. Whispering, at others, into their ears stories about barbarians both in Rome itself and abroad. It's not easy being a barbarian in Rome. The Romans rarely listen, but the barbarian has to keep it real.

Randa Jarrar was born in Chicago to an Egyptian-Greek mother and a Palestinian father, and is the author of the novel *A Map of Home*.

Arab-American literature today is distinctive for its diversity of voices, topics, genres, and purposes. We've got straight, queer, young, old, Christian, Muslim, and atheist Arab Americans writing about living in New York and Lebanon and everywhere in between. Want great poetry? There's still plenty of it (see under Hayan Charara, Khaled Mattawa, Suheir Hammad). Want plays? We've got 'em (see under Leila Buck). Want some nonfiction? Yup, it's here (see Moustafa Bayoumi and Alia Malek). Novels? They're getting better and better (I'm looking at you, Rabih Alameddine). Our past achievements were sometimes marred by self-exoticization: a focus on food ("Look, grape leaves! Baklava! Don't hate us—you love our food!") and the *Arabian Nights* ("Don't pay attention to these bearded weirdos—check out this hot chick in our past who told stories and saved one thousand and one virgins! Including herself! She rocks!"). I'm hoping we'll continue our path away from these themes; away from convincing people that we're "universal"—last I checked, Arab Americans are human beings and don't need to prove this fact to anyone.

The son of Palestinian refugees, Fady Joudah is the internationally recognized translator of Mahmoud Darwish and Ghassan Zaqtan, and the author of *The Light in the Attic, Alight*, and *Textu*. He has won the Yale Series of Younger Poets and the Griffin Poetry prizes.

Distinction is in the eyes of the beholder. The predominant vision is of those who see Arab-American poetry through the scope of the ethnic or the political, the topical and the thematic. And they will decide which poetry is Arabic enough or American enough, based on conscious or unconscious absorption of the cultural, and the othering of the culture. Of course there is little new in this trend. In the past such questions and categorizations were asked of and imposed on women, African Americans, etc. The presumption is that they were at a yet undifferentiated state (compared to American poetry or society at large) and now would be observed and encouraged to explore their multi-potentiality. Subcategories eventually reach a state where distinction is an academic imagination, an uninhibited mitosis of identities that consumes those who have entered it, and can only repeat itself when there's a new kid in town. And this newcomer must address the question of what it means to belong, a hegemonic matter more often than not. Arab-American poetry is and has been aesthetically as varied as any other American poetry, but that discussion still takes a back seat (in a minibus) today.

Marian Haddad is the author of *Somewhere Between Mexico and a River Called Home* **and** *Wildflower. Stone.* **She is of Syrian heritage, was born and raised in El Paso, Texas, and lives in San Antonio, Texas.**

There is nothing literary that characterizes the vast array of Arab-American writing appearing today, and this should not surprise anyone, since the Arab world itself is too vast and diverse to be reduced to clearly definable characteristics, and the culture of immigrants from the region is even further dispersed by the experience of migration. The only thing that really ties Arab Americans as a community today—and also distinguishes them from other hyphenated American communities—is a widespread dissident attitude regarding American foreign policy. Whereas other hyphenated American communities may form a semblance of a community identity through a shared experience of historical oppression inside the U.S. or a shared commitment to human rights, for Americans of Arab descent it is more often the experience of living in a "home" that has increasingly, over the past sixty years, constructed the "homeland" as its global other. The literary production of Americans of Arab descent is increasingly staggeringly diverse, with everything from long poems, novels, stories, memoirs, spoken word, and theater, to most recently film. But it is the marks left on our consciousness by this tension between the grand foreign policy narrative of "home" and the injustices visited upon "homeland" that connect these exciting new voices in American letters.

Philip Metres is the author of numerous books including *Behind the Lines: War Resistance Poetry on the American Homefront Since 1941*, co-translator of *Catalogue of Comedic Novelties: Selected Poems of Lev Rubinstein*, and co-editor of *Come Together: Imagine Peace*.

Though Arab-American writers have been around for over a century, the rise in readerly interest in Arab-American writing since 9/11 has dovetailed with what may be a literary renaissance. In every genre, Arab-American writers of real distinction have emerged to embody and represent the rich and complex textures of Arab-American and Arab life. With vibrant organizations like RAWI (Radius of Arab American Writers), and journals devoted to Arab-American arts and letters (*Mizna, Al-Jadid*), we have formed quasi-familial bonds and carried on critical and creative conversations in ways that echo the Harlem Renaissance, the Black Arts, and other key moments in ethnic American writing. Among the poets, Naomi Shihab Nye, Lawrence Joseph, Samuel Hazo, Fady Joudah, Khaled Mattawa, Hayan Charara, Deema Shehabi, and many others have inspired, instigated, and cajoled my own writing. We are building bridges between Arab literary and cultural traditions and American ones (through translation and original poetry), and addressing the depredations of U.S. foreign policy in the Middle East. Arab-American writers will continue to play a key role in braking (or least confronting) the imperial temperament, simply by constantly reminding us that the machinations of power are neither distant nor without consequence.

Hayan Charara's poetry collections include *The Alchemist's Diary* and *The Sadness of Others*, and he has edited *Inclined to Speak: An Anthology of Contemporary Arab American Poetry*. The son of Lebanese immigrants, Charara grew up in Detroit, and teaches at the University of Houston.

What most shapes my writing has a lot less to do with ethnicity than it does with language, structure, or story, or with imagining the world from another perspective. I spend more time than I care to admit figuring out rhetorical strategies, or looking at syntax, or trying out a dozen different ways to break a line or end a scene. On any given day, I think more about the placement of a period at the end of a sentence than I do my health or my marriage. Whether that's good or bad is up for grabs. But that's in part what it means to be a poet and writer, and every Arab poet and writer I know has these concerns. They are also each utterly unique, not only in how they write but also in what they write about and in the ways in which they make sense of the world. We aren't all the same.

Our work isn't all the same. In fact, about the only thing we have in common is our insistence on constantly challenging any singular notion of what it means to be Arab or Arab American. We're doing our best to help people out of the identity trap—to stop looking at us, and to look at our words.

Laila Halaby was born in Beirut to a Jordanian father and an American mother, and grew up in Arizona. She is the author of the PEN/Beyond Margins Award-winning novel *West of the Jordan* and another novel called *Once in a Promised Land*. She is also a poet and author of children's stories based on Palestinian folklore.

Arab-American literature has always bridged east and west and it does so now without losing its momentum or the power of its art by explaining itself or by talking too much about tabbouleh and other superficial cultural expectations. It has developed the confidence to be American—and this is important—to be American without having to apologize or explain itself; it has developed the confidence to be. Arab-American literature has stepped out of the margins and joined the ranks of the other Others that make up this country's literary body with a wide array of voices (some accented, some not) that tell classy stories and poems (especially poems) and write plays and nonfiction and sing (amazing) songs that reflect both the diversity of the Arab world (ethnically, religiously, politically, sexually) and the colorful immigrant threads that are such an integral part of the story. In short, Arab-American literature has stepped up to take its place in American literature as a large, powerful, lovely part of the whole body—an organ or blood rather than an unnecessary appendage.

Deema Shehabi is a widely published Kuwaiti-born poet of Palestinian heritage, and the vice president of the Radius of Arab American Writers (RAWI).

Any critical reader knows that Arab-American writing cannot be viewed through a monolithic lens. It is no secret that members of my generation categorically reject being placed into compartments. Our reasons for doing so are twofold: a desire to enter the mainstream canon in order to make our narratives part of a bigger "national" story and a desire for our work to stand alone under a discerning literary-aesthetics banner rather than on exclusionary constructs. Our themes are diverse, complex, irreducible, and wide. Our individual narratives and discourses culled from direct experience do, however, carry their particular preoccupations: a certain preoccupation with family, a serious social engagement with the politics of our time, a certain love/hate relationship with the literary canon that simultaneously compels us to reject and seek to (re-)enter it with vigor, an inheritance/remaking of the traditional lexicon of our ancestors as it has evolved through the generations, and a certain faithfulness to—and distaste for—memory and actual events. Ultimately, I believe that what is distinctive about Arab-American writing is the ambition of its scope, the humanism of its subject matter, and the potential it carries for formulating through language a hybrid, unclassifiable identity.

Nathalie Handal is a poet and playwright born in Haiti to Palestinian parents. Her books include *The Republics, Poet in Andalucía,* and *Love and Strange Horses.* She is the editor of *The Poetry of Arab Women* and co-editor of *Language for a New Century: Contemporary Poetry from the Middle East, Asia, and Beyond.*

The only real distinction is that these writers are originally Arab, and the United States is at war in the region. And of course, there is theme. When these writers' works are Arab-related what sets them apart is that they are writing from within that culture. I should point out that although Arab-American literature started with Kahlil Gibran, there is only a small number of recognized Arab-American writers. However, there is a growing number of writers from this community and it's promising. I will add that of the established authors such as Naomi Shihab Nye, Khaled Mattawa, and Diana Abu-Jaber, their experiences and influences are varied and their works are vastly different aesthetically, stylistically, and thematically. Most writers don't want to be classified and tend to agree that art transcends borders. Unfortunately, if you happen to be Arab, Middle Eastern, or Muslim, people often fixate on where you're from rather than the story or poem. The distinction lies not in the literature produced as much as in the responsibility that is often thrust on the author—one where he or she must explain or defend a region and its diverse people and cultures.

Plastic Realism:
The Rise of a New Style in American Fiction

The American novel has recently come to embody a striking reaction against not only modernism's skepticism with respect to epistemology (how we know) but also postmodernism's concern with ontology (what we are), in effect transcribing a desperate thrust toward narrative stability, taking on both epistemological and ontological worries but diluting and domesticating them.

Plastic realism, so vigorously marketed by the American publishing industry, is a formalistic structure that steals from earlier realism (and also at times from modernism and postmodernism) to construct something quite hollow of meaning. The 1980s and 1990s were decades of transition between the postmodernist innovation of the 1960s and 1970s and plastic realism. Raymond Carver's 1980s minimalism in particular initiated a revolt against postmodernism until plastic realism at last discovered the conditions to recreate nineteenth-century moralistic strictures in a hollow vein.

Plastic realism demolishes the unbearability of modernism and postmodernism so that linearity, closure, and determinacy are the new ideals, a turn reflected, for example, in the withering of digressive interior monologue in favor of "objectively" observed characters. Plastic realism is often couched in the panoramic style of George Eliot's *Middlemarch* (the quintessential Victorian realist novel) and takes its technical cues from Henry James and Gustave Flaubert, concealing its post-human content which is such a contrast to the liberal humanism of earlier forms of realism.

Realism, or mimesis, has been defined in the modern era by Erich Auerbach, Georg Lukács, Ian Watt, Michael McKeon, Wayne Booth, Theodor Adorno, Roland Barthes, and Mikhail Bakhtin. They would all agree on realism's typical features: objectivity, causality, plausibility, psychology; ordinary/typical/average/ nonheroical characters; and empirical/observational settings. The representational emphasis aims for "truth." Plastic realism seems to share in these characteristics, but actually flattens them all.

Bakhtin's concept of *heteroglossia*—or multiplicity of voices—is one of the defining markers of the modern novel, open-endedly contesting the determinacies of history, class, and psychology. But in plastic realism, instead of a multiplicity of classes (or voices) inhabiting the same narrative space, the narrator seeks to impose social stability. This is all the more true of recent American novels which make a show of wanting to flirt with indeterminacy.

The old bourgeois freedoms are gone, yet plastic realism pretends that they flourish. Bourgeois novelists like Balzac and Dickens were appreciated by Marxists critics like Lukács for honestly representing class conditions, and for being more revolutionary than the self-declared revolutionaries of Russian social realism, but plastic realism takes us in the opposite direction. Compared with Dickens's grotesque realism, Dostoevsky's fantastic realism, and Thackeray's satirical realism, plastic realism only plays a shell game with the conventions of realism and fails to illuminate social conditions.

Plastic realism is the dominant American aesthetic in fiction now. This is not to say that there aren't countervailing tendencies, but plastic realism is clearly in the ascendance. If we look at older writers who came to prominence before the rise of plastic realism, we notice that their work is also bending in that direction. This is true of Don DeLillo's *Cosmopolis* (2003), Cormac McCarthy's *The Road* (2006), and Richard Ford's *The Lay of the Land* (2006), which are by no means full-fledged works of plastic realism but share some of its features. The aesthetic is so pervasive that everyone has been affected.

The minimalism of the 1980s provided much of the philosophical ballast. But plastic realism has some unique features, enough so that it constitutes a definable movement with hierarchies, leaders and followers, support systems, and the desire to vanquish opposing aesthetics (see, for example, the essays of Jonathan Franzen and Zadie Smith).

The rise of plastic realism has a lot to do with the three interrelated and reinforcing factors of the hegemony of writing programs, the decline of literary readership, and the corporatization of publishing. For years many wondered what came after postmodernism, which was declared dead as early as the 1970s. It took a while for the dust to settle, but we now have our answer. Plastic realism it is.

I can think of many alternative labels that capture the movement. Mechanical realism, synthetic realism, textual realism, structured realism, formalized realism, anti-realism, pop realism, postmodern realism, fantastic realism, paranoid realism, sentimental realism, regressive realism, pedantic realism, institutional realism, artificial realism, market realism, and commodified realism all seem to capture aspects of the new movement, and any of these terms would do.

I prefer *plastic realism* because it suggests a certain flexibility in dealing with material reality, subject to arbitrarily shifting tastes. Plasticity also implies inauthenticity, and this occurs when the author is trying not to be an intermediary between reality and the reader, but only between competing texts. Impressionability, continuous deformation and regeneration, self-modeling, and superficiality are conveyed by the term, and I think these are all important aspects of the new ideal in American fiction writing.

Let us note what plastic realism is not. It is not an update of traditional realism—such as what John Updike practiced in the 1960s and later—to account for contemporary conditions. It is not postmodernism in a new guise. Postmodernism's self-doubt and irony are missing in the new formulation. It is not a retreat to the spirit of classical—i.e., nineteenth-century—realism either, though plastic realism borrows the template of classical realism to lend itself a veneer of authority. It is not an advancement over the minimalist fiction that served as bridge between postmodernism and plastic realism, though it does borrow some of its philosophical outlook. It is not a progressive movement, though its avatars do believe that they are moving forward, presenting pragmatic individualist solutions to insurmountable external challenges.

The following characteristics represent to me the most distinctive features of plastic realism:

1. Plastic realism is a mediated conversation between existing canonical texts, not a recreation of a reality uniquely perceived by the author, and has as its ultimate objective the desire to please institutional patrons rather than readers.

Institutions always, of course, intervene between writers and readers. There is no such thing as pure communication between the two, since different varieties of patrons always intervene. There is no writing without patronage. Yet the degree to which the marketplace figures in the equation is all-important. What if the market were cut out altogether? What if the author no longer had to worry about the marketplace as he or she wrote? What if worrying about the marketplace became, in fact, a detriment to professional advancement?

I would argue that we have actually come to this pass, and that the tendency will strengthen over time, as the hegemony of writing programs becomes complete, and older writers—Don DeLillo, Richard Ford, Thomas Pynchon,

Cormac McCarthy, Richard Russo, etc.—whom one doesn't think of as being the pure products of the academy cease their productivity. Younger writers of literary fiction originate almost entirely in the writing programs, which happens to be their ultimate audience as well. What is selling a few more books for a small percentage of the royalties compared to winning awards like the Guggenheim or receiving tenured teaching positions? The decision is a no-brainer.

But what if the writer could satisfy both constituencies? What if it were possible to write great works of fiction and be institutionally rewarded for it at the same time? I would say that there is a flaw in this argument, because what satisfies the academy is conformity to certain patterns. As time goes by, the patterns that win institutional recognition become more sharply defined, with limitations ascribed for each genre of literary fiction. The primary consumer of the work of fiction is the hypothetical award committee, and the primary screen for the book to get to that point is the editor of the publishing company. Their interests must not collide, their sensibilities must not be in conflict, there must be no daylight between them, or friction ensues. The process of editing (much of the function having been outsourced to agents these days) amounts these days to ending possibilities for friction. The marketplace is theoretically infinite; academic committees are preemptively finite.

Writers like Junot Diaz and Jhumpa Lahiri, masters of plastic realism, embody the process working at its most efficient, at every stage of management. Product branding, market rationale, niche placement, and consumer targeting are all in place. Both these writers address their works to previously unresolved issues in existing canonical works. They write additions to syllabuses, where they fit comfortably with, say, Amy Tan, Maxine Hong Kingston, Sandra Cisneros, and Julia Alvarez, works that exist not just in memory but in practice, at the curricular level. This results in a remarkable similarity of characters, events, speech, and settings until, over time, a monolith emerges that becomes acceptable as *writing*, and everything else that doesn't fit the pattern is not deemed writing.

The increasing precision of the canonical code in each of the genres of literary fiction is one of the major keys to plastic realism. Eventually the needs of readers become irrelevant to the equation. As the canonical standard inflates in importance, the writer suffers great diminishment as he or she is evaluated not according to the qualities of the work but according to its conformity to the living canon.

Another way of saying it is that plastic realism *addresses only the conditions of its own making.* The representational circuit is broken, and while all of realism's rhetorical strategies are adopted to bolster institutional and marketing support, the work addresses only how its creator responds to canonical inputs, picking and choosing as the mood strikes him, the sliver of choice his only claim to free agency.

2. Plastic realism often takes cues from nineteenth-century Victorian realism for moral authority, which constitutes an innovation of a kind, though an unwelcome one from the point of view of literary history.

When we think of Victorian realism we think of a panoramic view of society, where different social classes are assimilated in narratives propagating a generally progressive vision of history. Yes, there are those who are obtuse and unyielding, cruel and unfeeling, but history moves forward and conflict is dissolved toward greater harmony. The Victorian novel was perhaps the most powerful antidote to classical tragedy ever known. From the chaos of the industrial revolution emerged the minute articulation of bourgeois life, manners and codes incorporated in the kind of novel that sought to encompass the high and the low. Never before or since has the novelist's moral authority been so great.

Plastic realism aims to have the same kind of authority in the information age. But whereas Victorian realism was implicated in liberal political ideology and was part of the mental apparatus of thinkers of every stripe, plastic realism stands aside from public life, at a distinct remove, as though questioning its own veracity, its own truth-telling ability, its capacity to influence thinking. Plastic realism borrows from the Victorian novel authorial firmness, the desire to be all-encompassing, and the progress of the solitary soul in conflict with social intolerance, but the reader can rest assured that there is going to be no hectoring because the writer's job is not to advocate any particular form of morality.

Only the formal structure of the Victorian realist novel is perceptible then, not the philosophy animating it. Hardy and Dostoevsky took the nineteenth-century novel in the direction of tragedy, but this is not the kind of evolution plastic realism seeks to impart to the realism of Updike and his cohort.

The superficial Victorian template of plastic realism easily coexists with the transparent surfaces of postmodernism, as in Jennifer Egan, Dave Eggers, Michael Chabon, Gary Shteyngart, Jonathan Safran Foer, and so many others. Postmodernism has become reduced to a series of technical operations, minus the moral subversiveness of the 1960s and 1970s. Irony becomes merely a testament to the writer seeking to overcome the metaphysical challenges posed by postmodernism, not succumbing to them. When defamiliarizing techniques are employed, they only end up reinforcing the habits of the self whose every impulse and tendency is completely understood and explained.

Plastic realism allows postmodern irony to become deradicalized, domesticated, and reduced to comfort-giving ploy. At the same time it allows the writer to lay claim to being if not of the avant-garde then at least possessing a cool, inoffensive, nonideological personality that is the best marketing tool publishers and award committees possess in their arsenal to validate their own high self-esteem.

3. Plastic realism rejects romanticism, idealism, and utopia, regardless of whether it appears in maximalist or minimalist guise, and as such goes along very well with the passivist political tendencies of the time.

All fiction need not be utopian, and most of the time it isn't and shouldn't be. But for fiction to always spurn the slightest taint of utopia, always indulge in an ethics of pragmatism and compromise, and to shun the knowledge and efficacy of meta-narratives, that is distressing indeed. The innovation of plastic realism is that fiction is being reduced to the elements of craft, which are often very finely executed but add up to nothing larger. Part of it is workshop training, which results in fiction-by-consensus, writing that doesn't offend anyone. The publishing companies, subsidiaries of major entertainment conglomerates, won't abide utopianism either.

Plastic realism forces fiction writers to become part of the process of dumbing down politics. The political is now personal, all actions have narcissistic rather than collective roots. It is a glorification of a stark individualism, a privileging of the autonomous self, that Dreiser, Faulkner, and Hemingway, not to mention Lewis or Steinbeck or (Richard) Wright, would not have recognized. For the various forms of realism preceding plastic realism, the individual was part of the community not only in the sense that he found his identity within it and had to measure the consequences of actions with respect to it, but also in the sense that the community changed him just as he changed the community. The individual evolved organically with the community. Now the community stands apart from him, is not responsive to his needs as he is not responsive to its needs, and the chasm is unbridgeable. This is a characteristic we see again and again in plastic realism, and it appears in various distorted forms of reality, one variant of which is a wish-fulfilling heaven on earth where bourgeois privilege is unaffected by the neoliberal constrictions of the last thirty years (Alice Sebold, Chad Harbach, Jeffrey Eugenides, Foer, Chabon, and Egan are good examples).

Plastic realism has managed, with this ethic, to dissolve the differences between minimalism and maximalism. As we entered the turn of the century, on the one hand we had the spawn of Raymond Carver, writers like Tobias Wolff, Amy Hempel, and Frederick Barthelme, who refused to give way to emotion and expression, offering a dire interpretation of contemporary America as a land of soulless persons, indifferent to their own fate. On the other hand were the maximalists—exuberant, prolix, profound, even when addressing terrible subjects—like Gaddis and Pynchon and even Updike, trusting the overflow of words to do the job, proceeding by addition rather than subtraction.

What plastic realism does is to operate in either mode—or even switch fluidly between them, even within a particular work—without political charge, tending toward a passivity that has been rare in previous modes of realism. The current rage for memoir, and in poetry the dominance of watered-down confessionalism, reflects the same aesthetic. The subject—the writer's slightly sinister alter ego—resists public meaning, collective inference, totality of explanation. Narrative gets bogged down in the mechanics of narrative, events take on their own logic without circuit-breakers intruding from reality. The strange combination of expressive hyper-individualism—a prime imperative of the workshop ethic—and hyper-passivity is one of the most remarkable features of plastic realism, subsuming a variety of apparently diverse styles.

In essence, the subject is all dressed up with the paraphernalia of realism but has nowhere to go, no field of options upon which to exercise his intellect and will. The subject becomes self-consuming, devours his own lust, a standby entity whose precision can be admired from a distance but not loved up-close.

4. Plastic realism imposes a unilateral authorial voice to artificially mediate social conflict, compared to the free play of polyphonic voices that marks classical realism.

This links in particular to the second point about the pilferage of Victorian realism. The author's voice—or authority—is no different than the authority of other public figures: politicians, scientists, technocrats. In the postwar years, there was a crisis of political legitimacy that reached its peak in the 1960s and 1970s. Then there was a resurgence of moral authority, with both conservatives and liberals seeking to put the genie of disorder back in the bottle under a set of neoliberal prescriptions, and we have had more than three decades of diminishment of democracy as a result, precisely the elites' desired goal in the 1970s.

In a sense, the writer was questioning the veracity of his own voice during the 1950s, 1960s, and 1970s, until it petered out into a squeak and almost approached silence in the 1980s and 1990s. This was not necessarily bad, it was organic with the restriction of democratic input, the expansion of empire (even after Vietnam), and the encroachments of the state and corporations into private life. But the current resurgence of the authorial voice is something remarkable, a characteristic of plastic realism that denies organic continuation with immediately preceding literary history. It goes along with the reification of privilege in social life.

Social conflict in the age of globalization, with a vanishing middle class and a post-industrial economy, is not amenable to the kind of resolution Victorian realism provided. Modernism was an attempt to confront the fragmentation, and so was postmodernism, partly by seeking to outdo the level of fragmentation social life could throw at the individual. But just as the political system seemed to be exhausted in the 1960s as the demands of disenfranchized groups were nominally met, so was fiction exhausted after a certain level of fragmentation.

The great nineteenth-century realist/idealist novel, in the hands of Balzac or Dickens, sought to reconcile competing class values. It may appear at a superficial glance that plastic realism tries to do the same, but in fact the range of social classes represented is severely restricted, and when it does bring in different classes the firm authorial voice drowns them out in an aura of artificial domestic peace.

Characters, in other words, do not have freedom to take things where they will. This feature of plastic realism can be amply demonstrated in the major American novels of the present era. The author takes on an image of authority to hide his deep insecurity, catering to institutions that can pull the rug out from under him at any moment. Perhaps the multicultural novel—or as I call it, *the ecstatic novel of multiculturalism* (credit Zadie Smith with giving birth to it)—has been the most disappointing, untrue development in this regard. Immigrants and minorities are reflected back in the image of white bourgeois norms, and there is as little diversity of outcomes in fiction as there is in political life.

5. Plastic realism is a form of abstraction whose parameters depend on the needs of patron institutions, with displacement, nostalgia, sentimentalism, epiphany, and pseudo-confession—all of which I subsume under the label "pasteurized melancholia"—taking the place of representation of reality.

This point relates to the preceding one in particular. If plastic realism proceeds from the marketing demands of dominant institutions, and if writers are producing apolitical, passivist work, then a further corollary is that melancholia of a certain kind dominates narrative.

All the prominent literary works of the last decade, not limited to fiction, show this characteristic. The form of poetry taught in workshop, and deemed worthy of major award recognition, generally falls in the lyric tradition. What I've been saying about plastic realism in fiction applies with equal force to the situation in poetry. Lyric poetry stands in contrast to avant-garde poetry as a relic borrowing the dress of an earlier romantic tradition, yet pretending to embody the essence of human character today. Lyric poetry is as dead as omniscient, controlling, stabilizing Victorian realism, yet both are in the ascendance with patron institutions. Of the last ten poet laureates every single one has been in the lyric tradition, and the same is true of the last ten Pulitzer winners (with the sole exception of Rae Armantrout). This poetry offers confession that praises the superficiality of the self in a capitalist universe rather than destabilizing it.

Pasteurized melancholia—which often appears to struggle with death (a pervasive theme in American fiction of the last decade), but upon closer reading only at a superficial level, avoiding rather than dealing with the traumatic subject—appears everywhere in American literature today as a form of earnestness. Add this to passivity and one has a very clear summation of the aesthetic.

In fiction, narrative is often displaced to the recent (pre-neoliberal) past or to a slightly altered reality allowing pasteurized melancholia full scope to flourish, as in Jennifer Egan's envisioning of a becalmed New York of the near future in *A Visit to the Goon Squad* (2010) or Chad Harbach's creation of a modern liberal arts campus with a retro 1950s sensibility in *The Art of Fielding* (2011).[1] Nostalgia is pervasive, and it is closely allied with pseudo-epiphany, which describes lyric poetry as well.

None of this has much to do with the present social and economic reality, but everything to do with how institutions of patronage desire society to be reflected in literature, enforcing a kind of ideological hegemony.

6. Plastic realism demands that authors mold themselves into globally available market creatures abstracted from regional and political specificity, and that their biographies always be continuous with their work.

---

1 My essay, "Chad Harbach's *The Art of Fielding*: College Baseball as an Allegory for American National Greatness," published in *Cambridge Quarterly* in March 2014, is a detailed analysis of Harbach's assimilation of neoliberal ideology in the service of empire. Likewise, "Good Muslims Versus Bad Muslims: The Parochial Boundaries of Neoliberal Fictional Discourse," published in the *Antioch Review* in Spring 2013, compares Lahiri's fiction to Mohsin Hamid's, in particular, the latter being an exemplar of greater skepticism toward empire. I also looked at the uses and abuses of "realism" in Jonathan Franzen's *Freedom* in great detail here: http://www.huffington-post.com/anis-shivani/jonathan-franzen-freedom-overrated_b_819103.html.

All of the preceding points contribute to the kind of authorial persona desired by the institutions of patronage. The ideal author acts apolitically (or if he indulges in politics, it should reinforce the inevitability of present trends in political economy) when it comes to the large public issues of the day; admires the canon that immediately precedes him and writers who are employed by universities and produce writing just like his own; disavows interest in radical strategies of narration and character development, as though he were directly continuing Victorian metaphysical certainties, allowing no room for utopian impulses with regard to the business or content of writing; and embodies seamless professional and personal integration, an earnest persona given to a mild form of melancholia as a prerequisite of the artist's existence, disallowing any breach between the sentimental writing and the sentimental writer.

If you do all this, you have the ideal book club author, a la Egan, Diaz, Foer, or Lahiri. The formation of this author-persona, which is directly opposed to our impressions since the beginning of modernity of the author as rebel, outcast, and exile, or at the very least bohemian, is one of the great victories of late capitalist culture.

The author becomes someone in whom the events of the day disappear, as in a vortex, to be spun back to the public in palatable form. Laura Bush appears as a humanized Laura Bush in Curtis Sittenfeld's novel. The George Bush regime appears everywhere in plastic realism as a phenomenon we can comprehend and possibly even manage—very much as in the movies and television shows of the last decade. Empire appears as empirical fact, separated from individual responsibility, a behemoth that came from nowhere and is going nowhere, as in Denis Johnson and others. Economic inequality comes back distorted as the generally fair assign-ment of privilege, so that the losers appear as having deserved their fate. And the fairness of it all—just rewards accruing to the most deserving—is reflected in the author's own magnanimous persona, both grateful and detached at the same time.

In a sense, writers have become global corporate salesmen and saleswomen, selling a product that fits within the existing product line, their personal appearances geared toward deflecting any skepticism about the chosen canon. Lahiri, Diaz, and Egan remind one of nothing so much as corporate publicists, always able and willing to disarm and deprecate.

In conclusion, plastic realism explains why major American novelists today seem to mostly address each other, or to be more precise their institutional pa-trons, rather than any idealized readership. It explains why postmodern fiction peddled by small presses has become a safe minor brand not expected to shift the larger literary conversation. It explains the confusion over the moral consequences of minimalism versus maximalism, since plastic realism is the rubric that now encompasses both and emerges from the same cultural logic as neoliberalism. It explains why recent trends in cultural authoritarianism, nationalism, and militarism have been soaked into the fabric of writing without so much as a ripple.

Plastic realism is the new American mainstream literary style, and major recognition goes only to those who adhere to its rules. Both the writer and his fictional creations accept the ethic of untrammeled personal responsibility, and characters who fail on this measure are relegated to hells of their own making while those who show the diligence to learn therapeutic lessons are duly rewarded, as we can see clearly in the major American novels of the preceding decade and a half. All of this reinforces the belief of the ruling class that privilege is merited, success is always earned, and misery is not the natural human condition.

The author in plastic realism is simultaneously an emasculated creature (because he must show no freedom with regard to institutional rules) and a most exalted one (because he has been abstracted to the point where his real biography is beside the point), both prince and frog, propagating a philosophy where powerlessness is the ultimate power. From Sebold to Franzen to Egan to Lahiri to Diaz to Eggers to Eugenides to Chabon to Foer to Shteyngart to Harbach, there is agreement that the structures of society are independent from the techniques of the self. The main circuit of representation, the sine qua non of realism, has been broken.

In classical realism, the author shunned self-consciousness to present the community to itself without ifs and buts; in plastic realism, the author adopts faux self-consciousness to convince himself (or his institutional patrons) how the community should look like in accordance with the pleasures and conveniences of the reigning canon.

The rise of the novel encompassed the burgeoning discourses of journalism, social thought, autobiography, and historiography, whereas plastic realism signifies a *denovelization* of the culture as each of these discourses finds itself in disrepute. The novel, instead of assimilating new discourses, is shedding them. As the rise of the novel in seventeenth- and eighteenth-century England and France coincided with the inception of enlightenment, so does plastic realism enclose the end of enlightenment, with doubts about science, reason, and progress eroding the possibility of characters possessing free will. Unlike metafiction, however, this cynicism combines with the glorification of mimesis to yield a rearguard action against the liberating potential ensuing from the crisis of various discourses.

Plastic realism is characterized by its militant attitude against time-space complexity in narrative (Egan's and others' efforts in this regard only introduce linearity through the back door), seductive register of gentle irony reflecting lack of criticism of class relations, closure rather than openness (the text being readerly, not writerly, in Barthes's terms), and elimination of laughter, an anti-Menippean or anti-carnivalesque tendency (to use Bakhtin's terminology).

Plastic realism is the result of the convergence of parallel cultural and political tendencies. Classical realism's reaction against sentimentalism has collapsed, memoir is put on the same footing as the novel and distinctions between the two genres are blurred, the identity of privileged people is idealized while those not part of the elitist core group are excluded, and fiction is populated by consistent characters not made to suffer digressions and discrepancies, as is also true of the new biography. More or less the same authorial persona dominates plastic realism (enhancing an idealization of the white upper-middle-class, even in supposedly multicultural novels written by ethnic writers, contrasted to the opposition of William Dean Howells and other early American realists toward the upper classes); this conventional persona has disturbing consequences for the democracy of interests and passions.

The 2000s was a decade of violent reaction against fictional experiment in America, as the 1950s was in England. Plastic realism legislates a frantic search for renewed cultural authority. The old realist structure remains but harbors a new ideology, leading to schizoid, repressive texts. Plastic realism continually narrows subject matter, whereas realism had started off wanting to open up the novel to new subject matter. A veneer of naturalism saturates plastic realism, but it is planted in the guise of a new mystical mumbo-jumbo. Worldviews jostling for competition in the same text have been dispensed with, and ideological conflict has been eliminated in favor of the same meekly ironic voice acceptable to publishers.

Plastic realism reflects cynical acceptance of the reduced status of the human amidst restricted chances for mobility. It's the perfect aesthetic for the rise of right-wing economics accompanied by rhetorical paeans to pluralism and diversity (or class repression coinciding with superficial cultural broadening), leading to a weakened democracy. If forms of modern realism correspond to forms of capitalism, then plastic realism authorizes the most regressive form of post-industrial capitalism.

Symposium: Who is the Most Important Contemporary Fiction Writer?

Mona Simpson is the author of six novels, including *Anywhere But Here*, *The Lost Father*, and *Off Keck Road*.

I think I'm influenced by the writers I read, but not necessarily by the things I'd choose. When I first read Proust, I imbibed his melancholy, without gleaning the structural underpinnings he used to manage his great orchestral circus. For many reasons, my most important living writer is Alice Munro, for her apt, stylistic genius mostly restrained (she learned from *her* influences, the two Williamses, Maxwell and Trevor.) She uses time virtuosically, shuffling tenses within a paragraph to distinguish a moment from a habit. Writers everywhere study her stories to figure out just where and how they go so deep. Munro matters, too, because of her sustained fascination with female life, as the playing field, the parliament, the place where life is lived and history made. Virgina Woolf said that men write about women in certain colors and tempers of light. We had Leopold Bloom in the bathroom, but Woolf herself never took her fictional heroines into the bedroom or the bathroom, though she did wonder about the inner life of the char cleaning public stalls. Munro writes about sex, about bathrooms, about passion and class, and the ways they tease, trick, and determine each other. I often read hoping to absorb influences. Of late, I've been studying happy endings. As much for life as for art.

Michael Martone is the author of more than twenty-five books, including *Fort Wayne Is Seventh on Hitler's List*, *Unconventions: Attempting the Art of Craft and the Craft of Art*, and *Four for a Quarter: Fictions*.

William H. Gass. For me his story, "In the Heart of the Heart of the Country," demonstrated several things. First, that prose could be sustained without narrative. Second, that character need not be beholden to psychological "depth." Third, that juxtaposition is all, and that, yes, there is a world within a word. And fourth, that "Indiana" could be a subject. Published in the late 1950s, this fiction, I think, was eclipsed for decades by the hegemony of narrative realistic neo-Chekhovian stories, so I'm unsure how influential it was for other writers writing in the last half-century. For me, I held it silently in my heart: a story that is not a story, prose that is poetry, action that is static, character that is fields of language, flat fields of Indiana that are depthless. Gass did not so much write a story as create a complex space, an interesting environment, and invited me, the reader, into it to collaborate and contribute to its meaning. It is a frenetic performance where nothing happens. And that nothing was the everything I needed.

Francine Prose is the author of twenty books of fiction, including *Hungry Hearts, Primitive People*, and *Blue Angel*, and eight books of nonfiction.

Can I tweak the word influence? Let's say encouragement or energy. I don't sit down and say, Hey, I think I'll write a Philip Roth novel today. But I do think, The guy's been writing brilliant books with astonishingly beautiful sentences for all these years, it's inspirational. I can open his books at random and be sure I'll read something great. Likewise Stanley Elkin. The guy wrote as if he didn't give a shit about what anyone thought. No one else has written a tender sex scene with a bear that goes on for dozens of pages or a comic novel about a grief-stricken slob who takes terminally ill children to Disneyland. And obviously Grace Paley, the first writer I read whose characters talked like people I knew. If I listed the writers working now, just the ones of my generation, who influence me this way, it would take a long time and as always I'd forget the most important ones. They influence me every day. When I think of them, I think: Maybe I can do this, after all. I think I'll go back to my desk.

Ha Jin is an award-winning short story writer, novelist, poet, and essayist, whose books include *Ocean of Words, The Bridegroom, A Good Fall, Waiting, The Crazed*, and *A Free Life*.

I usually go by books, because no author can make every book of theirs a masterpiece. The contemporary writer who has influenced me the most, I would say, is V. S. Naipaul, particularly his *A Bend in the River*. I do not share most of his political views, but his writings have taught me how to look at things and how to reflect on my own situation. His prose is honest, supple, and without frills. His works are highly uneven, but he has written greats books, such as *A House for Mr. Biswas*, *A Bend in the River*, and *The Enigma of Arrival*. He will be remembered for those. Many young writers, especially those from a colonial background, regard him as a master, who has shown them how purely by the individual's effort and talent a writer can find his way in literature.

Arthur Phillips's novels include *Prague, The Egyptologist,* and *The Song is You.*

I'm afraid I smash into a lot of definition quibbles immediately, and wobble, stunned, disoriented. "Important": I can't think of what this word means in fiction except as "important to me." There's no other standard in literature that matters to me beyond the amount of pleasure I have enjoyed thanks to a particular writer. I can't be much happier than when I read the best of Martin Amis. "Contemporary": Dead but new work still published posthumously, i.e., David Foster Wallace? Alive, but not too productive, i.e., Kundera? "Fiction": Tom Stoppard is my choice for the best living writer of fiction, but I don't mean his one novel. "Influence on…others": Watching how the beneficial influence of my heroes is repressed, compressed, and expressed in my own work gives me not just pause but total paralysis at the thought of guessing how Coetzee or Munro might be affecting anyone else's work. I know that when I started writing, I was very conscious that writers about my age often cited Updike, DeLillo, Pynchon, and Roth as influences, and so I went to some trouble to read none of them for many years. I wouldn't dare say I know how anybody is influencing anyone.

David Leavitt's many books of fiction include *The Two Hotel Francforts, The Indian Clerk,* and *The Lost Language of Cranes.*

Cynthia Ozick's influence on contemporary literature is incalculable—literally, since so many writers have felt it without realizing that they have felt it. Writers of the last century (James and Forster especially) live in her. Yet she is in no sense "old-fashioned." On the contrary, her novels, stories, and essays form a roadmap of innovation. Her knowledge of the past—of history, religion, philosophy—is deeper than that of any living writer I can think of, yet she uses this knowledge not to pay homage to the past; she uses it to turn the past inside out. Consider *The Puttermesser Papers*, the heroine of which, a New York civil servant, crafts the first female golem in her living room. Or *Foreign Bodies*, for which James's

The Ambassadors provides the blueprint, and which is as much a slap in James's face as a paean to his genius. Or "The Shawl"—the most ruthless, the most heartbreaking, and (I would argue) the greatest story ever written about the Holocaust. In an interview with Bill Moyers, Ozick described herself as being at "heart and soul a rationalist." This oxymoron defines her. Here is her description of the roof of the Duomo in Milan, from the story "At Fumicaro": "What had looked, from the plaza below, like the frothiest lacework or egg-white spume here burst into solidity, weight, shadow, and dazzlement: a derangement of plenitude tumbling from a bloated cornucopia."

Jim Lynch is the author of the novels *Border Songs* and *The Highest Tide*.

How about Richard Price, the modern master of sociological crime fiction? He burst into the literary spotlight with *Clockers* (1992), a novel that so vividly captures the lives of cops and crackheads that you root for the troubled teen dealer every bit as much as the middle-aged detective. He backed that book up with two more daring urban novels and topped them with *Lush Life* (2008). Price is often praised for writing the best dialogue in America, but his biggest influence might be the way he creates palpable characters and scenes by riding along with cops and criminals. His immersion techniques inspire me and many others who build their novels with a mix of reportage and imagination. Price usually gets overlooked because he writes about crime and favors simple strong plot lines. But what he pulls off in scope and craft teaches literary writers about pace and realism and social observation. And he inspires screenwriters—HBO's *The Wire* was based, in part, on *Clockers*—to develop stronger character-driven cop dramas. Price also simply types some of the most spectacular sentences in fiction today. Crack open *Lush Life*, and you'll see what I mean.

Christopher Miller is the author of *The Cardboard Universe*.

Is Lydia Davis the most important contemporary fiction writer? I don't know, but for me she serves as an artistic conscience, a constant reminder that where prose is concerned, nothing is more beautiful than clarity, honesty, and accuracy. But she's barely a fiction writer at all nowadays, insofar as fiction assumes that what doesn't happen is more exciting than what does. When a writer ceases to believe that, when she takes to heart the dictum that truth is stranger than fiction, her unwillingness to fib can have stylistic consequences. Look at Davis's conjunctions. In *Almost No Memory*—her early collection and maybe her best—I count six pieces where the first word of the second sentence is "But." If there is, as Wittgenstein insisted, such a thing as a "but"-feeling, no one gives readers that feeling more promptly or reliably than Davis. Half her sentences serve to correct or retract preceding sentences, because none of our sentences ever points true north. Davis zigzags toward the truth by tacking now to the northeast and now to the northwest. One of the many kinds of fun her books afford is the almost kinesthetic pleasure of zigzagging with her.

David Bezmozgis is the author of *Natasha and Other Stories* and the novels *The Free World* and *The Betrayers*.

The most influential contemporary writer for me right now is J.M. Coetzee. I read his novel *Summertime* last year and have read *Disgrace* multiple times—along with almost everything else he has written. I admire the intelligence, directness, and economy of his prose, and also his willingness to continue to experiment formally. I admire his professionalism and productivity. He publishes novels with steady regularity while also being an excellent literary critic. As for his influence on the work of other contemporary writers—I don't think he's spawned a school of followers in the way of DeLillo or Pynchon or the late David Foster Wallace. Maybe it's because his style is more restrained, subtle, even severe. I admit, he doesn't crack many jokes.

Alan Cheuse[1] is the author of many story collections and novels, including *The Grandmothers' Club, Lost and Old Rivers: Stories*, and *Prayers for the Living*.

I can tell you whose work thrills me, and it's more than one writer. James Salter's and Richard Ford's stories set a high hurdle, and some pages by Jayne Anne Phillips and Stuart Dybek set my heart, and sometimes my hair, on fire. But this tells you more about the horizon point I trek toward in my own work rather than the wind at my back. If it comes down to me having to admit by whose notes I tune my own instrument, it's more modern poets than prose writers lining up in my mind: some of my contemporaries such as Robert Hass and Jane Hirshfield, Robert Pinsky, and before them Elizabeth Bishop and Pound and company. If it's prose, I make no great revelation when I say the sentences of Saul Bellow in his stories and some of the novels, and before him, Hemingway's sentences,

---

1. Cheuse died in July 2015.

and from there on it's looking back to the forceful creations of Thomas Hardy, D.H. Lawrence, James Joyce, and Virginia Woolf, and the great ocean of prose in our heritage: old Herman Melville. I don't mean to sound like something out of *My Fair Lady*, ranting about Shakespeare, Milton, and the Bible. Other writers among us may have other ideas.

Allan Gurganus's many books include *Oldest Living Confederate Widow Tells All, Plays Well with Others*, and *Local Souls*.

Alice Munro is alive, writing, and scaring me with all she is still learning, showing. How can tales so formally unpredictable seem, once inhabited, so intimately familiar? Munro's fascination with family disaster makes her our reliable broken-in life guide. This writer enjoys such a mercurial sense of time—she can compress a century to a page. Using her provincial Canadian past, she often sets raw working-class striving against the cosseted numbness of the upper-middle-class. She can recall a girlhood Christmas job, gutting turkeys. Her next story will empathize with some Toronto society hostess. In her scope of heart, in sheer narrative relish, she most resembles Chekhov. Munro's characters are sexually forthright. Their sense of humor runs to whatever's mordant yet fond. Her stories' precise language can leap from bone-plain to purest lyrical meringue, straight up in a single sentence. Munro's prose feels as fact-based as tombstone inscriptions. Like those, each sentence gets cut deep enough to outlive a hundred winters. I've read Alice Munro's every published word. Each stiffens my resolve with new permission. Each makes me want to try all that Munro (and the Bible) demand of us. "Speak the truth in Love."

David Ebershoff is the author of *The Danish Girl, The Rose City, Pasadena*, and *The 19th Wife*.

Is there any writer more important than the one you fall for at fifteen? For me, that was Edmund White. Sure there were others (the Brontës, Forster, Capote), but aren't you asking about writers alive today? Back then Edmund's novels gave me exactly what I was looking for: a reflection of myself on the page. Now, (many) years later, I can see his work in a larger sense. He's part of that very American tradition of writing honestly about the self. For Edmund, the truth is always beautiful. Of course he's a link in the daisy chain of gay American writers that includes Whitman, James, Williams, O'Hara, and Baldwin, but I also place him in that ferocious generation that has given us DeLillo, Morrison,

Oates, Pynchon, and Roth—all born in the 1930s—whose influence we're still working under today. White was born on January 13, 1940, two weeks late to fit neatly into this theory but close enough. Next year Edmund will publish his tenth novel.[2] It is the most honest look at the differences and similarities between gay and straight men I've ever read. I have to qualify all of this by telling you Edmund is now a friend of mine. Even so, history, I'm quite convinced, will be kind to Edmund White.

Mohammed Hanif is the author of *A Case of Exploding Mangoes* and *Our Lady of Alice Bhatti*.

I came to Hanif Kureishi through a short story called "With Your Tongue Down My Throat," partly set in Karachi. I thought I recognized some of the characters. Then I watched *My Beautiful Laundrette* (1985) which I couldn't identify with but loved the title and its strange energy. Later I read a piece of reportage by him in which he wrote about two girls of Pakistani origin who performed, for a living, a lesbian act at Asian weddings and parties in Britain. I found a VHS of his subjects' performance at a Karachi video shop. For the first time I realized what a writer does; he writes. I read his novels, his stories, and was always amazed by how unique his worldview was. He wrote *My Son the Fanatic* in the early 1990s, which, in retrospect, sounds quite prophetic. After moving to London I read his interviews and I liked the fact that like my favorite Urdu writer Manto (who also wrote fiction as well as screenplays) Kureishi made it a point to be identified as a sinner rather than a saint. At Karachi airport I picked up a book by him titled *Dreaming and Scheming*. I thought the title just about summed up a writer's job. When my first novel was about to be published, a Karachi wit said the publishers must have mistaken you for that other Hanif. I wish.

---

2. *Jack Holmes and His Friend*, published 2012.

The Pakistani Novel of Class Comes of Age

How to Get Filthy Rich in Rising Asia
By Mohsin Hamid
Riverhead, 2013. 230 pgs.

Mohsin Hamid has written a nearly flawless third novel, which begs to be seen as the concluding act of a trilogy. If his first novel, *Moth Smoke* (2000), was about Pakistani decadence prior to the calamitous changes brought on by the war on terror, and his second novel, *The Reluctant Fundamentalist* (2007), delved deep into the psychic foundation of those changes, the new novel builds on elements of both earlier books but is more of a look at the future than the immediate past.

How to Get Filthy Rich in Rising Asia recalls J. M. Coetzee more than any other writer, with the same detachment, suppressed rage at mortality, and constant ironic counterpoints that seem sufficient unto themselves, as in Coetzee's best work. It is high praise indeed to compare anyone to Coetzee, but Hamid's new novel is written very much in that vein, and shares much of Coetzee's tendency to allegorize as well.

The deep telescoping and the immense compression of events—natural to allegory—is what lend *Filthy Rich* its power. The setting, though unnamed, is of course Pakistan—mostly Lahore, but with also a subsidiary role for Karachi—and the journey of an ambitious man from bare subsistence in the village to outsized commercial success in the big city also takes place in recognizable Pakistan.

But there are ways in which this place threatens to leave the actual precincts of Pakistan, for example in the undying urge to freedom of the protagonist's love interest throughout the novel—the "pretty girl" from his poor neighborhood who will go on to become a successful fashion model, and whose life intersects with the protagonist's at various points in their lives.

Though the narrator marries another woman—with whom the romantic sparks never fly—the pretty girl is the true love of his life, and, in the end, destitute and frail, they do finally consummate, in a way, what was always meant to be their conjugal destiny. The pretty girl, with her distinctly existential norms, is just this side of believable, and sometimes not so at all, when she chooses uncertainty over security. It is an idealization of woman, whom riches ultimately fail to capture.

The book is part of the growing genre of "how they get rich" Asian novels, typified by Aravind Adiga above all, but rather inevitable considering South Asia's recent pell-mell plunge into hyperactive, postmodern globalization. Imposed upon ancient structures of tradition, the veneer of capitalist acquisitiveness sits uneasily, creating fertile material for the novelist. The situation is somewhat analogous to what William Dean Howells, Frank McTeague, Jack London, and Theodore Dreiser had to deal with when America rapidly transformed into an urban industrialized society at the turn of the twentieth century.

Human relations—their sanctity, their rootedness in idealism, their permanence—suffer when capitalism takes over, and this Hamid documents at various stages of transformation, compressing (often incongruously) a century or more of metamorphosis within the parameters of his narrator's lifetime.

Throughout, Hamid uses the second person to address would-be aspirants to success. The second person has recently been overutilized in American fiction, primarily because it is a handy gimmick in workshop, and it comes with its sweet set of built-in dangers. Hamid makes us forget that we're reading a manual for success, a book of advice for courtiers to courtiers, as the "you" in the narrative becomes increasingly less identified with the unnamed protagonist and more identified with the reader. The "you" in fact becomes an "I" (quite unnoticeably) which in turn becomes a "we" and finally a "he." "He" of course hides a lot; novelists deploy the default voice to maintain a measure of deniability. "You" can be simultaneously accusatory as well as exculpatory. Hamid excels at these seamless, almost unnoticeable transitions.

The short, pseudo-profound prefaces at the beginning of each of the twelve chapters—philosophy on the cheap, if you will, a twelve-step program for ruthless entrepreneurs—create an added element of tension between detachment and emotion, as we are invited each time to briefly float on a soothing stream of wise words, only to quickly emerge into the maelstrom, losing our bearings, such as happens after this quiet introduction to chapter six, "Work for Yourself," following which the narrator embarks on his entrepreneurial venture to sell polluted bottled water:

But when you read a book, what you see are black squiggles on pulped wood or, increasingly, dark pixels on a pale screen. To transform these icons into characters and events, you must imagine. And when you imagine, you create. It's in being read that a book becomes a book, and in each of a million different readings a book becomes one of a million different books, just as an egg becomes one of potentially a million different people when it's approached by a hard-swimming and frisky school of sperm.

The advice, the wisdom, the insight are all spurious, because there is in fact no way to get filthy rich in Asia without causing incalculable harm and violence.

So the novelist, in using these prefaces (authorial interventions) to perform other than their customary purpose (say, in the nineteenth-century novel of moral enlightenment), squarely aligns his authorship with the actual artistic function novels perform today. In the early twenty-first century milieu of globalized hypercapitalism with no palpable ideological alternatives, he dare not imagine for himself some worthy authorial stature that would be untrue to the facts of his situation in the institutional structure (this was a concern in *The Reluctant Fundamentalist* as well, but here it is almost the central preoccupation).

Self-help manuals try to put the unknowable mysteries of existence on practical footing, which makes them losing propositions by definition. A self-help manual can never be realized in practice; that is the broken promise we all prospectively accept. True philosophy, on the other hand, takes on this challenge differently, its ambiguity correlating with its richness.

As for the twenty-first-century novel, it finds itself falling between two chairs. When it tries to honestly narrativize the broken promises brought on by social transformation, the novel falls in the same category of genre as the hapless self-help book. The American realists of a century ago understood this, and Hamid and his fellow travelers in Asia are undermining romanticism in parallel gestures of futility. Hamid has taken self-consciousness toward the difficult situation of the novel of enlightenment in South Asia farther than any of his predecessors.

Moving through the chapters of this intentionally overschematic saga—the narrator's step-by-step conquest of the peculiarly Pakistani (and Asian) obstacles to success—is like rushing through the layers of an old-time newsreel, time flying by so swiftly that it stretches credibility. Yet in rising Asia this is precisely how fast things do take place (as was true of rising other continents in modernity).

Instead of epic scale, the novelist confronts the pace of change with mastery of characterization in miniature, with Nabokovian precision of description (as

Hamid applies it to each of his characters and places) without the spare time a Nabokov might have had for lavish exposition.

There simply isn't enough time. This is a dominant motif of the novel, almost the whole point of it, as old forms swiftly become unrecognizably new:

> Meanwhile similar attempts, both official and non, seem to be under way to try to desiccate society itself, through among other things creeping restrictions on festivals and the public pursuit of fun, with a similar result, cracks, those widening fissures evident between young people, who appear to you divided as never before, split into myriad, incomprehensible tribes, signaling their affiliations with an automobile sticker, a bare shoulder, or some arcane permutation in the possibilities of facial hair.

Freedom in this novel assumes fanciful new forms of self-imposed repression. There is no rising Asia, only sinking Asia: an old-fashioned trope like an absconding brother-in-law can sink the whole enterprise, decades of hard work and the care and feeding of the powers-that-be gone to waste in an instant. On the other hand, of course there is rising Asia, steeped in new technologies of communication and imitation, where everyone does have a chance to ascend.

To entangle these conflicting ideas in as short a space as Hamid does is what leads to an explosive dynamic of awareness, makes this a novel for the ages, with deserved comparisons to *The Great Gatsby*.

As *Filthy Rich* progresses, it acquires increasing layers of detachment, which, in Coetzeean fashion, somehow work to enhance emotional urgency.

In chapter Nine, "Patronize the Artists of War," Hamid describes the narrator's encounter with the head of a military-run corporation, eager to build a housing colony with a secure, permanent supply of pure water—water, that most precious of commodities in rising Asia, the narrator's lifelong means to riches, at first in the form of adulterated supply, but later more or less acceding to standards.

Here is Hamid's appropriation of the camera-eye technique to describe the insignificance of individuals in the global national security apparatus:

> A series of CCTV cameras observes various stages of your progress through the cantonment. Through their monochromatic optical sensors the expensive metallic finish of your sedan dulls to a ratty gray. Behind you are scenes little changed since Independence, images of well-manicured lawns, mess halls with regimental insignia, trees painted waist-high in skirts of white. Homes of the descendants of corps and division commanders abut those of oligarchical commercial magnates, and everywhere is a sense of unyielding order and arboreal grace increasingly

atypical of your city, much of the rest of which seethes outside this fortified garrison enclave like some great migratory horde besieging a royal castle.

When decline (in this bustling pre-apocalyptic expanse) comes, the zoo seems to be an apt concluding metaphor, and here is Hamid's precise description of this (antiquated) venue:

> You explore the city's main colonial-era museum and its pungently aromatic zoo, attractions you last visited when your son was a schoolboy. At the zoo you are surprised by how inexpensive tickets are, and further by the size of the facility, which seems bigger than you recall, though you had expected the opposite to be the case. The pretty girl marvels at the aviary, you at hippopotamuses slipping daintily into a mud pool from the grassy banks of their enclosure. She draws to your attention the large number of young men who are here, their accents and dialects often hailing from remote districts. They call to the animals in amusement and wonder, or sit in clusters on plentiful benches, taking advantage of the shade. The zoo has signs listing the daily dietary intake of its most prominent residents, and occasionally a literate visitor is to be heard reading to his fellows the prodigious quantities of food required to maintain such and such beast.

In its precision, lack of interest in romanticizing, and sensuous presence of mind that suggests Buddhist meditation, this passage, and many others like it, are nearly unmatched in new South Asian fiction.

There is something of the classic twentieth-century Japanese novelist's sage discernment in these descriptions, a desire to register minute gradations of feelings without getting carried away by the novelist's verbal skills, amounting to a deep, mature humility.

A similar vein of serene acceptance (which is almost inhuman in its dimensions, though no loss endearing for being so) familiar from Coetzee appears in a late passage when the narrator looks the other way as the pretty girl's servant, after her death, takes charge of his care:

> The factotum stays, in part out of loyalty to the pretty girl and in part because it is easy to skim money from you. You do not begrudge him this. You would do the same. You have done the same. It is a poor person's right. Instead you are grateful for his help, for his refusal to sever you from your few remaining possessions by violence.

Consider also this passage describing the pretty girl's last days:

Medications do not relieve her pain, but they make it less central, and in her center builds instead a desire to detach. It costs her to be touched, as she approaches her finish, companionship softly irritating her, like the remaining strand of flesh binding a loose milk tooth to its jaw.

This is as close to Coetzee as I have seen any modern novelist come, and it is not at all derivative either.

As one finishes *Filthy Rich*, the stink of death (or mortal corruption) retrospectively pervades everything one has read before, such as this earlier passage describing the narrator's visit to a politician to pay a bribe to facilitate his operations:

The politician's working environment is structured in the manner of the courts of princes of old, namely with one set of waiting rooms for commoners, another for those of rank, and an inner sanctum occupied by him and a contingent of his advisers. Your transaction is conducted simultaneously with multiple unrelated strands of endeavor, some public, some personal, and apparently without purpose, or rather with no purpose other than amusement. An extended lunch is under way, and so everything happens to the sounds of chewing and with repeated gestures that look like multi-fingered snaps but are in reality attempts to dislodge grease, rice, and bits of edible residue without the use of water or tissues.

This is Hamid's first truly mature book, and the confidence he shows in not desperately *needing* to represent Pakistan to any particular constituency is reflected in the form and structure. His first novel was a young man's overly jaded representation of his generation's depravities, in a transparent act of purging. The second novel was similarly purgative, as he sought to distance himself from his engagement with the West's capitalist project, punctuated by his return to Pakistan. In this third novel, he could care less about explicating modern Pakistan's pathologies, though that is ostensibly the scaffold.

The Coetzeean obsessions with mortality, aging, the stages of illness, the indignities of hospitalization and hospice attention, and the forever chastening chimera of unfulfilled desire, these can only be handled adeptly by the most mature of novelists.

Indeed, there seems to have been a quantum leap of wisdom between *The Reluctant Fundamentalist* and *Filthy Rich*, which can only be explained by the author's willingness to submerse himself in the vile sheath of corruption and uncertainty that is contemporary Pakistan. And he manages never to lose his sense of humor during all that. That alone is a monumental accomplishment.

Literary Escapism Toward the End of Empire:
Dave Eggers as a Representative Case

In his novel *A Hologram for the King* (McSweeney's, 2012), Dave Eggers has taken his skepticism toward whatever remains of the American dream to a deeper level than in his earlier book of imaginative reportage, *Zeitoun* (2009). In many ways, *Hologram* is Eggers's *Netherland* (2008), Joseph O'Neill's elegy for America, arguably the key novel of the last decade, a book which signaled the end of global expectations about America's goodness. But *Hologram* represents a benign acceptance of America's relative decline compared to the rest of the world, rather than a scathing indictment of the self-destructiveness that brought us to this low pass.

The plot is easily told. Alan Clay is a fifty-four-year-old American business executive who has been sent to the Kingdom of Saudi Arabia by his supervisor Eric Ingvall at Reliant Technologies ("the largest IT supplier in the world") to make a presentation to King Abdullah in order for Reliant to secure a contract to meet all the IT needs of the proposed King Abdullah Economic City (KAEC). Alan is accompanied from Reliant by three younger people, Brian, Rachel, and Cayley, and they travel back and forth from Jeddah to KAEC every day to wait in a tent adjoining a black building, ready for the moment the King might visit them. There's no knowing when that might happen: Alan is given the runaround, and the young Americans from Reliant acquire none too high an opinion of his capabilities. Alan has spent the majority of his career selling bicycles—Schwinns—but that career fizzles out because of globalization leading to cheaper bicycles being made abroad. It's important for Alan to succeed in Saudi Arabia because he is in a lot of debt and has to finance his daughter Kit's education.

There are two romantic interludes, one with Hanne, a Scandinavian consultant, and a more serious one with Alan's doctor, Zahra Hakem, with neither of whom Alan can rise to the occasion. Alan gets to know a young bored Saudi,

Yousef, who at first is his driver but soon becomes his friend; when Yousef is threatened by the husband of his former lover, Jameelah, because Jameelah is flirting with Yousef, Yousef makes a getaway to his father's mountain hideout, a fortress-like home, and takes Alan with him for a while.

As the days go by, Alan and his companions wonder if and when the King will ever show up. Will KAEC ever come to fruition? Why is it taking so long to build, when the King has the money to make it happen overnight should he want to? The hologram of the title is the fancy device whereby Reliant hopes to wow the King that Reliant has the technological capabilities to be trusted with the IT part of the infrastructure—that, and Alan's tenuous, twenty-year-old connection with the King's nephew.

The scaffold for the novel is the familiar one having to do with American expatriates floundering abroad. A disillusioned young man or woman on the cusp of maturity, or a disillusioned older man or woman on the cusp of mortality, travels to a foreign land where interactions with various exotic people make him or her reevaluate his whole life, assess mistakes and successes, and reconcile with realistic possibilities for the future. There is a tendency in this genre for the exotic foreign locale to be represented merely as a tool in the service of the expatriate as trigger for memories, and for the people the American meets to amount to little more than testing-out possibilities for romantic entanglement. Both place and people come across as secondary to the purposes of the hero's narrative. This genre, then, is problematic, and there are few instances where objectification, simplification, and romanticization have been minimized in execution.

To the extent that Eggers relies on the familiar plot mechanism, he remains strictly within realistic territory. The narrative must move forward somehow, and constant worries about what he has left behind (which isn't much) serve as the anchor. This part is the least interesting, and also the least convincing. If someone really wants to go to college in America, even today financial aid can be had; but it's a convenient hook. So Alan's constant abortive letters to his daughter Kim—often accompanied by sadness at his failed marriage with the activist go-getter Ruby, altogether too much of a handful for him—do not generate emotional heat. We're always more interested in the endless wait for the King; even the mute business focus of the three young people accompanying Alan, caught in an anodyne alien environment, holds more interest.

The hero—like America, whose symbol he is in so many such novels these days—finds himself in an extended moment of paralysis, unable to move forward. And if the hero himself is primarily a symbol, then it's a safe bet that the narrative will come freighted with numerous other symbols pointing to his predicament.

There is the ominous growth on Alan's neck, which when he's drunk on Hanne's moonshine he tries to rip apart with a serrated knife in his hotel room. It's this growth whose successful extraction by Dr. Zahra Hakem leads to his revealing romantic encounter with her. The growth—not cancerous, but definitely not something to be lived with—represents everything America doesn't know about its own body, its own physique and limitations, its self-destructive tendencies and feelings of melodramatic hypochondria.

Similarly for the tent. The tent, of course, is tenuous. The glory years of the neoconservative empire-making project have come to an end, and American power is forced to take up abode in a temporary shelter, not knowing whether it will be successful relative to aggressive competitors like China, able to get protection in the sturdy Black Box building.

Similarly, the Red Sea, the desert, the blue water in which Zahra and Alan go snorkeling, and the mountaintop fortress where Yousef takes Alan, all of these are loaded with overt symbolism, which Eggers often spells out.

Of the Red Sea, Alan meditates:

The sea ahead of him was unbroken by the mast of any sailboat, any vessel of any kind. This seemed a remarkably underused body of water, at least what he'd seen of it. In the eighty or so miles they'd driven to get here Alan hadn't seen much in the way of development. How could so much coastline go so little exploited? He thought about buying one of the properties here. He could buy one or two, rent them out half the year and still come out ahead. He was in the middle of the calculations when he realized he was not the man who could do such things. He had nothing to spend.

But what meaning does the symbolism in the end add up to? The adept twenty-first century reader of novels is apt to discount all such symbolism and become impatient to move forward. Eggers might be better served with plots not reliant on such heavy symbolism. But this would require Eggers to take a closer look at his whole project of mild-mannered irony—which is where he is mostly content to stay in *Hologram*. And which is where the contrast with *Netherland* is so sharp.

Eggers writes not as a harsh critic of his own country's faults but as someone not yet, or not quite, able to let go of some of the quintessential American illusions. There is the idea of romantic fulfillment across cultures. I don't think Eggers has completely given up on that. There is the idea of friendship as a bridge between very different cultures. Eggers hasn't given up on that either. There is the idea of the natural enlightenment of decent, well-meaning, pragmatic young people—Eggers's own generation—whether Saudis like Yousef and Salem, or the young Reliant representatives. The Reliant people, no matter how boring they may be in interacting with Alan, at least end up doing the right thing by eventually conducting a threesome in the tent.

So *Hologram* is an elegy for the end of American power, but the book doesn't necessarily suggest that we need to spend all that much time lamenting what's been lost—whereas in *Netherland*, the sense of loss is overpowering, behind which is the immigrant's conviction that America was the world's last great hope.

Eggers's generation and the one that came after it—as was demonstrated during the Arab Spring—is notoriously partisan to this value system: leave ideology alone, work around it, pretend it doesn't exist, act as if the physical reality, the material definitions of power, are all that matter. Occupy Wall Street represents a similar masked move.

Yousef, Alan's confidant in Saudi Arabia, is bored, there's nothing to do in Saudi Arabia, yet in a pinch we can easily see him functioning quite well in any American or European city—or as a protestor in the Arab Spring or Occupy movements. Yousef has already spent a little time studying in America, and has an American accent. But so does nearly everyone worth knowing in the far reaches of empire these days (as Eggers confirms), and this goes along with education in the ice-cool morality of the post-baby boom generations. Yousef is actually Eggers's idealization of the way it ought to all work out in the Arab and Muslim worlds if he had his way; this generation can be cool, like the generation that took *A Heartbreaking Work of Staggering Genius* so much to heart, a generation for whom war and revolution and politics and empire have nothing like the meaning they did for previous generations.

And again, this is supposed to be all to the good, if I'm reading Eggers correctly. If one idea is becoming superfluous—the idea of empire as America practiced it from around 1941 to 2008, with a massive rupture in the mid-1970s—then what is replacing it is supposedly a new form of consciousness. Now, every generation seems to think that's its own special privilege. The 1968 generation felt that way, as no doubt did the 1956 generation, and the 1979 generation, and the 1933 generation, and so on. Behind the cuteness of the hologram in Eggers's book is a larger truth, and that is the abiding, even inno-cent, faith of the younger generation that everything will work out in the end.

I don't think Eggers suggests that this is a complete illusion; he leaves it open-ended. America cannot compete on the old battlefields of business and war as it used to, but that's not to say that it doesn't still have the human resource potential to reinvent itself. Alan (America) may have passed on—he is impotent on both sexual occasions, with Hanne and with Zahra, despite being excited and cooking up a storm of sentiment (as America always does before firing up a war or any grandiose scheme)—but the future of America is not necessarily to fear. This is the kind of divided loyalty—or uncertainty—we simply don't see in *Netherland*, for example, or Mohsin Hamid's *The Reluctant Fundamentalist* (2007).

Eggers, in short, hasn't gone so far as to try to deal a death blow to the novel of expatriation. He keeps enough tension in the narrative to keep hope alive for Alan, until almost the very end—and the end comes abruptly, in a surprising reversal, when we think at last things might be turning around for Alan.

We might call Eggers's continuing aesthetic since the beginning of his career *romantic cool*, based as it is on a certain conviction of rightness or virtue about his generation. The superfluous generation is the older one, the solid heart of the baby boom generation. The cluelessness isn't true of Eggers's own generation, wised up to the power dynamics of the new world order.

Now for some larger points that beg to be made. During the last decade and a half, as the war on terror raged on and Muslims and Arabs came in for special scrutiny, American novelists decided to make this population a particular area of inquiry. I never thought I'd say this—since I'm firmly against the kind of belief inculcated in writing programs about each group having the right to speak only about its own members—but it's time to note what this authority signifies.

True, Eggers doesn't speak in the voice of a Saudi, but he does embody the hopes and worries of the younger generation of Saudis, in Yousef, Salem, and even Zahra. In the last few years in America we've had white novelists representing Muslims and Arabs more prominently than Muslims or Arabs have in their own writing. They seem fair game for everyone: Amy Waldman, for example, in *The Submission* (2011), or Nell Freudenberger in *The Newlyweds* (2012).

What we're seeing is perhaps a particular form of Orientalism, only pitched at a higher, more refined, more politically correct level. The other can't be demonized, of course—that's the business of bureaucrats propagating the endless campaign against terror, or unreconstructed neoconservative types—but whereas Eggers may be offering something of a critique of neoliberalism in economic terms, his overall venture in *Hologram* accords quite well with neoliberalism's position with respect to countries on the periphery.

For neoliberalism, countries like Saudi Arabia are the subject of particular discourse formations, and I don't think Eggers deviates too far from this discourse because he too, after all, breathes the same intellectual air.

Let me explain this a bit. I don't want to suggest that Eggers doesn't depict Saudis sympathetically—he does—but the *kind* of sympathy he represents is precisely the problem. The opposite of the demonized terrorist is the bored cool millennial person, the negation of any ideological threat. Neither is more than an abstraction.

There's no denying that Eggers may have met many cool Saudis like Yousef and Salem and Zahra, but why has it suddenly become a predominant business of white American novelists to represent the deepest hopes and ambitions of Bangladeshis and Egyptians and Saudis and Pakistanis to America and the rest of the world?

It is, by definition, a colonial project of a kind, since it wants to fix character in certain ways. And let's be clear, in Eggers's vision if America (in the guise of Alan) is redundant, so is Saudi Arabia (in the guise of everyone Alan encounters in the Kingdom), and by implication, all the oil-rich Arab peoples. They're reduced to mere consumers of supplies from other people, and thus linked with America in an endless chain of (neoliberal) sympathy. The *real devils* (not that Eggers has anything like that attitude) are the Chinese (but let's hear Donald Trump speak to that). Also Indians who work too hard, but the Chinese above all. They'll take over everything. Their way is the superior one, at least for the early twenty-first century.

Consider Alan's consternation when he realizes at last that Reliant had no chance to begin with compared to the Chinese, who're now the most favored nation, if you will (Alan's team has been given just a few minutes to present the hologram to the King, and Alan didn't have a chance to speak to the King at all):

> Alan watched as they drove up the road, but not far. They disappeared into the garage below the Black Box. Outside the building, Alan saw three white vans parked in a tidy row. There had never been any vehicles like that parked outside the building in all the time he'd been there, so he went to get a closer look. On each van, there were two rows of type on the side, the first in Arabic, the second in Chinese. Alan couldn't read either.

> He waited outside the building, trying not to attract notice, for almost two hours, until the King emerged with his men and a contingent of Chinese men in business attire. They all shook hands, smiling warmly. The King returned to the Black Box, and a few minutes later his motorcade emerged from the garage and left the city. The Chinese businessmen got in their vans and departed, too, leaving a wall of dust that took hours to settle.

I suggest that to buy into the premises of Eggers's formulation, as viewed through Alan's eyes, is unavoidably to enter some zero-sum calculations. And *Hologram* is in many ways—curiously enough for a book by one of the founding members of the first fully networked generation—a zero-sum book, where to add something is always to subtract something from somewhere else, where positive feedback effects due to pervasive networking and infinitely open exchange might as well be pure abstractions.

For example, Alan is confronted with the failure of Schwinn by one of his Saudi hosts, who has already encountered the company in a case study:

> Always the case studies…. Was it a mistake to have shopped out all the labor to China? This coming from kids whose experience with business was summer lawn-cutting. How did your suppliers become your competitors? That was a rhetorical question. You want your unit cost down, you manufacture in Asia, but pretty soon the suppliers don't need you, do they? Teach a man to fish. Now the Chinese know how to fish, and ninety-nine percent of all bicycles are being made there, in one province.

In another example of the anxiety prompted by the zero-sum game, one of Alan's (similarly redundant) friends offers this example of the Chinese displacing American ingenuity:

> But then there was a kicker, a big one: the Chinese glass maker was using a PPG patent. PPG had developed the glass, applied for and gotten a patent, and shortly before the bidding began, they'd licensed the patent to firms around the world. And one of those firms was Sanxin Façade, based on the South China Sea. And Sanxin Façade, it turned out, would be the firm building the glass in Freedom Tower. So PPG had invented a new type of blast-resistant glass, only to have a Chinese company use that technology to build the glass, cheaper, and sell it back to the Port Authority, which was attempting, at least, to resurrect something like pride and resilience in the center of the white-hot center of everything American.

Here Eggers isn't neutral. His sympathies are clearly with the American manufacturer; it's probably an inexorable process that can't be stopped, but America has *lost* something.

So the Chinese are coming! Just as when the Japanese were coming in the 1980s, we got movies like *Gung Ho* (1986)—though that was a great feel-good movie. In a sense, Alan's early experiences with Schwinn are the stuff *Gung Ho* was made of, but neoliberalism's current zero-sum game makes conceiving a pragmatic, transactional, win-win situation like *Gung Ho* impossible, and that is the true subject of *Hologram*.

America can't get away with trickery and fakery (relying on the hologram) anymore, but there's nothing else left for it to do. I suggest that this insinuation of defeat (or impotence, as Alan repeatedly manifests) is a pretty pure abstraction too, one that neoliberalism, with its lack of national allegiance, would find little trouble with.

There are any number of alternatives to orthodox capitalist economics—which actually determines our whole way of life (and death)—which are not explored in mainstream discussion, alternatives falling under the rubric of down-shifting or the post-work economy or collaborative economics. Eggers is to be given credit for taking on big subjects, when the predominant bulk of American literary fiction insists on living in a world of nostalgia and psychosis. But at the same time, Eggers's vision is strictly limited to the mainstream options on the table.

He might counter that his job is to depict reality as it is, but I would say that a novelist should generally try to do more than faithfully represent the mainstream view of things. Why does Alan have to be in so much debt? Why is paying for Kit's education such an issue? Why does Alan have to be impotent and unhappy after his divorce from Ruby? Deeply skeptical answers, which do not accept present reality as etched in stone, are possible to each of these questions, and if a novelist were to have that kind of worldview, then Eggers's plot—based on the superfluous American salesman—wouldn't be possible, because the re-dundant Alan wouldn't be redundant, he would find other ways to conceptualize himself than the one capitalism has offered him (now we harken back to Defoe and other writers imagining the liberal-capitalist-individualist into being, and how that enlightenment era project has unraveled and seemingly come to an end in both the literary and the real world).

Alan is a far-fetched conceit in any case, not an entirely honest representation of reality. The novelist always runs into the difficulty of depicting the thought pro-cesses of anyone not belonging to the culturally creative class—writers and artists and academics and so on—because the thoughts of people who aren't creative are going to be less complex. They—the rest of humanity—presumably don't think in pretty metaphors or have a grip on the big economic picture or contemplate mor-tality too much, though this may well be the ultimate illusion of the creative class.

If you imagine a character like Alan, you give credence to the very neoliberalism you're seeking to assail—after all, you, as a member of the younger generations, were sympathetic to the 1999 WTO protests and the 2011 Occupy movement—because you don't get carried away by sweeping alternatives. And so *Hologram* ends up being uncomfortably close to the familiar novel of middle-class, middle-age stasis and bankruptcy, emotional and financial. It's just that it takes place in Saudi Arabia, a land where the ruling elite gets away with pretty much anything it wants—drinking, promiscuity, self-criticism, you name it.

I'm not expecting Eggers to be an economic philosopher; he is, however, enough of a student of the history of the novel not to want to push his fiction in a more questioning direction.

Hologram is a highly readable novel of late globalization, and is bound to spark conflicting thoughts no matter one's persuasion on the merits of globalization. If it suffers from faint-heartedness, it's because it's difficult to work with a character like Alan and do much more than live within the constraints of reality. Once you start with someone like Alan, the end is pretty much determined, and the novel ends up not making a substantial advance over journalism. It's difficult to have deep sympathy for a sorry white male character associated with a particularly self-satisfied stage of capitalism—John Updike, Arthur Miller, and Tennessee Williams covered that territory very well, and it's not clear if the exotic new place adds substantially to the meaning.

The paradox millennial writers would be well-served to explore in more depth is that globalization disrupts traditional ways of doing things, yet it also helps produce uniformity of psychology and motives (or at least the appearance of such) so that human beings across cultures communicate more easily. The loss of local tradition, in other words, comes with the gain of better communication, but the cost is greater mediocrity across the board.

The way out of that bind is one of the biggest cultural challenges globalization faces, but a novel with a quintessential American like Alan at its center of consciousness is ill-equipped to explore this conflict.

Neoliberal faith in markets as the universal solvent is something that's actually confirmed by Eggers's narrative—since Alan can even sympathize with the entrepreneurial abilities of Yousef's shoe-selling father—but Eggers doesn't seem to have completely understood its pernicious effects. What kind of humanization discourse—the universal consumer manipulated by the sign of the commodity?—is predicated under neoliberalism, and does Eggers's humanization of Saudis ever amount to more than this?

Hologram—like others of its class—is a realist novel of the post-ideological vein, from a card-carrying member of the coolest generation, a point emphasized by the incredibly diverse range of creative people mentioned in the acknowledgments, as though the book had been processed and approved by every shade of conviction, and had bypassed the taint of specific ideology. A touch of anger would have done this novel a world of good.

Symposium: *Who is the Most Important Contemporary Poet?*

Harvey L. Hix's many books of poetry include *Incident Light, Legible Heavens*, and *Chromatic*, for which he was a National Book Award finalist.

In asking "Who is the most important contemporary poet?" Anis knows his question cannot be about ranking poets, as polls rank sports teams. The superlative in "Which is the best college football team this year?" is unconditional and exclusive. "Best" in relation to football teams means "would win against any other team," so there can be only one best team, and the question is about identifying that team. But "most important" in relation to poets might mean any number of things—having the widest influence, being allied with the most powerful person, having the largest audience—so the question is *not* about identifying which poet is most important, but about stipulating which meaning of "most important" is at stake. An answer doesn't give information about the poet, but about the meaning of the term "most important."

In naming Adrienne Rich, then, when any number of names come to mind as apt answers, how do I mean the term "most important"? I mean most consistent and effective, over the longest period of time, at defying "Poetry makes nothing happen." I mean demonstrating how a capacious body of work can shape an elevating vision, and be shaped by an elevated vision, of humanity and justice and peace and respect. I mean living up to her own standard that poetry be "liberatory at its core," asking herself and her readers, and challenging us to answer with our better rather than our worse selves, the question "With whom do you believe your lot is cast?"

Rigoberto Gonzalez's poetry books include *Unpeopled Eden* and *Black Blossoms*.

Though I would like to champion more than one poet, today I will single out Benjamin Alire Sáenz, who has been fearless in politicizing his verse. His last two poetry books, *The Book of What Remains* (2010)[1] and *Dreaming the End of War* (2006), have been unwavering in their pro-border, pro-human rights, and pro-peace stance, without compromising the integrity of what the apolitical poets call craft. I'm more engaged, however, by his vision of a better world, where poetry builds and hopes. Sáenz has been a longtime hero of mine because he is also an accomplished prose writer and children's book author, but I always go back to his poetry, particularly his first collection, *Calendar of Dust* (1991), which won an American Book Award when I was just beginning graduate school. This incredible book explored my community's history and Southwestern landscape, the complexities of our troubled families—it gave me permission to imagine that the people I knew and the places I came from could become the ink on a page. So many books later he continues to inspire me.

Marilyn Hacker's many books of poetry include *Presentation Piece* and *Love, Death, and the Changing of the Seasons*.

Let me praise here a poet who has been present in my life since I was sixteen, Marie Ponsot, whose critical and lyrical intelligence I could only wish to inform my own poetic practice. A bilingual writer, with France and varied North American landscapes significant in her work, Ponsot remains one of the most eloquent poets of New York City, one whom I'd not hesitate to place alongside Crane, Rukeyser, and O'Hara in her realization of an urban poetics, in the way in which her work inhabits and is inhabited by this city. Her poetry negotiates an edgy territory of loss and discovers it to share a border with the breathtaking landscape of intellectual freedom. The skill in her deployment of prosody is such that one need not remark upon it. A careful reader notices that her words mean what they have always said: every inflection and connotation rippling through the common usage from a point of origin has been accounted for. She teaches us thought's verbal anatomies, not from a syllabus, but in the context of conversation, storytelling, even admonition: loving discourse. Ponsot's poetry is

---

1. My review of *The Book of What Remains* was published in the *Austin American-Statesman*, and can be found at http://www.statesman.com/news/entertainment/books-literature/two-poets-of-southwestern-alienation/nRwX6/.

always demanding, but it is never "difficult" in the contemporary critical sense. Rigorous and generous with readers, it is unsparing in what it indicates as it shares what it loves.

John Matthias has published some twenty-five books of poetry, criticism, scholarship, and translation, including *Kedging* and *Trigons*.

In the spirit of this game—and it can't be more than that; "greatest" is impossible to ferret out among contemporaries—I would feel obliged to say Geoffrey Hill. My reading of Hill goes back to 1957 when I was still in high school and discovered him in the two much-maligned Hall, Pack, and Simpson anthologies.[2] By the mid-1960s I was living in England and had read *King Log*, and, a little later, *Mercian Hymns*. These, I thought, were very great books, and *Mercian Hymns* sent me back to David Jones, whose work I later edited and whose influence on my work is probably greater than Hill's. While I do not admire all of Hill's work equally—and while there is no indication that he is even aware of my own—I have come to value particularly the books that many of his commentators seem to feel are the most problematic, the quartet of volumes from his "American" period that began in 1997 with *Canaan*. In rapid succession, *The Triumph of Love, Speech! Speech!*, and *The Orchards of Syon* appeared. These are all book-length poems of enormous ambition, which take tremendous risks. While I was reading these books I was working on four long poems of my own, *A Gathering of Ways, Pages: From a Book of Years, Automystifistical Plaice*, and *Kedging*. I'm sure that an astute reader could spot some debts. The closest approximation we have to Geoffrey Hill in the U.S. is the profoundly underestimated John Peck. Peck's learning, gravity, allusiveness, density, and music make his poetry, at its best, the equal of Hill's own. The book of Peck's to begin with is *Red Strawberry Leaf*.

Mary Jo Bang won the National Book Critics Circle award for *Elegy*.

What if you were asked to name the most important contemporary musician? Could you argue for a family tree that traces everything, hip-hop to Portishead, back to a single figure? Wouldn't that risk overestimating a favorite while reducing the others to mere followers. Who is the most important contemporary poet? It's too easy to point to Ashbery as the single reason high modernism slid into

---

2. *The New Poets of England and America*, edited by Donald Hall, Robert Pack, and Louis Simpson, with an introduction by Robert Frost, published by Meridian Books in 1957 and 1962.

postmodernism so gracefully we still can't find a seam. However, his influence was coincidental with a long moment that included the 1960s, Vietnam, feminism, semiotics, Oulipo, the L=A=N=G=U=A=G=E movement, Lyn Hejinian breathing new life into Gertrude Stein on her way to writing *My Life* (her disjunctive retelling of how she learned to speak), Susan Howe's poetic mash-ups (lyric history discourse), and Rae Armantrout's wry tangential minimalism. On the lyric side, we'd have to discredit Charles Simic, James Tate, and cross out Lucie Brock-Broido's "brocade apostrophes" (Bonnie Costello, reviewing *The Master Letters*), Louise Glück's *Meadowlands*, and Jorie Graham's *Materialism*. Poetic history mirrors real history (tanks and such, plus ideas). To try to pin that much credit (or blame) on one person suggests the world doesn't exist. All of these poets, Ashbery among them, practice a poetic that combines earnestness and irony, the exact ratio of which is dictated by the poet's personality and personal encounters with history. All prefer collage over linear cohesion. Collage takes us back to Surrealism and to early Eliot, and Rimbaud before that. Maybe we have to go back that far to credit someone with being the most important poet.

Juan Felipe Herrera was named U.S. poet laureate in 2015.

I'd say Tadeusz Różewicz—his ability to speak of transcendence and brutality, of slaughter and being; all within ten to fifteen lines. Every line a history without a historian, as if breaking back to us through rubble. Decades ago, after one of my friends, Victor Martinez, mentioned Różewicz to me, I began to reexamine my penchant for collage and dream-flow. For Różewicz this was ornament, impasto. Even punctuation was extra. How could he speak of the Holocaust without summoning thick description, the surreal, I asked? I began to pare down the artificial within the artificial, rather than look for essence within the radius of surface. Sincerity, simplicity—those minty twins that all wannabe rebel poets deride; how can I write this? Darwish, Parra, and Levine seem to be there. What to do with today's poetry as noise, disruption, spoken loops and/or "illegal" hybrid, cross-border, cross-genre sampling? Maybe we have moved from the text to an audience without a name where what the poet is after (if we can still call her a "poet") is explosive dissolution, a kind of sizzling trespass, an "instant message" into "everywhere." Różewicz escorts us to the boundary between the heart-felt "I" and the net "I-Poem."

Eileen Myles is the author of more than a dozen books of poetry and fiction, including *Not Me* and *Chelsea Girls*.

C. A. Conrad is approximately fifty years old, from Philly, queer, and author of the groundbreaking *The Book of Frank* (Wave Books, 2010). The book is the product of fourteen years of wild dedication to making this haiku accumulation of trippy sexual cultural critique that zings into the Disney protoplasm of the public American imagination. He invests a character "Frank" with the capacity to have all sexes, genders, and class sympathies. He's a poet for our time like Ginsberg was for his. Conrad is also instigator of Somatic Poetics which is a series of canny exercises for transmuting dark cul-de-sacs of knowledge and fear into playful and resilient arenas of desiring and feast. Go to http://SomaticPoetryExercises.blogspot.com to see what I mean. His *Advanced Elvis Course* (Soft Skull, 2009) is a compendium of prose poems about the King that radiate improvisational intelligence and wit. C.A. Conrad readings are events in themselves. He's a large man with long hair and prone to wearing glitter on his nails. His presence both alarms and disarms the space of the poetry world by his reedy and generous delivery of a constantly moving poetic that dismisses no topic or approach to being human and artist both.

David Biespiel's books of poetry include *Shattering Air* and *The Book of Men and Women*.

Though he died five years ago, the Polish poet Czeslaw Milosz gets my vote today for the most important contemporary poet. In an age of horror and wonder, Milosz comes as close as any poet in the last fifty years to synthesizing those opposites into a single vision that includes both introspection and public judgment. His poetry is a fusion of multiple poetic crossroads—each essential in their way and each influential to generations of poets across the world. His lyric gifts display a tremendous urgency of emotion, image, and occasion. His moral vision is profound and unyielding, a mixture of faith and skepticism that is characterized by a rare clarity of spiritual interrogation. His historic insights are non-partisan and non-aestheticized. Instead, his sense of history is fashioned in his poems as macro- and micro-narratives of complex and contradictory human behavior—in his case a reaction to the bleak twentieth-century void that living in Poland meant through the Nazi invasion, the Second World War, fascism, genocide, the collapse of independent Poland, and the crushing consequences of totalitarianism. It would be impossible to select a single poem that exemplifies

Milosz's art as a grand vision of the lyric, the moral, and the historical. A sample of a half-dozen might include: "A Poor Christian Looks at the Ghetto," "Campo dei Fiori," "City Without a Name," "Dedication," "A Song on the End of the World," and "And the City Stood in Its Brightness." Milosz's influence on other major poets of influence has been elegant and undeniable: Seamus Heaney's haunting portraits of religious violence, Joseph Brodsky's cool interpretations of public hypocrisy, to name two non-Americans. As well as on American poets, such as W. S. Merwin's velocities into soul and self, C. D. Wright's historical unveiling of the American South, and C. K. Williams's skepticism toward political leadership, to name just three. His influence upon poets of every stripe and aesthetic is not debatable. I can't quantify the influence he has had on my work except to say that he inspires me, each time I write, to make poems where all the poetic thrusters are running at maximum and at once—and to consider that the lyric is hollow without the social, the self is incorporated in the community, and the subjects of time and faith are the heartbeat of poetic expression.

Michael McClure's books of poetry over the past sixty years include *The New Book/A Book of Torture*, *Rebel Lions*, and *Mysteriosos and Other Poems*.

In Diane di Prima's luminous poetry, wars are against the flesh of living beings, the socially and personally enslaved, and consciousness itself. "Revolutionary Letter #75: Rant" begins, "You cannot write a single line without a cosmology / a cosmogony / laid out before all eyes." Soon Rant becomes "THE ONLY WAR THAT MATTERS IS THE WAR AGAINST THE IMAGINATION / ALL OTHER WARS ARE SUBSUMED IN IT." Though Captain Ahab failed at it, di Prima has struck through the mask. This is poetry of bio-wisdom—a part of a great-hearted consciousness. It is one with body and mind. It is warm-blooded spirit from a human mammal. Di Prima sees history and future as shapes that we create with shoulders and breasts and hands. Her music on the page reverberates in the voice and the mind. Her poetry ranges from grand, as in the epic poem *Loba*, to small, floating, sometimes abstract verses. Book-length *Loba* is the incarnation of being female in all worlds, places, and mythologies. Begun in the late 1960s, *Revolutionary Letters* is a growing chronicle of the unstoppable revolution. Her impelling systems are in alchemical practices and science, as well as the core of Zen and Tibetan practices. There is no other poet like Diane di Prima.

Kelly Cherry is a novelist, poet, essayist, and former poet laureate of Virginia. Her sixteen books of poetry include *The Retreats of Thought: Poems* and *Hazard and Prospect: New and Selected Poems*.

Fred Chappell's manifold awards include the Bollingen Prize, the Prix du Meilleur Livre Étranger, the T. S. Eliot Prize, an award in literature from the National Institute of Arts and Letters, and the Mihai Eminescu Medal from the Republic of Moldova. Considering that Moldovans are aware of his poetry, it's odd that not more Americans are, but if his work is not better known, it is because (a) he prefers a low profile, and (b) he lives in the South. He has published thirty full-length books, including sixteen volumes of poetry; and four chapbooks. I am inspired daily by the purity of his intention, his devotion to literature, his unremitting allegiance to the highest standards, and his hard work on behalf of students and his native state of North Carolina. I once heard him say that his chief aim in life is to get out of it without causing harm: that's Chappell, through and through. Those who don't know his poetry might start with *Shadow Box, Backsass, Family Gathering, Source,* or the bewitchingly beautiful *Castle Tzingal.* His voice is by turns intimate and public, serious and playful, and he uses it to think about things that matter.

Jay Parini is a poet, novelist, biographer, and critic, whose six books of poetry include *Anthracite Country* and *The Art of Subtraction: New and Selected Poems*.

It's a mug's game, as T.S. Eliot once said of poetry. What he may have meant is that it's almost impossible to rank poets, and the game itself somehow takes poetry into a realm where it will always live uncomfortably. Nevertheless, over many years, I've gravitated to a handful of contemporary poets: Seamus Heaney, Philip Levine, Charles Wright, and Charles Simic. Of these, I would probably have to say that Simic has been most important to me in the past decade. Born in Belgrade in 1938, he understands viscerally about war, oppression, despair, and—in the midst of these bad things—hope. In "Explaining a Few Things," for instance, he writes: "It's raining. In spite of their huge armies / What can the ants do?" The cycle of nature holds us in its mighty grip, no matter what. In my view, Simic is our primary poet, with his finger exactly on the pulse of our cultural despair, our giddiness, our sense of language being the last resource of the broken spirit. His darkness is ours, but it's backlight. There is massive sunshine in his poems, too, as in "Summer Morning," which celebrates listening, merely being in the world.

Clayton Eshleman is noted for his translations of César Vallejo and has received the National Book Award for his work. He has been publishing books of poetry for almost sixty years, including, recently, *The Essential Poetry: 1960-2015* (Black Widow Press).

The poetry of the Martinican Aimé Césaire (1913-2008) symbolizes and sums up what is probably the twentieth century's most important phenomenon: the powerful surge next to the old and the new world of a third world both very new and very old. Animistically dense, charged with eroticism and blasphemy, and imbued with African and Vodun spirituality, Césaire's poetry takes the French surrealist adventure to new heights and depths. A Césaire poem is a crisscrossing intersection where metaphoric traceries create historically-aware nexuses of thought and experience, jagged solidarity, apocalyptic surgery, and solar dynamite. As in the case of César Vallejo, translating Césaire's poetry taught me that ambivalence and contradiction are facets of metaphoric probing, and he gave me permission to try anything in my quest for an authentic alternative world in poetry. Césaire is the primary influence on two of our finest contemporary American poets: Jayne Cortez and Will Alexander.

Fady Joudah's *The Earth in the Attic* won the Yale Series of Younger Poets prize. His translation of Mahmoud Darwish's poetry, *If I Were Another*, received the PEN USA Literary Award for Translation.

Mahmoud Darwish would have to be that poet for me. He was a poet of stages, of perpetual metamorphosis, insistent on changing his aesthetic each time he achieved a new height within it. He moved from the political poem to the witness and documentary poem; from the collective lyric to the personal lyric; from the historical poem to the quotidian, the daily; from the epic to the dramatist; from monologue to dialogue; from prosody to prose poems. He always oscillated between representation and becoming. He also developed his private lexicon and continued to expand it not only beyond a fixed set of signifiers but also beyond signification at times. He created a dictionary for his own texts through which a reader's imagination roams free of the contemporary limitations of specificity as we have come to insist on it. He also wrote fantastic prose narratives—three of which exhibit his journey from journal or essay to memoir, from memoir to simply "text," free of naming. He is a poet ahead of his time, despite his "celebrity," and he will come to be fully read later on, like the best of wines.

Bill Zavatsky's books include *Theories of Rain and Other Poems* and *Where X Marks the Spot*.

Ron Padgett has been a favorite poet of mine since the 1960s, when I first encountered his work. His verbal daring, his humor, his sense of life as a landscape of mystery and joy, his honesty and humaneness, and the emotional deepening of his work as he goes forward draw me to his books again and again. Padgett's genius is to follow his thought no matter where it leads him. He is less concerned with making an old-fashioned shapely poem than he is with the movement of a shapely mind, and in that regard he joins ranks with other poets who have broken new ground. There are plenty of twists, turns, and unexpected moments in Padgett's work, but this feeling of excitement is exactly why I want to read him. Sometimes his work is straightforward, sometimes it is roller-coaster wild, but he never trades in obscurity. I often find myself wishing that I had written all of his poems. Of Padgett's plethora of books you might begin by reading his recent large collection, *How to Be Perfect* (Coffee House Press), and his next book, *How Long*, from the same publisher.

Kevin Prufer's six books of poetry include *Churches, In a Beautiful Country*, and *National Anthem*.

There is a certain elasticity in great (i.e. "important") poetry that allows it to be meaningful not only to the poet's contemporaries, but to those who follow through the ages, who read the work from different contexts and ever-shifting concerns. In this way, we cannot read Homer as ancient Greeks, nor can we read Shakespeare as sixteenth-century Londoners, though their work, never entirely grounded in the past, unfolds in our present in new and thrilling ways. From the limitations of where I stand, then, I can't know who is "important," though Robert Hass is important to me. In his best poems, he creates intricate, complex, restless narratives like no other poet—but it is the anxious mind beneath them that I admire more, the mind that tries (and often fails) to make sense of the complicated world, to express the nuances of lived experience, to understand both the artifice of the poem and the truth it would communicate to us. I'd like one day to achieve something like his illusions of narrative and his sense of a fine, intricate mind at work on complex problems. I hope his work affects my peers in the same way.

Campbell McGrath's numerous books of poetry include *Capitalism, American Noise, Florida Poems, Pax Atomica,* and *Seven Notebooks.*

The most important poet? A multitude of names springs to mind, of which I might pick five—Louise Glück, Robert Hass, Galway Kinnell, Yusef Komunyakaa, and C.K. Williams—each of whom has, at some point in the last thirty years, been our very best poet, the one writing at the almost magical spot where personal vision and the power of the tradition intersect. Looking to the future, I can only say, all hail the Dark Room Collective! Has there ever been a movement or school in American poetry with more raw talent than the poets who have emerged from this Cambridge-based poetry confab of the 1980s and 1990s, among them Elizabeth Alexander, Major Jackson, Tracy K. Smith, Natasha Tretheway, and Kevin Young? Dark Room writers have already begun to win major awards and will undoubtedly impact our literature for decades to come. Having praised American poetry sufficiently, let me conclude with the assertion that the single obvious master poet of our era is Seamus Heaney, whose depth of feeling, historical vision, linguistic dexterity, formal range, and musical ear are unmatched on our side of the Atlantic.

Bob Hicok's books include *Animal Soul, Insomnia Diary,* and *Elegy Owed.*

If I popped open a dozen lit mags, the poet I'm most likely to feel ghosting the poems is still John Ashbery. His devotion to his mind's peregrinations has been like a French kiss with the zeitgeist. The era's dominant notions have led to artistries driven by epistemological suspicion and shaped significantly by pastiche and collage. The play and breeze in his work suit the times and jibe with the po-mo love of insouciance, as well as a widely held belief in mind as the true subject of art. His poems feel like performances, like they're written river-quick and with honest appreciation for the opportunity the particular writing moment has to offer. This is a gift to poets told they must revise, revise, revise and cut their poems from stone, which has led to a lot of stone-dead poems. However, this associative vitality is hard to channel into a felt sense of overall purpose or meaning, even for Ashbery. The downside of his influence is the downside of influence generally: borrowers tend to evince more of the limitations of a style than its strengths. Poets who try to wear Ashbery's head tend to write poems that are so coy about their purpose as to have little or none. This says less about his poems and more about how we teach writing.

Forrest Gander's books include *Eye Against Eye, Torn Awake*, and *Science and Steepleflower*.

The most important North American poet? John Ashbery of course. If he doesn't win the Nobel Prize in Literature, it will be a crying shame. Like his books or not, it's almost impossible to read or write poetry anywhere in the world and not take into account Ashbery's legacy. Ashbery is avant-garde. His book *The Tennis Court Oath* is radically disjunctive. Ashbery is formal. He writes centos and double sestinas. He's a lyric poet whose *Notes from the Air* includes some of the shapeliest sentencing and loveliest rhythms in our language. His long prose passages in *Three Poems* blazed a new genre in English, tipping a hat to France. France?! Ashbery so capaciously samples a demotic American English that he's captured, more than anyone else, how we sound to our century. He's hilarious and will sigh, apropos of nothing, "Oh nargileh!" He's a philosophical poet who considers that "to leave all out" may be a truer mode of expression than any attempt to channel story. His lines erotically resist resolution. Loss haunts his work; poems (and whole books like *Girls on the Run*) go bottomlessly poignant. He's still doing it, up on the one, nailing keepers. Hallelujah!

David Young's books include *Field of Light and Shadow* and *The Planet on the Desk: Selected and New Poems 1960-1990*.

I think I would have to say William Stafford. No doubt he wrote too much and was reluctant to revise and refine his poems, but he seems to me to continue something in American poetry that was fostered by Dickinson and Williams, an openness to experience, a habit of poetry that wove it in and through the textures of ordinary life and thought. Also, for poets like me (a kid from Nebraska/Iowa/Minnesota), he opened up the territories of the Midwest and the West as valid locales for poets and poems. Then too, in his life and his personal integrity, he set an example for a new generation of poets, a way of being a poet that didn't necessarily involve alcoholism, infidelity, depression, competitive behavior, and suicide. Poets as different as Robert Bly, Gary Snyder, Charles Wright, Denise Levertov, Ted Kooser, and W.S. Merwin seem to me to have profited from his example, eschewing rhetoric in the interest of making poetry into something it has most often been in the Asian tradition: a natural part of life, a practice that has spiritual implications, a way of being that belongs to all of us, at least in our best moments.

Jean Valentine is the author of over a dozen books of poetry, including *Break the Glass* and *Shirt in Heaven*.

I first found Eleanor Ross Taylor's work back when her first book, *Wilderness of Ladies*, came out, in 1960; she was forty. At the time, some of the good poets I knew said her poetry was hard to understand; reading it now, it might be hard to think why. But she was a woman, and completely original, and she chose to work far away from the "engine room" of literary life, and that combination may have made for some of the resistance. Her intelligence, song, and the reach of her narratives contain, without a hair of pretension, her exploration of the spirit's fate, spoken by a wild collection of captive voices. Taylor did not choose a "career," but she did what she could: she chose a faithful life in writing. My hunch is that somewhere inside her, she knows who she is. In any case, this has always been one reason her life in poetry gives me faith, and hope: she has let her poetry flower without much of any public light (though now it is good to see that she has gotten some). Her husband, the novelist Peter Taylor, once told me that Randall Jarrell, a very close friend of the Taylor family, who first got Eleanor's poetry into print, had said about Eleanor: "She works at the bottom of the ocean, without a diving bell."

Thoughts for AWP Week:
The Glut in Creative Writing Is the Reverse Side
of the Drought in Humanities

This week in Seattle,[1] at the annual AWP (Association of Writers & Writing Programs) conference, anywhere from ten to fifteen thousand writers will congregate in what has become the largest such literary gathering in America. There will be more than four hundred and fifty panels on every aspect of professional advancement, and a bookfair hosting more than six hundred and fifty exhibitors, each of whom will pay a hefty fee to be seen among fellow indie presses. A parallel conference of countless off-site events will occur simultaneously, so that anyone with any gumption *will* have an opportunity to read and promote themselves.

Fifteen thousand, you say? Does that boggle the mind? Do the colossal numbers to which this professional guild has grown signify the health or sickness of writing?

Alas, discussion of the ultimate goals of literature will not be part of the official record at AWP, since out of the hundreds of panels none seem to be devoted to asking such worrisome questions. Instead, the panels repeat a few characteristic anxieties: how to convert autobiographical experience within particular identity niches into saleable memoir, how to get funding and recognition for one's writing program at different levels, how to reach into new constituencies like prisoners and high-school students and mental patients, how to exploit social media from Facebook to Twitter to promote one's press or individual work, and how to write the kinds of books that win contests or awards leading to secure jobs.

---

1. February 26 to March 1, 2014.

The titles of some of the panels testify to the obsession with professional success within extremely narrow boundaries, rather than any transcendent concerns about literature:

- Put Your Shit on Paper: Two Chicago-Based Writing Programs on Running Trauma-Informed High School Workshops
- The Author's Children: The Intersection of Art, Advocacy, and Ethics in Writing About Your Kids
- Beef Jerky, Bras, and Car Parts: What We Write About When We Write for Money
- Taking Literature off the Page: How to Be a More Attractive Job Candidate
- Family Trouble: Memoirists on the Hazards and Rewards of Revealing Family
- Poetry and the Online Community: Using Digital Media to Build Audience
- Independent Bookselling: Opportunities for Authors
- Verses Versus Verses: Perspectives on Poetry Contests
- Writing Inside Out: Authors' Day Jobs
- Full Disclosure: How to Spill Your Guts without Making a Mess
- Applying for a National Endowment for the Arts Creative Writing Fellowship
- All Publishers Great and Small: Reexamining the Book Business in the Twenty-First Century
- How Twitter Works (and Doesn't Work) For Writers
- #interaction: How Social Media Changed the Conversation Between Audience and Author
- From Thesis to Book: The Stretch Run
- Gaming Social Media
- A Family Affair: Family Structure as Narrative Structure
- Calling all Poets! You've Found Your Voice; Now Find Your Audience
- To Wear Every Color of the Heart: Going Beyond Craft to Teach Youth in Hospital Settings
- The Parent-Writer: Can We Really Have It All?
- Crossing the Veil: Engaging the Editor Who Rejects Your Work
- Beg, Borrow, Steal: Twenty-five Best Teaching Practices from Teachers Who Write for Writers Who Teach
- From Finding Your Muse to Finding Your Readers: Book Promotion in the Twenty-first Century

- MFA Students as TAs at Community College: Two Models
- Lead from the Front: Best Practices for Working with Veterans in the Writing Classroom
- News from Nowhere: Writing Through Difficulty with Marginalized Middle and High-School Populations
- The Business of Literary Publishing in the Twenty-First Century
- What's a Creative Writing PhD Worth?
- The Irony of the Internet: Reevaluating & Redefining Business & Creativity in the Digital Age
- Advice to Nonprofit Organizations Seeking Funding from the NEA
- Amazon for Authors
- Brave New Media: The Promises and Pitfalls of Teaching Creative Writing for Digital Environments
- and last but not least, Best Practices for Submitting an AWP Panel Proposal (hint: read the above panel titles!)

Is your head spinning yet? Notice that the profession presents itself as so totally victorious over literature that it need not ask any questions beyond process and mechanics: every panel seems preoccupied with "best practices." It also becomes clear that autobiographical/therapeutic/memoiristic writing—the foundation of workshop pedagogy—is essentially what most literary writing boils down to today.

The defenders of creative writing programs have a lot of explaining to do. Their rationales for the mind-boggling proliferation of MFA programs at American universities over the last three decades reveal a self-serving vocational bias, immune to criticisms with legitimate historical and philosophical grounding.

As a result, critics like myself—or in earlier periods, Donald Hall, Greg Kuzma, Vernon Shetley, Joseph Epstein, John Aldridge, Kurt Vonnegut, and many others—tend to be dismissed as motivated by sour grapes if they're writers themselves or lacking practical knowledge of the profession if they're primarily scholars. Rarely is the substance of our criticisms addressed in the increasingly desperate apologias mounted on behalf of a bureaucracy that has exceeded all expectations since the AWP was founded with modest aims in the late 1960s. Today one goes to AWP not for criticism but for self-validation.

A recent defensive screed, appearing in *Inside Higher Ed* on July 5, 2013, reveals the usual problems of deflection and subterfuge. A phenomenon cannot be justified as morally sound because of its prevalence. Just because hundreds of writing programs have recently cropped up in American universities, and just because they are financially successful for institutions, does not mean that they are good for *writing*. The false promise held out by a gathering of AWP's magnitude has real consequences for how genuine writing is received in the world.

In *Against the Workshop: Provocations, Polemics, Controversies* (Texas Review Press, 2011) and elsewhere, I have described creative writing programs as primarily therapeutic rather than motivated by traditional notions of creativity and inspiration. I would add that therapy in these programs functions within a narrow range of white middle-class norms, so it is not surprising that the typical MFA student also comes from a narrow background.[2] Sheer numbers cannot hide this fact.

Certainly, minorities are increasingly found in writing programs, but any observer of the scene will note the tremendous pressure to conform. When so-called "silenced voices" find expression within this mode of organized creativity, what often results is an apolitical product that leaves the institutional bases of oppression and tyranny untouched because of the writing workshop's false—neoliberal—credo that all psychological problems are self-created and subject to individual, not collective, responses. This is why there is so much interest in memoir as originating from the self's own conundrums, in essence a privatization of social instinct.

The workshop is a great model for teaching economic citizenship within a narrow spectrum, so the apparently diverse student recruitment in writing programs doesn't really reflect the constraints put upon voice and discovery.

Criticism in this vein, the defenders of creative writing should note, is not new, going back to Mas'ud Zavarzadeh's critique of the ideology of the workshop, while any number of other critics over the decades have taken the Iowa Writers Workshop model to task for the banality and programmatic lack of innovation it engenders. The idea that workshop pedagogy leads to conservative outcomes should not sound surprising to anyone with knowledge of literary theory, but the profession acts in shock when any such proposition is advanced.

It's not coincidental that defenders of the system leap most aggressively to defense of the *workshop* itself, because the present hegemony in writing instruction is inconceivable without this centerpiece of faux democracy which is actually a cover for ideological conformity. Without workshop, one starts allowing literary history and literary criticism—that is to say, the institutional context of writing both past and present—into the classroom, but this is verboten because it would make the current model collapse.

---

2 I explicitly compare writing workshop with therapy modalities in my essay "Creative Writing Is Therapy, Even If the Pedagogues Won't Admit It," published in *Boulevard* in Fall 2012.

Despite what the "Five Creative Writing Professors" I mentioned earlier would have you believe, my books are in conversation with three preceding important evaluations of the workshop system—namely, D. G. Myers's *The Elephants Teach: Creative Writing Since 1880* (1996), Paul Dawson's *Creative Writing and the New Humanities* (2005), and Mark McGurl's *The Program Era: Postwar Fiction and the Rise of Creative Writing* (2009)—which show a progressive degree of acceptance of workshop from the earliest to the latest book. This fatalism—for example toward the behemoth known as AWP—seems most unfortunate to me.

In *Against the Workshop*, I specifically question McGurl for his functionalist endorsement of workshop as the pedagogy we must accept simply because it dominates. It is the apologists, in fact, who act as if workshop persists in an ideological vacuum, as though there can be no other method to train writers.

Similarly, a vast literature exists to show the parallels between therapy and writing workshops, a body of work I explicitly recognize and assess, whereas this particular set of defenders of workshop makes no recognition of this internal critique from within the profession. The charge is often made simultaneously that my ideas are so well-known as to be unoriginal and that they are so radical as to be unsubstantiable; both cannot be true. Furthermore, being able to reach a broad audience does not make one a talk show host. The interest of the designated apologists is to silence dissenting voices at all costs.

There is the larger question of the crisis in the humanities, of which scholarly skepticism toward the humanities' function and worth because of theory's assault is one aspect, and the loss of direction of students exposed to the humanities in their current state of self-doubt is another. Does the atmosphere at AWP evoke the humanities as a live phenomenon, able to speak to issues of concern to the public at large, or does it speak of a radical diminishment of ideas liable to be dangerous if they get out?

After all, who wants to undergo the rigors of studying history or philosophy when the very idea of liberal education under humanistic premises has been shown to be a sham? Doesn't expressing one's purely subjective concerns become a valid alternative under such conditions, especially if great numbers of people are seen as following the same path? And furthermore, isn't it something that everyone can potentially do, because after all everyone has a life story to tell, rather than get into the weeds of fussy scholarship?

But if large numbers of those who used to pursue traditional humanistic disciplines as valid creative endeavors choose to become "creative writers," then there is an oversupply of creativity, or what substitutes for creativity, and therefore a debasement of the whole creative venture. Art is served poorly when it is made a fetish outside time and space, outside the history which always makes it real and pertinent. The severance of literature and criticism is a reality with terrible consequences the defenders of workshop are at pains to ignore.

All is not well in writing and publishing, the claims of the AWP hierarchy notwithstanding. I would pose the following questions as starters toward a productive conversation which looks beyond the knee-jerk defense of a system that has assumed all the airs of a sacred theology:

- What is the ideological dimension of the MFA system when it comes to the class interests it protects and serves?
- If the system is predicated on replication and uniformity—as must be the case when the numbers involved are so great—then is there anything teachers can do to provoke genuine inspiration and innovation?
- How can the chasm between creative writing and literary criticism be bridged, assuming that this is a destructive tendency making both sides hunker down in further isolation?
- If workshop presents itself as the exclusive path to glory, then how can it be truly democratic? Are the boosters willing to recognize the new means of exclusion and delegitimation that have been put in place to counter those not inclined to follow the favored professional track?
- At what point is anarchic breakdown within the hegemonic system actually a service rather than a disservice to writing? What would be the conditions inviting such a breakdown?

In short, is it fair to see writing as a commodity, a business, or a credential? If the answer is no, then how can writing teachers—i.e., writers—justify spending all their energies on the validation of these inevitable outcomes of workshop?

If writing today is homogenous, it is because the teaching method has become homogenous. Almost the totality of young American writers are encouraged to approach their vocation now through the institutional system firmly in place. Even if they're not naturally inclined to pursue the favored path, they clearly see the disadvantages of not allying with the methodology producing nearly all literary writers, so they don't see a choice. Debt and disappointment are often the results, except perhaps for those lucky enough to find spots in the most prestigious schools and thereafter jobs teaching writing to others.

Literary writing has become almost completely assimilated inside academia.

Nearly all writers are professors first and writers second. Is this a healthy situation, especially if one narrow pedagogy—the peer-oriented workshop—dominates teaching? What effects does this have on the forward advancement of literature? This, it seems to me, is the question to answer, rather than carping at critics who point out the obvious. And it seems strange indeed that not a single panel out of hundreds at AWP is devoted to addressing this ultimate question.

The bunker mentality of the defenders of creative writing prevents them from seeing that their profession has evolved as a result of the long-maturing crisis in the humanities. Creative writing is a curious apparition, having split off from the traditional humanities to permit self-expression without depth of knowledge; in effect, it is a pastiche of the humanities, the credential without the foundation. It happens to produce outsized financial rewards for universities because of the elastic supply of substitutable instructors, providing a model of low-stakes instruction that avoids the scrutiny of measurement otherwise obsessing academia only because it wears a fuzzy cloak of outcomes.

The humanities have taken a body blow in recent decades because of accusations of lack of utilitarian value in a technocracy, and part of the response has been for creative writing to step into the breach to produce a culture that makes virtues out of the original flaws, doubling down on all that is perceived to be wrong with the humanities.

The economic grievances of endless surplus academic labor in the new corporate university have become redirected toward harmless memoirist expression within identity niches, an arrangement quite satisfactory to those in control of the purse strings. Increasingly, the justifications offered for creative writing are the ones that used to be offered for liberal education in general, except in watered-down form and without any specific promises.

For the defenders of workshop, there is no crisis in the humanities (because previously suppressed voices are supposedly finding self-expression), there is no crisis in writing, there is no crisis of any kind. But the truth is that serious fiction and poetry have hardly any audience outside academia today, a result that came about deliberately rather than coincidentally.

One can imagine the degree of professional competitiveness—for the few lucrative spots on publishers' lists or for plum teaching positions—that must rage at AWP, whereas the official presentation of the conference is as a mediator of the networks of mutual recognition that lead to advancement within the parameters of the profession. Each year, as comparison of this year's sixty-one page schedule in fine print testifies, these parameters get elaborated to more and more absurd levels, getting articulated in increasingly obsessive detail. Deviation from these standards then becomes an impossibility, because the sheer weight of opposition grows too large to be countered by any individual.

It has become an amazingly collectivist enterprise, which seems the whole point of the official conference as well as the parallel off-site networking that only confirms the formal tendencies. There was a big fuss among exhibitors this year when it looked like the bookfair wasn't going to be open to the public on Saturday as in previous years; eventually the conference relented, but the ruckus only emphasized the incestuous nature of the whole event: it's all about writers branding one another within a self-contained guild, not reaching out to the public anyway. The public (even if allowed into the bookfair for a look-see on a single day) is quite beside the point, it's not why writers become writers these days; they do it so they can teach and get funded.

One notices too that despite the hundreds of panels, the same limited number of individuals seems repetitively prominent, and that the count stays more or less stable from year to year. Growth is rampant and obscene, but in the end peripheral, since opportunity for any real literary success simply cannot be accommodated in such volume; this leads to the inevitable paradox of writing being deflected from its true goals and becoming obsessed with justifying the reach of existing practice.

Serious writing has become like a magic art with secret practitioners and overlords with mystical powers. Meanwhile, it is hard to convince scholars outside the creative writing vocation (not to mention the public) that the profession serves any humanistic function, when the writing is so class-bound, therapeutic, mediocre, and self-serving. To assert this is not to air dirty laundry, exposing the profession to an unnecessary hostile gaze; it is to ask the profession to look closely at the ways economic constraints and class biases blind us to the more utopian dimensions of writing.

Or one can just go to AWP and get with the program.

The Writer as Confidence Man:
James Magnuson's Wily Novel of Creative Writing

James Magnuson's *Famous Writers I Have Known* (*FWIHK*)[1] meets all the expectations of the campus novel genre and then some: the creation of art has obviously become bureaucratized, but the satirist's conundrum is that critique itself must be articulated within the formal terms set by the bureaucratization. Magnuson—as director of the Michener Center for Writers at the University of Texas at Austin—understands this paradox all too well and exploits it for maximum impact throughout this very enjoyable novel.[2]

Writers are famously preoccupied with the anxiety of influence: what is authentic, and what is mere imitation? Magnuson makes this the central theme in the dynamic between his protagonist, Frank Abandonato, an East Coast con man who finds himself taking the place of famous reclusive writer V. S. Mohle (think J. D. Salinger) hired by the world's best-selling writer Rex Schoeninger (modeled on James Michener) to teach pampered students at the Fiction Institute (standing in for the Michener Center) for the hefty sum of seventy-five thousand dollars. It becomes difficult after a while to distinguish the con man from the genuine aspirant, a confusion that escalates all the way to the inevitable denouement.

Magnuson deftly maneuvers Abandonato into adopting the identity of Mohle, as a result of a botched fake lottery ticket scheme that involves a mobster

---

1. W. W. Norton, 2014. An entirely separate radio interview, which I conducted with James Magnuson for Observer Radio on March 24, 2014 (Episode 49), can be heard here: https://www.texasobserver.org/observer-radio-episode-49-laying-prisoners-rest-huntsville/.

2. A related interview which I had to exclude from this book, but which fits very well into the context, is the extended conversation I had with John McNally, about his own satirical novel *After the Workshop* (2010), set at the Iowa Writers Workshop and having a lot of fun with the inanities of the workshop setting and the writing life in general. I found McNally's discussion of the unfortunate hierarchies that still prevail at institutions like Iowa particularly helpful. The full interview with McNally is here: http://www.huffingtonpost.com/anis-shivani/iowa-writers-workshop-gra_b_578258.html.

from the feared Cannetti family. When his accomplice Barry is killed by mafia goons, Frank, while making his getaway, observes a man who looks very much like him—Mohle—change his mind about boarding a flight to Austin to take on the aforementioned teaching position. Once he reaches Austin, Frank is mistakenly greeted as Mohle by dashing female MFA students, taken under the wings by Wayne, the institute director, and deposited at the isolated house meant for Mohle. The actual workshop teaching turns out to be easy enough to improvise, so there's no turning back.

Schoeninger has called Mohle to Austin because of a lingering sense of hurt going back twenty-five years ago to their fisticuffs on the Dick Cavett show, following which Schoeninger sued Mohle into bankruptcy and abandoning writing. Schoeninger—like Michener—is the author of numerous thousand-page novels, chockful of information about esoteric subjects but lacking any literary merit; Mohle, in contrast, is the author of a single slim book, *Eat Your Wheaties*, which has ensured his literary reputation (much like *The Catcher in the Rye*). It is Schoeninger, however, who wins the Pulitzer Prize, causing the long-ago estrangement.

Schoeninger's dark secret is that he once had a child whom he refused to raise, although he is an orphan himself; Frank is also an orphan, as is Mohle. The eighty-five-year-old Schoeninger—like Michener—is busily giving away his fortune, to the tune of a hundred million dollars, and Frank hopes to get a few million under the pretenses of a philanthropy for poor children. But an even more accomplished con artist, Dudley Stainforth, an Ivy League scholar and founder of a phony literary award, shows up to scam Schoeninger out of five million dollars. Frank's moral dilemma is whether to tell Schoeninger the secret of Stainforth's identity and deprive the dying benefactor of a final literary consolation, or to let Schoeninger fade out with illusions of grandeur.

With this basic setup Magnuson is able to let complex moral tensions play out. For example, the fake Mohle is much better at forgiveness than the real Mohle; it's true that Frank has nothing personal at stake, but we also observe a degree of human feeling rare in the hypercompetitive literary world.

Similarly, the advice Frank gives his students in workshop is far superior to that provided in real workshop, because of Frank's ability to filter through the literary bullshit his earnest students are producing to curry favor.

Frank also inspires Wayne to quit his mind-deadening administrative job and leave his family for the proverbial cabin in Montana to give his moribund novel a last shot; it's not likely to come to anything, but Frank's insincere advice is actually a great deal more sincere than what is ordinarily seen in the writing community.

If all Magnuson had accomplished was to skewer the fatuosities of workshop, it wouldn't have been particularly memorable since the genre is well covered. Certainly, Magnuson is excellent at capturing the absurdity of organized creativity, as when Frank comments on a student's work:

"I think it would be a big help if you went back to read some early de Maupassant. . . . And that scene in Grand Central . . . how late is it? Maybe our hero gets pickpocketed. Every other goddamned thing happens to him, why not? . . . I'm not trying to rewrite your story for you, but late at night at Grand Central, there are some real sleazeballs out there . . ."

This drivel is familiar enough from workshop, but the added charge here is that the con man speaks the lingo better than the pros.

But Magnuson has larger fish to fry than the obvious satire. Whereas Schoeninger's novels are based on voluminous research, Mohle only had the one autobiographical story in him. This represents the conflict between the current workshop credo of "write what you know" versus the social documentarian impulse of the nineteenth-century novelist, but it also extends to the struggle over the nature of morality: should it be based on feelings or rationality? The crafty old Schoeninger stands for abstract reasoning, whereas both Mohles abide on the pole of emotionalism. Magnuson's narrative skill consists in never allowing us to commit clearly in either direction.

In a world of profound duplicity—the writing world—the counterfeit Mohle raises the stakes. It takes a cultural ignoramus like Frank—with his bare-minimum knowledge of the Western canon and basic techniques of writing—to come to genuine cultural insight; by the end Frank is more committed to artistic purity than the real Mohle ever was in pristine isolation on his Maine island. As Frank notes, "I hate it when people think they can take advantage of us writers. They think we're naive, that we have our heads in the clouds, that we're so hungry for any crumb of praise they can treat us like children."

The crisis of the humanities is a crisis of the bureaucratization of thought and feeling: how are breakthroughs possible when even philanthropy—such as the Michener/Schoeninger impulse—is conformist? Magnuson understands that communities solidify themselves by repeated self-affirmation until they lose all touch with founding motivations, becoming parodies of themselves.

But the next parody that comes along—such as Magnuson's novel—becomes instantly absorbed in the community's self-rationalization and is therefore rendered immediately harmless. Magnuson has no answer to this, but he's smart enough to appreciate the impossibility of effective critique. Real art isn't forged inside workshop, yet outside workshop there's no legitimacy; neither Schoeninger nor Mohle, as unpampered autodidacts, would be relevant today.

The infinite progression of parody reigns supreme, so it is fitting that Frank composes the book we're reading in a comfortable "prison" where writing is offered as therapy, and where other con men from business and government are similarly composing saleable narratives. It is fitting too that his former students at the fiction institute have gone on to big success, while his own final attempt to retrieve the Cannetti mobster's money from his locker comes to nothing.

Writing fiction can be the source of orgasmic pleasure, but along with this come demons who discredit the activity every step of the way. Whatever confidence exists in the profession is precarious, which makes sincere relationships difficult. So the material for Magnuson's satire is readily available, yet he does an astonishing amount with it.

I was fascinated by your description of Rex Schoeninger as a way of understanding James Michener. What kind of relationship did you have with the late Michener, and what did you learn from him?

I would say that our relationship was mutually respectful. He was anything but a glad-hander. I quickly learned that the last thing you should do with Michener was ask him for something. He was a very shrewd man and knew when he was being worked.

The founders of some of the generously endowed writing programs and residencies would perhaps not recognize the degree to which their original function and rationale have become altered. What do you think have been the biggest changes with Stegner, Yaddo, FAWC, etc., and what would surprise the founders the most?

I'm no expert on the history of writing programs, but I have seen how the Michener Center has changed. Twenty years ago we were the new kids on the creative writing block and a bit of an oddity, because we were interdisciplinary. We made lots of mistakes in the beginning, corrected them as best we were able to. Because of the success of a number of the students, we are certainly viewed in a very different way now. That can be unnerving. I've tried very hard to keep us from getting too fancy.

In FWIHK the writing workshop students have a decent recognition of theory. That may be true on an individual level, but my understanding is that on a more systemic level theory and creative writing function in isolation, even antagonism, believing that one doesn't have a lot to teach the other. Do you regret the passing of humanist criticism in favor of the technocratic language of theory?

When someone showed me a Walter Benjamin article in the 1970s, it felt like a total revelation. A few years later, critical theory was spreading like kudzu. What had seemed so electrifying soon became doctrinaire and dispiriting, particularly to writers. You're right about the antagonism. It does exist. I do still seek out eccentric and suggestive criticism written by writers like D.H. Lawrence and William Carlos Williams. Zadie Smith is superb writing about books. But I confess, sometimes I will read a book like *Shamanism, Colonialism, and The Wild Man.*

What parts of writing can be taught? What can't be taught? Are we under a mass illusion when it comes to the teaching of writing, or is something helpful being done with instruction? Do you think the age of great original writers is over?

I think you can teach a young writer to spot and destroy the most egregious clichés, how to use point of view in a consistent way, how to develop a bit of an eye for the telling detail. You can get them excited about reading. You can teach them to prune dead language, even if you can't really teach them how to make language come alive. But the storytelling instinct is either there or it isn't. You have it or you don't, and there's not much a teacher can do.

What do you think is the biggest con as far as the writing industry is concerned?

A tough question. I think it's probably instilling false hope. I wince at this, because I'm a natural encourager. But sustaining a writing career is so difficult. My greatest nightmare is telling someone he's a genius, because I want him to feel better, and then he ends up wasting the next decade of his life.

I like the degree of moral overlap between Frank as con man and the similar feelings of anxiety and self-doubt—if not feelings of outright fakery—most writers experience. Was the character of Frank the original germ of the story, or was there some other starting point?

I appreciate your point. I spent eight years working on this novel and it was turned down by thirty publishers before it was finally taken. I absolutely felt like a fraud for a substantial part of that time.

As far as the germ of the novel goes, the book sprang from two very different notions. On the one hand I was intrigued by the idea of a lowlife passing himself as a world-class writer. I've always taken pleasure in farce, in those Danish plays where the beggar wakes up in the king's bed and everyone treats him as royalty.

But the other seed of the novel was planted as I watched so many people circling James Michener at the end of his life, angling for the remainder of his fortune. My wicked thought was, who could come along to ace them all out?

Did you have any difficulty settling on the tone for the novel?

Getting the tone just right was the hardest thing, and the most crucial. I had to take the utmost care not to impose my literary opinions on Frankie. In one sense I had to dumb him down (smart as he is). I went through and meticulously deleted all the words that I would use and he wouldn't. I also had to keep from becoming too fair-minded and kind for as long as I could.

We seem to be well past the age where a literary dispute could mean anything to the culture at large, as with the case of Mohle and Schoeninger's spat on national television, with dire consequences for both. Yet writers are eagerly enlisting in the latest phase of their own cultural emasculation—namely participation in social media, which really amounts to substituting a fake brand for any sense of individuality. What are your feelings toward the impact of technology on various aspects of writers' self-understanding?

I'm bewildered by all this. I'm one of the late adapters, one of those people who can never remember their password. It's a little unnerving. On the one hand, I find some great literary things on the internet I would never find any other way. But I wonder if it's turning all of us nerdy literary types into something we're not. A friend of mine says she feels like one of those clowns with the balloons out in front of Jiffy Lube, hopping up and down, shouting, "Look at me! Look at me!"

What are some of your favorite campus novels?

I love the David Lodge novels, Kingsley Amis's *Lucky Jim*, Richard Russo's *Straight Man*, and Michael Chabon's *Wonder Boys*.

Me too! It seems to me that Schoeninger—with his research orientation—does have a glimmer of truth in his possession, as far as the future of the global novel is concerned, even if his execution, and those of others like him, lacks much literary merit. Have you incorporated research in any of your novels? Do you think there can be a balance between the genuinely autobiographical (represented by Mohle) and the sociological approach (represented by Schoe-ninger)? Are there writers today who successfully integrate both elements, the autobiographical and the sociological?

I used to do a lot of research for my novels. I loved to go out into the world with a small spiral notebook in my back pocket and just look at things. I learned about rat-baiting in nineteenth-century New York, the layout of major-league ballparks, the whereabouts of anti-war radicals in the mountains of New Mexico. But then a family and a job curtailed my roaming. I made adjustments.

I love novels with reach and ambition. It seems to me as if a lot of contemporary fiction is way too cautious, as if it's been put through the rinse cycle one too many times. Peter Carey's novels are wonderful in the way they blend history and the very idiosyncratically personal. What Salman Rushdie pulled off in *Midnight's Children* was amazing. And don't forget Doris Lessing and the way she shuttled back and forth between the autobiographical and the political in *The Golden Notebook*. Will there be another Tolstoy? I don't know. I'd be happy with another Dos Passos.

Poetry Book Contests Should Be Abolished: Why Contests Are the Most Irrational Way to Publish First Books

Poetry contests are about the only remaining way to publish a first poetry book. And that's one way poetry is being killed in this country, reduced to consensus-by-committee, stripped of individual vision, yielding vast parchments of conformity and mediocrity, worthy only as boosters to resumes and means of landing academic jobs. Our poetry is haunted today by a blind adherence to lack of ambition—and the poetry contest model is part of the problem.

Nearly all independent and university-affiliated presses have converted to this model, which includes a poet submitting a manuscript to many different contests, paying typically twenty-five dollars[1] for the privilege, and being part of a pool of anywhere from a few hundred to more than a thousand manuscripts judged "blindly"—we'll soon see what that means in poetry contest parlance. The winner gets about a thousand dollars along with publication, and publicity in cloistered academic poetry circles. The nine hundred and ninety-nine losers print out another copy of the manuscript and write another check to yet another contest, never giving up hope.

Is this the best way to discover new poetry talent in the country? What happens to editorial judgment, consistent aesthetic vision, commitment to particular values, building a movement, advocating for a particular style, and creating a critical mass of new writing if the contest model is allegedly based

---

1. $25 is on the low side now; the rates are going up. A more serious issue is the rapid normalization of the standard $3.00 (or up) fee to read submissions, which creates a significant financial barrier to publication. To submit a poem or story to just ten journals would cost $30, or to twenty journals $60; this is an exclusionary model that hurts writers. In conversations I've had with journal editors, the fees are openly justified as going directly to the subsistence of the journal staff, not necessarily to the benefit of the journal itself. I am as opposed in principle to journals charging fees to read submissions as I am to paying contest fees for book entries.

on "impartiality" and "blindness"—in other words, the exemplar of democracy, egalitarianism, and disavowal of values? Has institutionalization gone too far? Would we all be better off—far-fetched as it sounds—if the contest model were eliminated and consistent editorial judgment were allowed to enter into the process of first book publication again?

Once upon a time, the contest model wasn't predominant, but along with the explosive growth in MFA programs and the thorough institutionalization of literary writing under the academy's auspices, small publishers who used to read submissions (without a fee, without a contest) have become almost completely extinct. A few remain, but they're so overwhelmed with commitments to long-term authors that new poets can't usually look to them as a viable option. They're a drop in the bucket, drowned by the overwhelming scale of the contest phenomenon.

The May/June 2011 *Poets & Writers* has a feature on writing contests. Editor Kevin Larimer (all credit to him for asking the right questions) interviews four poetry first book contest administrators, Stephanie G'Schwind (director of the Center for Literary Publishing and editor of *Colorado Review*), Michael Collier (director of the Bread Loaf Writers' Conference), Camille Rankine (program and communications coordinator at Cave Canem Foundation), and Beth Harrison (associate director of the Academy of American Poets and administrator of the Walt Whitman Award), discussing issues of fairness, impartiality, process, revenues, and results. (Full Disclosure: I've been published in *Colorado Review* and consider G'Schwind an excellent editor; and I know Collier from Bread Loaf).

Publishing new writing by way of contests implies a certain metaphysical attitude: what is a contest but belief in randomness, divisibility, fragmentation, unknowability, nondeterminism, perfected and ground through a process of rationalization to what we can only presume are the opposites of these conditions? Something that starts out as fluid and yielding is supposed to gel into a final judgment. The contradictions are rife. Victory in a poetry contest is never unequivocal—hence the (sometimes inordinately) long lists of runners-up, finalists, and honorable mentions, as though any of these could easily have been the victor. There is a victor, and yet there isn't. The illusion must be perpetuated that everyone always has an equal shot at winning the contest. All books are potentially publishable.

Much of Larimer's interview focuses on the mechanics of judging contests, from the point of view of these four administrators. How do the contests get the submissions, who screens them, how is impartiality ensured, etc. However, the way the questions are framed presumes the fairness of the system, delving instead into the nitty-gritty. This serves to sideline the larger political and philosophical implications of the idea of publishing books by contest. Discussing tactics, or occasionally strategy, but not philosophy, is a way to defuse the angst and enhance existing legitimacy for the benefit of the system.

For instance, Harrison tells Larimer: "The Academy [of American Poets] has on staff three part-timers who are MFA candidates at Columbia University; they do a first screening of manuscripts. . . . If none of the screeners is particularly moved by a manuscript, but the person who's submitting has a ton of publication credits, it moves along to the judge anyway." Not all of them allow screeners to read publication credits. G'Schwind adds: "They [the screeners] each get between a hundred and fifty and two hundred manuscripts. I always have three screening judges and I just divide the pile up."

So the crucial work of initial screening of manuscripts is outsourced to lowly MFA candidates, themselves desperately trying to get a book published, preempting and anticipating what the judge might like or not like. Notice how a philosophical/aesthetic question has been broken down into a procedural one. Contests go out of their way to emphasize the fairness of their procedures, which is a convenient way out of the bigger issue. The reality is that only a certain sensibility will get through in a given contest.

Typically there are two types of aesthetics (following the MFA division of poetry into two major camps): the narrative/formally uninventive/epiphany-based confessional or memoiristic short poem, and the experimental/avant-garde/language poetry camp, which takes its inspiration from deconstruction and makes a fetish of the insensibility of ordinary language. A judge from one camp is never going to pick a book from another camp; it just doesn't happen. The screeners know it, and hopefully the submitters know it too (unless they're really stupid). Already a great deal of self-screening has taken place, which rapidly amplifies during the early stages of screening.

So what is going through the minds of the poor MFA screeners? They're guessing the sensibility that will most please the judge. There can be little question of independent assertion of aesthetic judgment, since the screener is neither qualified nor willing to exercise such judgment. Does the manuscript look like something the judge and the contest would feel authorized to endorse? The screener cannot be deeply engaged with the manuscript if she's looking at two hundred manuscripts. What she can do, with speed and efficiency, is to get a general feel for appearance, sifting out the ones least likely to get the screener in trouble for being "outlandish" or "inappropriate," given the biases of the judge and the contest's recent winners.

It's also interesting—but what else do we expect in the politically correct academy?—that diversity of the judges is broken down by gender and geography.

The administrators of the contests are keen to emphasize such diversity, as though this were the main issue with the quality of first poetry books. Note the shifting logic: from evading the question of what kind of poetry is being published to the number of manuscripts handled by screeners to the diversity of judges by politically correct criteria!

Rankine elaborates: "We tend to alternate between a man and a woman every year, and I think we do choose judges who have name recognition and will draw a lot of submissions." Similarly, Collier: "I rely a lot on Bread Loaf faculty, which is very diverse; they represent, I think a pretty good cross section of what's going on in contemporary American literary culture." The Bread Loaf faculty has its recurrent stars, returning year after year, a highly select coterie advancing each other's causes (these are the poetry superstars who give each other awards of huge sums of money, for which there is no nomination process). Bread Loaf has in place a sophisticated multilayered screening process, so anyone not fully beholden to reigning aesthetics is unlikely to make it to a waiter's position—let alone faculty member! Gender and geographic diversity is a red herring in this sense. In fact, the article includes a sidebar, "The Anatomy of Awards," where the one hundred and twenty-nine book contest winners announced the previous year in *Poets & Writers* are broken down by gender, age, genre, education, residence, and ethnic background. The amazing thing is that decomposing things in this census-like manner seems like the most natural thing to an academic.

What kind of money is involved? The Walt Whitman Award, according to Harrison, gets 1,245 entries at $25 a shot: that's $31,125. Thirty thousand dollars is a lot of money. The publishers justify the take as going toward "administrative costs," including paying screeners and judges. For much less than thirty thousand dollars a publisher could solicit books from poets already being published in the best literary journals, or keep an eye out for burgeoning talent and encourage and promote them to put together a book. The way it used to work, before contests took over. Any amount of money, even fifty thousand dollars, can be justified as being eaten up in administrative costs; costs will expand in relation to the amount being collected, which in turn is dependent on brand-name judges drawing in large numbers of submissions. Collier says that "the screeners and the judges cost almost ten thousand." That's a great deal of money to pay one's fellow Bread Loaf judges—the money stays in-house, within the circle, so to speak.

The most interesting part of the interview revolves around conflicts of interest. In the mid-2000s, Foetry.com exposed a number of egregious conflicts of interest. For example, Jorie Graham awarded the University of Georgia Press's

Contemporary Poetry Series award to her husband and Harvard colleague, Peter Sacks.[2] At some level, the work of those who are regular conference-goers and part of the higher echelons of the MFA system is well-known to each other. There is only a slight leap involved from master and apprentice to judge and winning contestant.

I have a soft spot for Tony Hoagland, as a poet and as a person, and have had occasion for some wonderful conversations with him, but in 2008 he picked Matthew Dickman for the *American Poetry Review*/Honickman Prize—leading to the explosive rise in Dickman's career. Hoagland is an admirable poet, Dickman a mediocre one; more to the point, Hoagland regularly teaches at Bread Loaf, where Dickman is a frequent attendee. Surely Hoagland recognized Dickman's poetry when he came across the manuscript passed on to him? Perhaps Hoagland would have picked him anyway—but this raises the larger issue of contests serving as seamless ways to satisfy judges' preferences. What should Hoagland have done when he recognized Dickman's writing? Out of the apparent chaos of randomness in contests, order is being retrieved, in ways that accord with the traditional method—except that the new method comes dressed in the paraphernalia of democracy, almost the connotations of a lottery, which it most definitely is not.

There was a time, around 2005 to 2008, when I used to regularly scrutinize the results of poetry book awards in *Poets & Writers*, and just googling the names of the judge and the winner typically revealed some obvious connection—a common MFA program was the most recurrent flag. I gave up this exercise, and, I suspect, based on Larimer's interview, that contests are more careful these days about allowing such obvious connections out into the open. They must have tightened up the appearance of conflict of interest, so that simply googling two people doesn't necessarily yield an instant relationship. Still, pursuing the old habit, I checked at random a book award in the new issue of *Poets & Writers*—Lory Bedikian, winner of the 2010 Philip Levine Prize from Cal State Fresno—and found out that both she and judge Brian Turner attended the University of Oregon MFA program. Do the two know each other? Just coincidence? It would be enlightening to get a response from them.[3]

Larimer and the four publishers reduce the issue of conflict of interest to adopting the CLMP (Council of Literary Magazines and Presses) Code of Ethics. Collier says: "We're very clear with the judges and the screeners that if

---

2 For some examples of Graham's indiscretions, see: http://foetry.com/wp/?page_id=85.

3 My open invitation to respond stirred up a furious backlash on the internet, with certain prominent judges—whose incestuous link to contest winners or finalists has been obvious for a time—rising to the unmitigated defense of the accused, and vouching for the purity of the contest system as a whole.

they recognize the manuscript or if they have a relationship with the writer, we ask them to not advance it." One fails to understand, despite the vast documentation of overt corruption, how Collier can say even about the past: "By and large . . . the system ran pretty well without any real, let's say, policing, or scrutiny. But now it's just more explicit and it's tightened things up, and I think that's really good."

G'Schwind, on the other hand, recognizes that there was a big problem, but puts it clearly in the past: "The problem was that judges were picking students . . . people they knew. . . . The claim was that students were being picked by the judges. And they were." So there is admission here of corruption—violating the terms of ethics governing contests—in the past. The larger philosophical issue remains: the likelihood that the manuscripts that advance are the kinds that the judge's favorite students would be producing anyway. And no formal code of ethics is going to address the issue of narrow boundaries of selection, since this is inherent in the process itself.

The four administrators dislike the fact that Foetry was washing dirty laundry in public; after those revelations, the entire contest system should have been delegitimized and dismantled, and a new process should have been discovered and followed. But then there is the MFA beast to satisfy: where are tens of thousands of "poets" to sustain the illusion that every time they shell out twenty-five dollars they're in the running for the Whitman award? There's too much supply of copy—paper has to be kept churning, and proliferating contests are one way to accomplish that.

Both genres of poetry, under the contest regime, have degenerated into a parody of poetry. The domestic grief/loss/illness/ethnicity/migration/sexuality/race narrative is put together in a very structured way, designed to maximize the chances of getting through the early screeners. One gets the sense that there is a formal universal design to how poets put manuscripts together, how they hit the high and low notes with prologue and epilogue, how they check the different politically correct boxes, how they strike the right tone in terms of earnest personal striving (which is also quite depoliticized at the same time). It's an interesting exercise to pick, at random, contest-winning books and notice the similar patterns of structuring (in fact, in the March/April 2011 issue, *Poets & Writers* published an article by April Ossmann advising how to order a collection to maximize the chances of winning). Increasingly, winning manuscripts are coordinated in the form of prosy verse novels—with the same arcs of storytelling familiar from workshop instruction in fiction writing.

I picked three recent book contest winners and picked a poem each, completely randomly. Notice any similarity in tone in the beginnings of these poems?

1. A Beautiful Life

I'll steal a stare across your thigh
and trace the small flaws that freckle
toward your heavenly hips.
I'll follow the implicit aroma
of you and whisper something
to stir the rich syrup inside.
You'll laugh at the absurdity of it,
yet you'll come wearing a summer
dress—the random color of dawn—
hiding the soft down of flesh underneath.

(Gary Jackson, *Missing You, Metropolis*, Graywolf Press, winner of the Cave Canem Poetry Prize selected by Yusef Komunyakaa)

2. Available Resource

When the clapping dies
down, I step up to the mic-
rophone. Because of the
lightning, it's hard to see
the crowd, but most (I assume)
are hoping for a mishap. With
the help of my assistant, I go on
to explain the act.

(Daniel Khalastchi, *Manoleria*, winner of the Tupelo Press/*Crazyhorse* Award)

3. Before Memory

As an infant, my eyes
wouldn't stay—
only ever looked up.

Good as lakes
for lenses, good as pennies.
I'm not supposed to remember this.
In flashbulbs
they went owlish,
lacquered in oil blue.

(Molly Brodak, *A Little Middle of the Night*, winner of the Iowa Poetry Prize)

Go ahead, do the experiment for yourself. It's as if the same person(a) wrote all the books. If there are differences, they're minor ones among family members. Now how's this for a different sensibility altogether:

"The poet,"
Charles Olson writes,
"cannot afford to traffic in any other *sign* than his one"
"his self," he says, "the man
or woman he is" Who? Rodia
   at 81 is through work.
Whatever man or woman he is,
   he is a tower, three towers,
a trinity upraised by himself.
   "Otherwise God does rush in."

This is Robert Duncan from "Nel Mezzo del Cammin di Nostra Vita," from *Roots and Branches* (1964). Now here's a poet of ambition, striding like a colossus across the tradition of English poetry, daring to make it his own in his own way, not giving a damn about readers and audience—or petty screeners at some MFA program! This is a challenging sensibility.

The heavy costs of this institutionalization of poetry are rather cavalierly ignored by the interviewed contest managers. Larimer again poses the right question: "How do you all see contests changing the publishing landscape? It's changed how poets, certainly, view getting their books published. It's a viable publishing model, but what may be lost in it is the idea of a sustained poet-publisher relationship." Larimer is smart—he's hinting toward the same strong editorial vision I've been harping on. Harrison offers the irrelevant response: "I don't know that the multiple-books deal at the larger houses is quite so common, if extant at all." Larimer—and I—are not talking about the multiple-book deal, for heaven's sake. We're talking about building a relationship, such as Milkweed or Coffee House Press do in encouraging poets over the duration of their careers. G'Schwind's answer is, unfortunately, circular: "My sense is that it's getting really hard to send unsolicited poetry manuscripts to publishers, and this is one opportunity where you still can." Well, maybe if there weren't contests! They've crowded out the non-contest model.

Collier ultimately gives away the philosophical sleight of hand behind the model: "It really is a facet of the democratization of the arts to be able to just send a manuscript out somewhere and know that, okay, you have to pay a fee, but you know it's going to be read, it's going to be considered. You don't have to have an agent; you don't have to know anybody." What Collier is implying is the emerging concept of "teamwork" in writing: whereas literary writing used to be solitary, now writers solicit input from those comparable to their eventual readers and publishers, modeling their writing according to what's successful in the market; a few do get published; and how democratic that we don't need to conduct this process through an agent! Agents who charge reading fees are suspect; shouldn't the same be true of contests? Opposition, originality, resistance, and dynamic movement are being bred out of poetry, and it is very much what the guild masters want.

Everyone, including aspiring poets, including even those stuck in the MFA system, would be better off if the contest system were abolished, and publishers once again took responsibility for promoting individual strong aesthetics, rather than outsourcing the decision at every stage, and supporting safe conformist meeting room-style outcomes. A different model is that followed by, for instance, Canarium Books, whose editor Joshua Edwards has a vision, and whose recent books, by Suzanne Buffam, Paul Killebrew, John Beer, and others all impress me; the same goes for Anna Moschovakis and her fellow editors at Ugly Duckling Presse, whose prolific output of books always captures me. It doesn't have to be avant-garde poetry; from the formalist direction, Robert McDowell's (now defunct) Story Line Press set an example of promoting narrative poetry of a high order. At least there was a specific editorial vision, year after year, and the editors had the cojones to back up their vision. But to do this, you have to be a strong poet yourself, not an administrator/manager of contests. There are other small presses following the non-contest model, but they are distinctly in the minority, and the greater prestige, unfortunately, rests with the big contest winners: apprentices picked in the exact image of the all-knowing name-brand judge (whose number, by the way, is tiny and recirculating).

To sum up, the contest system is at least partially responsible for:

1. A halt to aesthetic progression, or the emergence of strong schools of thought contesting with each other, as was true before the rise of the MFA system. Those who hit the jackpot winning a first poetry book then enter their manuscripts in contests for follow-up books, where they're likely to stay close to the winning aesthetic, to perpetuate their "brand" and not create any surprises among future selectors. Thus conversation between poetry schools comes to an end, as everyone gets distracted by the business of publishing more and more books designed to get tenure and promotion.

2. An encouragement of mediocrity and ambition, since by definition anything that stands out is less likely to get through. This is only human nature. Only strong poets can recognize and admire other strong poets. It's not probable that the apprentice at the lower level is going to get blown away by radically new work; it's more likely that she'll get intimidated and put it aside. Besides, the entire contest system would get corrupted philosophically if outliers and risk-takers were encouraged—it would mess up the system of feedback and expectations, whose ultimate manifestation is low expectation in workshop itself. It begins there, and it ends in contest victory.

3. A corruption of the poetic process itself—insight and inspiration and habits of writing and revision—since the goal is already in mind, and it is a large and looming one from the earliest stages (at least for the smart careerists). Is the formalized apprentice model (including entering contests to earn beauty pageant approval—for that is what it amounts to) the best way to find great poetry? Or is the system an absolute negation of how we should conceptualize poetry's role in the larger society? If the young poet addresses the potential judge always on his mind, how can he possibly seek a strong audience (which may not exist yet)? Thus the tautological excuse that there is no audience for poetry except other MFA students; of course, since that is the premise of the poetry being written.

O ye oppressed contest-submitters of the MFA world, throw away your shackles and start your own collective with like-minded friends, publish poetry that will immortalize you, not poetry with the maximum chance of pleasing screeners and judges! Start your own press! If nothing else, write on scrap paper and share it with your wife and dog, but don't dilute your work to win contests! It doesn't cost $30,000 to publish a book of poetry. Maybe it doesn't even cost $3! Just as it doesn't cost $100,000 to "*buy* two years of time" to get feedback on your writing in an MFA program—maybe it just costs a library card.

The Entire Publishing Model Should Be Scrapped: Five Principles for a Sustainable Publishing Industry

You, the reader, walk into the nearest Knopf outlet[1]—it's an unassuming building, with few bells and whistles, looking like a combination of an unkempt public library and a 1970s health food store. There are no sections for you to find books in your niche. The place appears like the epitome of chaos, with nobody apparently in charge. In one corner, a bunch of writers are having coffee and talking about sex books—which have become so philosophically astute that the genre could use some vulgarization. Perhaps some of them are part-time "bookstore" employees—one hesitates to call the convivial, communal place by this name—with a share in the profits. Some of them might be editors, but if they are, they bear no distinguishing traits. The name Knopf is an evocation of times past, almost a mockery of the bad old days of dinosaur publishing, but its nostalgic value can't entirely be discounted.

There are no closing hours to the store; night owls are welcome to read whenever they wish; many have taken to this habit over the endless dark seductions of social media. There is no pressure to buy. One can even print and check out books, just as at a public library. Most people do buy books though, because they're so cheap. There are no massive inventories of books, no frivolous sections of cookbooks and self-help manuals and illness treatises—all of which lost their popularity over time. Major fields in modern publishing simply fell away, once publicity departments were abolished and the book was typically

---

1. Nearly five years after this thought piece was written, Milkweed Press announced in May 2016 that it was opening its own bookstore in Minneapolis; see here for details: http://www.publishersweekly.com/pw/by-topic/industry-news/publisher-news/article/70313-milkweed-editions-to-open-indie-bookstore.html. In the same month, Penguin Random House also backed a pilot bookstore in Puerto Rico. I suspect that this will become standard industry practice over time.

priced at five dollars—or less, if it was a work of fiction or poetry and didn't have illustrations or photos.

Authors may drop by anytime—they frequently do. There are no "readings" as such, but it's common to find authors chatting with readers. There's a fine line between respecting readers and surrendering to them, and it's something every author has to work out for himself. If the author doesn't want to make himself visible, he doesn't have to. The market for books, with the complete globalization of literary production, is incalculable—hundreds of millions of people in India, China, Africa, and Latin America are eager to follow authors they first got to know online, or in versions of Knopf bookstores in their own countries. The bookstores convey the same charm around the world. Readers browse for as long as they want to on reading devices, and they can print out a book for two to five dollars.

It turns out that a few literary stars—very difficult, obscure, visionary authors, whom one wouldn't have pegged for this role—are the ones whose oeuvres fill the physical inventory; it's difficult to classify this new breed of enormously popular and powerful global writer who bears all the trappings of high modernism, or even postmodernism, yet manages to appeal to audiences so large their magnitude has been a revelation. Already there are rumblings among the self-declared "proles" of writing that the superstars suck up all the energy and money and attention: did the revolution occur just to reconstitute the star system in another form? But there's enough money to go around, and once you've established credibility as an author, reputation feeds on itself and it's difficult to fall below a certain level of income. Unless you totally goof off.

Far-fetched? Ridiculously utopian? But which do you like, this scenario, or going into a Barnes & Noble and shelling out thirty dollars for a book the store has decided is good for you, which is why it's front and center and screaming for your attention? Did you ever come out of a Barnes & Noble feeling uplifted and rewarded? You've spent too much money. You doubt the value of the books you've just bought. You wish you could borrow the books and return them, but you can't. Something is missing, the whole transaction is crass and commercial, and you suspect there has to be a better way than this. On the way out you're greeted by a wall of discounted cookbooks and illustrated travel books. No one wants to buy them. The fiction section in the front looks more anemic than ever. There's not a single book that stands out. Yet they all come with glorious blurbs. How do you decide what's good and what's just hype? It's all too overwhelming, and you feel depressed when you realize there's no one you can trust.

It's a little different at the independent bookstore—if you have any left in your town—but you're still limited by the top-down model of publishing, which decides what you should read. You're not an active member of the literary community. You determine whether to read a book—by the day's Franzen or Egan—based on what the newspaper reviewers have said and whether the book has generated buzz. It's too depressing.

The current model is doomed. The idea that there should be centralized, massively consolidated, bureaucratic organizations known as the major trade houses, with multiple layers of editors, vast publicity departments, and books fed to them by an entity known as literary agents, only to take repeated losses and rely on a few stars to help them break even, is bound for extinction.

What I have outlined may not necessarily come true in its specifics—this is a speculative exercise after all—but if book publishing is to survive, something close to it will have to occur. The technology already exists to make publishing a democratic venture, driven from the bottom up rather than the other way around. The real constraint at this point is that any such revolution in the culture industry must be predicated on transformation in the economic base—and that's a much harder change to foresee, given the sclerotic political system which doesn't respond to the need for a more egalitarian economy. None of the major changes can occur short of a transformation to a more humane economy, which allows more time for leisure, de-emphasizes consumption for its own sake, and reduces massive inequalities in income and wealth.

The discussion of the crisis of publishing persists mostly at a pedestrian or superficial level. The crisis is enormous, almost unprecedented, yet the alternatives offered are minor fixes, taking basic production, distribution, and consumption methodologies for granted. We don't need to figure out how to maximize sales with the latest e-reader. We need to reconceive the whole concept of writing, editing, and reading, and subject every one of the institutional components to radical critique. It isn't a question anymore of which reading device is best, or how publishers will make up for the loss of Borders outlets, or how they can somehow squeeze more money out of the present distribution model.

The crisis of publishing is really the crisis of writing and reading. The publishing industry as it exists in America today generally obstructs the free flow of energies between readers and writers. It is a broker for celebrity authors, or authors with commercial possibilities, taking the entire literary culture on a downward slope because the definition of "commercial" is constantly being dumbed down. Hence, cookie-cutter books, formulaic sensations, highly publicized advances, the anachronistic book tour, and literary stars with all the trappings of their brethren in the movie and fashion industries.

Rather than pushing more of the product that publishers already offer—which clearly most people aren't interested in buying, or are buying in numbers too small to satisfy—the nature of the product itself must be changed. Yes, there is a crisis in publishing, but that is a very desirable thing, because it means that despite all the publicity and promotion efforts, the public isn't buying the hype. The structures of distribution are not written in stone—why must there be so many layers of intermediaries, all of which the final product must survive to make itself visible?

I propose the following key principles for a major restructuring of the publishing industry:

1. Decentralization.

Even within existing economic and social conditions, it makes no sense to have giant conglomerates located in New York and making all the major decisions about publishing. Decentralization should cover every aspect of publishing, including acquisition. The big publishers are going to have to break up into smaller units, and address the real needs of real markets, not cater to advertising-created images of "national" readers. Regionalism in publishing can be a great spur to revitalization of reading. To some extent, what I'm calling for is already being followed by independent literary presses and university presses,[2] except it would be on a far more radical scale. The elite gatekeeping function of a highly centralized elite, with common educational and class backgrounds, is a barrier to the flourishing of vital writing. All of the apparatuses of centralization need to be subject to reconsideration.

2. Autonomy (of readers, writers, editors).

Instead of a literary product that ensues from every actor along the line—writer, editor, sales representative, reader—fulfilling his or her expected role in the

---

2. Yet another interview that I wish had been part of this book is the one I did with Princeton University Press director Peter Dougherty, with a look behind the scenes of how a university press operates, how they too are coping with technological and economic changes as are small presses specializing in poetry and fiction, and how they too are adopting a global outlook, in terms of reach and readership. I have always been an unstinting supporter of university presses for being the obvious fount of the most important books published in the humanities and social sciences, though they rarely ever get their deserved share of review coverage. I wish more writing students would consider working at a university press as a viable career option. The full interview with Dougherty is here: http://www.huffingtonpost.com/anis-shivani/university-presses_b_939697.html.

continuum, according to grand marketing plans and corporate strategies, each of these actors needs to be freed, in order to assume responsibility for the acts of writing and editing and selling and reading. This would mean, for example, that an editor edits again, instead of being an administrator who has farmed out his real work to sub-literate agents. It would mean that a writer reconceives himself differently as someone appealing to audiences that perhaps don't fully exist yet but that might come into being with enough chutzpah; to cater to existing audiences, to write to constituencies that can be shown to exist, is the death of writing. It would mean that the sales function is broadly diffused across the organization so that it becomes a more organic idea than something to which everyone must submit their visionary ideas. And it would mean that readers take responsibility for what they are reading, because they would be actively solicited as integral components of publishing, not remain as afterthoughts.

3. Responsiveness (to market, demography, new needs).

Are readers dumb? Is the market an inert force to be manipulated and fooled and exploited, to deprive it of hard-earned cash? Are needs to be imposed from above, rather than felt from below? Such would definitely seem to be the mindset in this most elitist of industries, and the results are there for all to see. With the hundreds of thousands of books being published each year, what is the net cultural contribution of publishers? The exceptions are the few truly innovative small presses and university presses (which, of course, don't receive much notice from the mainstream reviewing establishment), but almost the entirety of what the major trade houses put out is junk. These are not books I want to have on my shelf, these are not classics, these are not books I can't do without. These are creations of marketing strategies, the internalized focus group screaming in the writer's and editor's and sales representative's head, instead of taking advantage of always-shifting possibilities for creation.

4. Smallness (end hierarchy).

Bigness is the bane of any creative or responsive activity and publishing is no exception. There are simply too many books being produced by too many giant organizations that have little connection with reality anymore, except in terms of abstract conceptions of the reader and the marketplace. The situation needs to evolve to the point of radical flatness within organizations, so that the editor-in-chief should be someone who sees himself as more or less on the same plane as the lowliest employee. Literary writing has become corrupted as a result of the pervasive hierarchies. The writer desires to be at the top of the hierarchy too, on par with the top people at the publishing firms, instead of visualizing himself outside the system, in tune with it but never quite belonging to it. The bigness has reached obscene proportions.

5. Risk.

The preceding disabilities prevent publishing houses from taking necessary risks. In literary culture, risk is always overestimated. The safest thing is to go with the existing formula, which means that like newspapers, the trade houses have become prone to offering few new ideas, lagging behind events and reacting to them rather than offering visionary alternatives to burgeoning challenges (again, the best among the university presses like Princeton and Yale are a notable exception to this rule, because their mission and their process of acquisition and editing militates against the corrupt model familiar from the major New York houses). Publishers would become profitable in short order if entrenched agents and editors weren't allowed to have veto power over innovative proposals, running their jaded, cynical eyes on every hint of freshness, trained in being subservient lapdogs to the master strategists holding the keys to the riches.

In short, writing needs to be reader and community driven, hierarchies need to be radically flattened, creativity needs to be diffused at the local level, and globalization needs to reactivate literary worth. But more than likely, nothing substantial changes and we muddle along, except with new technologies lending some momentary glamour to the diminished act of reading, creating the illusion of democracy, when in fact there is none. More than likely, the system continues as before, with corporate strategists, bloated editorial teams, and well-trained loyalists screening out the barbarians despite further economic deterioration.

But if things don't change, it's not because the concepts or the technology or the means aren't there to make publishing exciting and profitable and culturally worthwhile again; it's because the overlords don't want to change, even if it means they go down and take reading and writing with them.

Reading and Writing in the Digital Age: Interview with Richard Eoin Nash, Publishing Visionary

I've been intrigued by Richard Eoin Nash since the time he ran the indie press Soft Skull in the 2000s. His new enterprise is Red Lemonade/Cursor, a reader/ participant-oriented publishing venture hoping to take full advantage of the social potential of new media. I talked to him about the future of publishing in a rapidly changing landscape.

Let's speculate about a revolution in publishing. Scrap the existing model. Is the technology already there to do it? What further technological advances are required? What would such a revolution mean in practical terms?

Well, certain aspects of the existing infrastructure are ideal for certain purposes, so what I describe will partly sound like the old system. OK, so what we need to do is have a large ecosystem of publishing communities (large = one hundred thousand-plus worldwide). Each community ought to operate by permitting people to upload their work to the publisher's website, subject perhaps to some conditions, which should be spelled out transparently. Users can designate their work for review whereupon the entire community can respond to the work. By some reasonably transparent mechanism, one or more of the site's operators makes a decision about one or more projects to get behind, to "publish." The site's operators, aka the Publisher, or Editor in Chief, or Community Moderator, or Mayor give the project editorial resources and marketing resources—they invest time and money in it. They use a reasonable array of best current practices to hustle the book. In particular, by having already engaged the community in selecting the project for support, they engage the entire community in the pro- cess. This is part of the implicit social contract in publishing—you give us your feedback, we use it to help make decisions and pick dynamic writing that best expresses the vision of the community, you give the writing your support in the larger world (via your on- and offline voice) because the writing is a powerful representative of the kind of writing you believe in. That hustling involves the social media we currently know of, and stuff to come. You just use all your tools, your voice, your texts in all senses. One thing this happens to still entail, though, is bricks-and-mortar bookselling—as we see in fashion, in pharmaceuticals, in furniture, the ability to showcase product and gather experts on products under one roof is very important. Bookstores and libraries are hotspots of the kind of knowledge contained in the staff and in the regular customers. That system is not a way for a publisher to make money, but it is a way to market your products and your vision. Bookstore clerks and readers' advisory librarians are critical components of the total book ecosystem—we have to stop thinking of ourselves as their suppliers, and instead look at them as contributors.

The technology for the foregoing all already exists (as one of our team remarked, not only is there a lot of writing out there, there is a lot of code out there too). But not much of it has been orchestrated in the way I describe. There are tweaks to be done, and a lot of streamlining to be done, and a lot of integration to be done. And the target will always be moving as more technology and more uses of technology arise. (In practice, when we talk about technology, we're really talking about new uses of technology.) And Cursor will be a leader in doing all of this.

The implications? Most writers will want to be a part of these kinds of communities because they will grow as writers and grow in their readership by working alongside writers who inspire, support, and sometimes challenge them, and will gain the readerships of the fans of their fellow writers. This means that those writers will leave those publishers who rely mostly on scale of distribution infrastructure, rather than on intimate communities to grow their readership. Writers with very large established readerships will likely remain with big publishers since what they need is infrastructure to deliver their work to existing readers and fairly mass medium methods of informing and galvanizing that readership.

How should publishers think of readers? How should they reorganize themselves to come closer to readers? Can you be as far-fetched as possible in pursuing this speculative exercise?

Publishers need to not even think of readers as readers. We need to go straight from recognizing their existence to recognizing that they are active participants in the making of culture, not just passive consumers, and the publisher needs to actively engage them in that, not just finally grasp they're important and start grabbing their email addresses. Engaged reading, after all, produces writing, like your criticism, or like anyone tweeting a book rec, and doing #FridayReads. We should support reading, but I almost think we need to skip right past recognizing readers to recognizing we're facilitating engaged writing and reading coming from an array of creators, some writing books, some trying to write books, some writing about books, some writing literally and metaphorically on books, etc. A publisher should be convening them all, not merely selling the work of the few to extract money out of the pockets of the many.

How about readers? Do they have a new role and responsibility in finding good books?

Yup. No one gets a free ride in this system. I'm deeply influenced by Clay Shirky and am very lucky to have him as an advisor for Cursor. Clay is mistakenly viewed as a techno-utopian whereas in fact Clay merely notes that the internet helps solve collective action problems. Just like nuclear physics, this can be used for good or ill. The internet enables participation, but if you don't participate, you gain nothing. As in any civil society, you have to read, you have to speak, you have to vote.

How should books be priced? Is there something wrong with pricing today?

Everything is wrong, with the pricing and the product. All kinds of things need to happen at once, above all to diversify the product range. Not just hard, and paper, and digital, and not just books. To start with, we need options that allow people to buy at very limited risk, that is, for free or close to it. The reason being that the reader has to pay with hours of her life just to sample the book. Once a reader is hooked on a writer, the fear of wasting one's time is gone. The notion that we're "devaluing" a product by charging less for it is hokum—we do far more devaluing of books by publishing sequels, knockoffs, celebrity memoirs, etc. People pay twenty-five thousand dollars a year to do an MFA—I don't think there's a problem with the loss of cultural value around books. So limiting the range of means by which writing and reading connect to books priced fifteen to twenty-five dollars is economic and cultural suicide. Already in music and in journalism and in nonprofit publishing we're seeing participation through cruises, conferences, cocktail parties, foundations, patronage, dinner parties, seminars, limited editions, festivals—things that are unhackable, things that are priceless to some, things that collapse distance, things that bring you closer to your peers. A quick glance at Kickstarter will show you the kind of diverse products and pricing that is not just possible but necessary.

Will present distributional methods completely collapse as a result of new technologies?

Not completely, but there has been some dramatic shrinking and that shrinking will continue. However other channels are arising, for the various products and experiences I described above. Bricks-and-mortar stores still serve a valuable marketing force and we will still need some infrastructure to effectively supply them.

Do you have a grand theory of how publishing has shaken out in response to economic change over the last few decades, and how continuing economic change will push the model toward further change?

Well, the supply chain as a method of connecting writers and readers is an artifact of the Industrial Revolution. And it will prove to be an anomaly. We are returning to something like the coffeehouse culture of the seventeenth and eighteenth centuries, to the culture from whence the novel, the pamphlet, the newspaper arose. In my lifetime, changes in manufacturing technology have already started to bring about a less uniform, more customized approach to supplying goods and services in a lot of sectors. The book industry lagged greatly here—brands proliferated across retail capitalism, but not in books. The areas of capitalism that maintained the Industrial Revolution focus on economics of scale—in the U.S. Wal-Mart and Costco, in the U.K., Tesco, Sainsbury's—those were whom publishers focused on, places that were relentlessly focused on cost, on making things cheap, instead of focusing on the fashion sector, say, which focused on identity, storytelling, difference. Manufacturing is about to enter a golden era of customization though 3D printing like MakerBot. The publishing industry, as it diversifies into a service business (serving writer and readers), will still do some manufacturing but it will be much more bespoke.

Is there anything in the present publishing model that you would like to see retained? Can there be substitutes for those functions nonetheless—cheaper, more efficient, more responsive substitutes?

I don't see much *substitution* going on in our society. Things mostly *coexist*. The world is a pretty Creole place, we have wheelchairs to take people onto airplanes, we have bicycles and motorized rickshaws, we have knives and rifles and lasers all coexisting. Most of what needs to change isn't the thingness of publishing: the books, the design—or the social dimension: the editorial, the parties, the readings, the Twittering—but rather the mentality. We're all making culture together, and our job is to serve.

What will be the most surprising thing about publishing in the near future that none of us is thinking about? What has already surprised you most over the last ten years?

Lordie, that's hard to say. I think it'd surprise people if Cursor became a billion-dollar business, but, it will, over seven years, though, not three. (If it doesn't, then someone will be making a billion dollars doing something similar to what Cursor would have been doing.) I also think some people will be surprised by the rate at which the book business will grow in the developing world. Novels are critical to an emergent middle class, and at least a billion people are entering the middle class worldwide, and their kids will be writing the great novels of their respective cultures as their leisure time and access to intellectual capital increases. In the West, we'll see the aging of literature as society itself ages and as leisure time grows primarily amongst the over-sixty-fives as life expectancy heads toward one hundred and over. Demographics are on our side. Of course we'll produce ever vaster quantities of shit, but we always have, and we always will. What has surprised me? That indie publishing works, albeit for reasons I didn't understand at the time.

What institutional factors do you hold responsible for the cultural irrelevance of literary writing today? How should publishers at different levels of size and reach correct these factors?

Well, it begs the question: compared to what? All cultural forms struggle with irrelevance, ditto their individual practitioners. Network TV, newspapers, arena rock bands, AOL, MySpace, all fret about cultural irrelevance. I actually don't think literature has that much to worry about. The time you fall into cultural irrelevance is when you stop worrying about it. You're a Cassandra, Anis, you act to ensure we don't stop worrying.

Symposium:
Can America's Little Magazines Survive the New Economic and Technological Regime?

Literary journals are one of America's most precious institutions. Emerging writers typically make their mark here first. Unlike commercial publishers, literary journals tend to push the boundaries of writing, and don't get as carried away by literary fashions. Their long perspective is indispensable in maintaining a necessary balance. We have more of them in this country than perhaps the rest of the world combined. Some of them have kept stellar reputations for decades, while new ones, adventurous and refreshing, crop up every day.

How are the literary journals faring amidst the rise of the internet? Are they suffering from the current cost-cutting mania in higher education? Can this venerable American literary institution survive—or even thrive—despite new technologies and new economic realities?

Dan Latimer, editor of *Southern Humanities Review*

It is astonishing to learn that the journals that spread Modernism over the globe rarely had a circulation over a thousand. *The Dial* was an exception. Yet they had their impact before they ran out of steam around 1940. Today there are formidable forces arrayed again against the little magazine, not the least of which is the U.S. Postal Service, which continues to raise its prices for presorted mail. Yet electronic internet publication does not have the longevity of paper and print, which can languish in your magazine rack until you realize, I should have read that! Or, What was that again?! One would think that a liberal arts dean would be a bastion of dependability at such times, and there may indeed be some who are. Yet an editor knows that a visit to the dean's office, hat in hand, is the most melancholy visit that he can ever make. With the adoption of the business model for the university, beauty seems far less crucial than contracts for asphalt, or outlandish administrator salaries, which have not yet reached the level of Wall Street opulence, or for that matter arthropodal proliferation of the administrator class as a whole, whose top-down style seems to function mainly to terrorize faculty with post-tenure review and to cut the budgets of editors. And yet if you look at the list of literary journals in *NewPages,* you can see the Philistines still have quite a few little voices to exterminate before there is total silence.

Russell Scott Valentino, editor of *The Iowa Review*

I think the answer is similar to the old Soviet joke about whether there will be money in the coming communist society: Yugoslav deviationists say, yes, there will indeed be money; Chinese dogmatists say, no, there will not be any money. We take a dialectical approach. We say: for some there will be money, for others there will not. Some print lit mags will thrive, but it won't be for ideological reasons. It will be because they have a viable business model; a strong organization supporting them; a solid network of high-quality contributors; a smart, talented, and hardworking staff; top-notch design and layout; zero tolerance for crap between their covers; and, very likely, an online presence that complements what they do in print, and vice versa. They will make use of the available tech without kowtowing to it, recognizing that, just as print enables and encourages certain modes of representation and expression, so do digital technologies, and not necessarily the same ones. And in the end, the dogmatists and the deviationists will fall by the wayside, leaving only prognosticating dialecticians in their wake.

Wendy Lesser, editor of *The Threepenny Review*

At *The Threepenny Review*, we figure we can lick them *and* join them. That is, we've published a literary magazine in print format for almost forty years, but recently we've also added a digital edition, available through Zinio.com. Now that the digital version can exactly replicate the look of our printed page, as Zinio's does, I am willing to allow a digital version to exist, though I certainly don't intend to read that way myself. Why should people keep reading literary magazines in the internet age? Here are five possible reasons: 1) They have attention spans longer than thirty seconds. 2) Their heroes are Tolstoy, Proust, Dickens, and James, not the latest graphic novelist or best-selling author. 3) They like the idea of an editor who will carefully select things for them, so they don't have to sort through the whole universe of dreck to get at the good stuff. 4) They love the feel of paper in their hands, the look of photographs on a printed page, the cumulative experience of encountering the perfect poem placed next to the perfect article. 5) They think that computer screens are for work but reading is for pleasure.

Sven Birkerts, editor of *AGNI*

All of us who edit literary journals are living with this question. The key word, as I read it, is "thrive." Not survive—*thrive*. For a thousand obvious practical reasons, the answer is no. Or, not long. But thankfully the whole of our world is not yet ruled by the obvious and the practical. Yes, the literary journal (as opposed to *literary journals* as a class) can thrive, but the new thriving will be different than the old thriving. The new print journal must exploit to the full its means, its strengths, which is to say that it must present itself as a total artifact, a made thing in which the parts announce an organic relation to the whole (not possible on the web), as a deliberated item of beauty that not only presents, but *represents* its vision of literary excellence. It must be worthy of the posterity that print is now coming to symbolize. To thrive the journal must be a thing not merely read, but reread. And read not just in a sitting or two, but over time, in the way the best journals are read—one day this, another day that. The reader must covet it, view it as a resource of the inner life, not just an episode in the morning's screen sweep.

Robert Boyers, editor of *Salmagundi*

Most literary journals have tiny circulations and very modest readerships. They may be said to "thrive" only in the sense that their sponsors continue to provide adequate subsidies which allow the magazines to offer what such publications alone can offer. At a time when even the best mainstream publications cater to the limited attention spans of their average readers, the best literary journals frequently publish demanding work and do not worry overmuch about the willingness of their hypothetically "average" readers to be stretched and tested. At *Salmagundi* magazine we do not at all object to a novella-length fiction by Andrea Barrett, or a lengthy, somewhat theoretical, email exchange between J. M. Coetzee and an Australian psychotherapist—two features contained in our present issue. We thrive because we are committed to publishing work that cannot appear in *The Atlantic* or *The New Yorker*, work that will often seem far too eccentric and rigorous for online publications. How can we say with confidence that we thrive? Simply because we have a few thousand very good and loyal readers and because the best writers in the country continue to send us their work for publication. When Michael Kinsley writes, in *The Atlantic*, that what appears in newspapers and magazines is too lengthy and demands too much of readers who are rightly looking to get in and out of an article as quickly as possible, we say as loudly as we can that the work of literary journals—what we prefer to call "little magazines"—is too important to be abandoned or consigned to irrelevance.

J. D. McClatchy, editor of *The Yale Review*

Little magazines have thrived on the brink of extinction for decades now. They come, they go; they make a splash, they sink. (*The Yale Review*, I should quickly add, has been around since 1819—there *are* exceptions.) It is more useful to look at the phenomenon than at individual examples of it. "Little" doesn't only refer to a magazine's circulation. All too often the term could refer to the staff, the budget, and the business savvy. But they have bravely persisted, discovering new writers, catering to an unquenchable appetite for strong, original work. What does not seem to have survived as long are disciplined habits of reading. Sidebars, cable chatter, blogs and tweets, the "updating" of educational curricula…all of this attention-deficit evidence is the most serious threat to little magazines, which makes them more valuable and necessary. Yes, it will always be a niche—like philately, chess clubs, opera subscribers. But in a land of quick fixes and short views and in a time of increasingly commercial publishing, the little magazine has an authority that derives from its commitment to both established writers and promising newcomers, to both challenging literary work and a range of essays and reviews that can explore the connections between the imagination and the broader movements in American society, thought, and culture. With independence and boldness, with a concern for issues and ideas, and with a respect for the mind's capacity to be surprised by speculation and delighted by elegance, it will continue—possibly only online, but I hope not. I like the feel and smell of their pages and print.

Robert S. Fogarty, editor of *The Antioch Review*

Too much is usually made of technological advances that create an "either/or" scenario. At the moment there is, first, a "delivery system" (online/digitized) and then, more important, the "product." In an amicus brief in the Google copyright case, the French government called a book a "product" unlike other products because of its capacity to elevate human consciousness, while the German brief spoke, according to Robert Darnton, Harvard's librarian, in the "name of the land of poets and thinkers." That is the land that literary magazines dwell in and there is no reason that they cannot survive in the new internet world. Numerous universities and philanthropies still support the French/German model of culture rather than simply adhering to a bottom-line approach. There is a place in the modern world for institutions like All Souls College at Oxford and the Institute for Advanced Study at Princeton and for small independent-minded print literary journals like *The Antioch Review* in Yellow Springs and *Areté* in Oxford. All are small and intimate. Print journals are the literary equivalent of the slow food movement: satisfying and good for you. In short, they strive to excel rather than consume. Most print literary magazines have small staffs, small audiences, small budgets (unlike mass-marketed commercial magazines), and appeal to a discrete and cultivated readership that is willing to pay less than ten dollars for a paperback (the average issue of *The Antioch Review* is two hundred pages) that offers both a tactile and aesthetic experience. Production and distribution costs have, in fact, gone down in the past ten years. Not everyone (contrary to the flack generated by both companies) wants their delivery system to be a Kindle or a Nook book and many (including young readers) prefer to read just like their parents and grandparents did and choose not to confine themselves to their inbox. Cultivate them.

David H. Lynn, editor of *The Kenyon Review*

I think it's very much an open question whether the literary journal in print will long survive in the age of the internet. When asked how long there would be a print version of *The Kenyon Review*, I used to answer "as long as I'm editor." I no longer make that promise. Anyone who makes predictions about where literary publishing will be in more than two or three years is either a fool or a liar. On the other hand, our culture continues to fragment into ever more "niches," where considerable numbers of people invest their time, money, and self-identity, whether in expensive bicycles or equally expensive big-screen televisions. My strong suspicion is that there will be a considerable niche of readers who remain loyal to the print literary journal. These people appreciate the thinginess of the artifact, the feel of the paper, the care of the design, as well as the achievement of the contents. The danger for print journals, however, is that they may come to be seen as anomalies or anachronisms, out of touch with the contemporary world.

This is one reason why we launched *KROnline*, an electronic literary journal for the internet, designed as a complement to the print *Kenyon Review*, rather than its replacement or reproduction. It has its own aesthetic as well, attempting to reach a different, larger, younger, more international "niche" of readers.

Charles Alcorn, editor of *American Book Review*

No . . . and unequivocally, yes. In fact, a literary journal such as the *American Book Review*, which has frankly struggled throughout its forty-year history to gain and hold distribution/shelf space in traditional bricks-and-mortar book-stores, benefits greatly from the increased readership provided by the more easily accessible internet. In addition, *ABR* is able to take advantage of the vastly improved graphics capability afforded web-based journals and provide digital content designed to attract the cyberliterate. That said, our distribution is traditionally subscription-based and I would venture that the vast majority of our customers prefer holding and reading the tangible tabloid. Of course, with the digital consumer—readers comfortable and accustomed to accessing content online—*ABR* is obliged to develop compelling web-based frames that value textual compression and graphic punch. The twenty-first century challenge for *ABR* editors is to retain our original print-biased customers and entice a new generation of online readers. As with any literary enterprise this is accomplished by actualizing, in every issue, the age-old recipe: a liberal mix of insightful, well-written reviews and features delivered piping hot in presentations that evolve at the pace of reading culture.

William O'Rourke, editor of *Notre Dame Review*

When have literary journals thrived? During the golden age of reading, through the mid-1970s, I suppose, before the various thieves of time, first VCRs, cable TV, then DVDs, the world wide web, and now the vast universe of digitized electronic media, began to consume whatever spare minutes are left to the literate reader. It's an aural-visual world today, not a literate one. (Though, just as the rich are getting richer, there remains a small cohort of piping hot folks out there—and Out There takes on planetary size.) Stores like Borders[1] and Barnes & Noble are galleries of books, where they are viewed and displayed. In a sour irony, books have become art objects and high literature is as rare as the

---

1. Borders closed shop in September 2011.

masterpieces that hang in museums. (Though not rare in numbers, since everything written, thanks to digitization, now exists simultaneously.) Nonetheless, most literary journals these days have a web presence and as their print versions lose readers, they have, paradoxically, an instantly archived life history, as long as they go undeleted. They exist online, but aren't necessarily read. The *Notre Dame Review's* online companion is different than the print edition, filled with more to see, as well as read. Given the circumstances (the overall decline of print sales), it is good the journals are there in cyberspace. But, again, those online are looked at first, read second. Electronic media has changed and will change the literary culture. It is now a Babel of competition. And thousands of eyeballs can dance on the head of a pin, a web address. Poetry might well profit over time, given its usual length, size; but not, alas, I think, fiction.

Carolyn Kuebler, editor of *New England Review*

The internet is an efficient conveyer of words and is, of course, incredibly useful for information-gathering or skimming or sampling. But it's also efficient at distraction, and therefore not the best backdrop for reading longer works, literary works, or any writing that attempts to remove the reader to a different space altogether. Print books, or offline e-books, are better for the type of writing that has nothing to do with efficiency or information gathering, and that requires a longer attention span than most people can sustain on the internet. Paper offers a different reading experience and different design and tactile qualities than a screen and always will. Even young people who've had internet access for as long as they've been reading still often prefer print. But eventually print will be reserved only for things that are best suited to its particular charms—literary magazines among them—rather than the assumed medium of choice. Literary journals have always thrived in an economically threadbare way, and the internet won't change that. Print journals will simply exist alongside journals in electronic formats; they might cost a little more, but in turn you can take them as far out of range as you want, and, of course, the software won't ever be obsolete.

Jonathan Freedman, editor of *Michigan Quarterly Review*

There are two simple equally persuasive answers to this question. I have no idea which one is an accurate forecast of the future. 1) No. The economics of publishing a literary journal in print have always been dicey. By definition, literary magazines attract small, if intensely loyal, audiences—but we can't charge too much (not that we want to). Many of us rely on library subscriptions to augment our base, but these have been slowly, if steadily, declining as library budgets get cut mercilessly by universities, and the cost of scientific and engineering journals goes through the roof. And many of us rely, as well, on universities for support, either in the form of direct subvention funds or in office space and staff—or, more commonly, both. Although we represent a pittance in the budget, we're increasingly being found irrelevant and hence easily choppable in this intensely budget-cutting era. Venerable and wonderful journals—*The Southern Review, New England Review, Triquarterly*[2]—have been under threat from their institutions, and the future for all of these as print journals is cloudy at best. Put it all together, and there is no economic model—none—under which literary journals can thrive. (And going online is not a panacea; printing costs are going down every year. The main expense is human capital: copyeditors, people to read the unmanageable flood of submissions for the editor in chief, etc. 2) Yes. There are many, many, many thousands of writers in the U.S., all eager to see their poetry, prose, and nonfiction appear in the prestigious and semi-permanent form of print rather than in the fluid, amorphous, still-to-be rationalized world of online publication. There are fewer, but still a number of, people who prefer the reading experience made possible by paper and print. We don't need them all to subscribe to our journals to continue to make a go of it—just some (if some more). We shall see what the future will bring.

Wayne Miller, editor of *Pleiades*

"Thrive" is a pretty subjective term. Even powerhouses—such as *The Paris Review* and *Partisan Review*—that led the narrow field of the 1950s had relatively small circulations. I don't think the internet *hurts* print journals—mostly, it offers new possibilities for exposure (think Facebook, *NewPages*, and *Poetry Daily*). Among writers of my generation, there's still a sense that the really important publications are presented primarily through print. (For example, I've had friends who have been disappointed to have a poem accepted by *AGNI Online* rather than by *AGNI* "proper.") The fact that online publications tend to be free and immediately available gives them something of a competitive edge over print journals, but that's offset somewhat by the latter's historical prestige and/or tactile pleasure. I think the larger challenge the internet poses is the same as that posed by the advent of desktop publishing: diffusion. As more people put

2. In 2010, *Triquarterly* relaunched as an online-only journal.

out literary publications—and the internet makes this even easier, since online magazines don't need to secure distribution—it becomes increasingly difficult to capture the attention of an audience that's naturally limited in size. I don't think the internet shrinks or grows that audience significantly, it just spreads it even thinner.

Stephen Corey, editor of *The Georgia Review*

One is driven to seek the right analogy, as if doing so would transform one's desire into fact: Do we lose our need to see Rodin's sculptures or Monet's paintings up close in museum galleries because we can see them on a computer monitor—or in a book? Do we cease seeking fine restaurants because we have omnipresent fast-food chains? Is touch in all its forms subsumable to mere looking? Are reflection and savoring now to be defined as equivalent to rushing and ever-changing? But these comparisons are not right enough. They have counterparts ready to drag them back into the naiveté, the Luddism, whence many would say they arise. Where are the monk scribes of yesteryear, toiling in the shadow of Gutenberg they could not see for the dimness of their stone cubicles? Given the chance, would you take a stagecoach from Chicago to San Francisco? But these are not right enough, either. The internet is a steamroller, an insufficiently tested drug: bull force and flashy first impressions and quick shifts do not a Brave New World make. I believe in physical touch, in accruing knowledge and wisdom—and in the value of a certain privacy during one's experience of both: the magazine, the book, in my hands.

Jeanne Leiby,[3] editor of *The Southern Review*

Yes, I fully believe that literary journals can survive (and thrive) in the age of the internet; at least, they can survive (and thrive) as well as they have since literary journals first came into being. Let's be honest: this has never been a multimillion dollar industry. Maybe this hopeful sentiment is an expression of my deep love for printed matter, or maybe it is my naive hope that well-edited print journals will continue to flourish, or my profound belief that there is a large (and, in fact, growing) audience of readers who want books and not screens. If I have any proof to offer, it's that over the last two years, our subscription base has grown—not decreased. In large part, this is because of the internet and social networking

---

3. Jeanne Leiby died in April 2011.

websites. With the internet, it is easier—and less expensive—to advertise, to broaden our audience, and to entice people to *The Southern Review*'s printed pages. I'm not saying that I think online literary journals don't have a place or are in any way lesser than print journals—only that the two things need not be mutually exclusive. I think there is audience enough for all of us.

Richard Burgin, editor of *Boulevard*

It's difficult to predict the future, even the immediate future, of anything when so much is determined by economic factors virtually none of us can foresee. My semi-educated (at best) guess would be that more and more literary publishing will take place on the internet but that literary print magazines will survive and hold their own, much as the radio survived despite television, and movie theaters have flourished despite DVDs. It seems to me that the inventions which dominate their environment to the point where they obliterate the competition are those that accelerate the tempo of life. In a word, it's survival of the fastest. The typewriter obliterated writing by hand because you could write and read faster with it, just as the computer later obliterated the typewriter. Despite these relentless Darwinian truths, and despite how antique print magazines may seem in other respects, one can still read a print magazine or book at least as fast and accurately as one can read the same material on a screen. Also, because literature exists in our minds in a deeper way than most internet material does, reading a print journal is at least as satisfying an experience as reading a screen and in some ways more satisfying. Literary journals (and books) offer the subtle pleasures of touch, portability, and visibility—that strange delight their writers, and readers too, feel in seeing books physically exist in a bookstore or other public place—that the internet can't yet duplicate. Maybe that's why most of the best and most prestigious literary magazines are still the print ones and why most writers I know would still rather publish in them than on the internet.

Jackson Lears, editor of *Raritan: A Quarterly Review*

The short answer is: yes, indeed. No one would deny the power, reach, and value of digital publishing. But the imperative to "go digital" depends on a technological determinism that imagines digital publishing must sweep all before it, and that sanctions a certain indifference to the actual experience of reading and thinking at the core of our common intellectual life—the experience provided by *Raritan* and its peer journals. One of the rewards of reading *Raritan* is that the magazine offers material space for reflection and inquiry. The sheer physicality of the thing itself—everything from typeface to texture to the heft of the book in your hand—promotes sensitivity to ambiguities and shades of meaning. This kind of reading repays a sustained investment of time, which is one reason serious writers like to write for *Raritan*: they want serious readers. The Web, by contrast, is a superb medium for transferring information, or for the short, tight argument of an op-ed piece. But reading on the Web focuses a reader's attention in ways that are different and often more ephemeral than those offered by journals like *Raritan*. The shift to predominantly digital publishing should not demand the erasure of all older alternatives, especially if they continue to play a vital cultural role. *Raritan* has every intention of doing precisely that.

Symposium: Have Online Literary Journals Come of Age?

After two decades of sustained presence, what can we say about the status of journals that promote literature online? I asked the editors of some of the oldest online journals, as well as some new ones, these questions: What are online literary journals doing that print journals are failing to do? Have online journals come of age yet? Can you point to specific examples of areas where online literary journals are in a league of their own?

Rick Rofihe, publisher and editor in chief, *Anderbo.com*

I was a hardcopy book publisher many years ago, and I am somewhat affiliated with a hardcopy literary publisher even now—certainly the pleasures of holding a well-printed, well-bound volume in one's hands are undeniable. Yet a poem or story online needs not only neither ink nor paper, it also doesn't need warehousing, shipping, billing, etc. As a writer myself, of course I'm interested in money, but, as an experiment, I decided a few years ago to put nine short stories of mine, each of which originally appeared in *The New Yorker* magazine, together as a "book," under the title "BOYS who DO the BOP," and make it easily and freely available in e-form at *Anderbo.com*, so anyone, anywhere, anytime could read it on a computer (or, more recently, on a smartphone.) Now, while I can't really make any money off such a venture, I don't really lose any either. So, yes, there was a time when I was paid twenty-five hundred dollars-plus by *The New Yorker* for my fictions, but, as an editor there at the time, Daniel Menaker, said to me, "You can't expect to make a living selling short stories." This, I think, is and will be increasingly true, both for writers and for publishers.

Colleen M. Ryor, founding editor, *The Adirondack Review*

Online literary journals are bringing poetry to a wider, more international audience in a way that would be highly impractical, if not impossible, for print journals to do. Because readers can now print out their favorite poems with the click of a button, and writers can reach a much wider audience than was previously possible, it's difficult for print journals to compete with that immediacy and convenience. Another very important aspect of online literary publishing is the level of creative flexibility that editors and designers have when working with visual artists in producing the issues of the magazine. I see the internet as being nothing but a catalyst for the dissemination of art for all. I see a scenario in which a teenager may be searching the internet for lyrics to her favorite song, or something about a movie she wants to see, and then surreptitiously happens upon a poem in the search results that has been published in an online literary journal. She loves it and shares it with her closest friends. Would this happen with a dusty literary magazine sitting in her local library with a circulation of ten thousand at best? What I see for the future is more online publishing of single poems and stories culminating in traditional printed books to celebrate and preserve in tangible form what writers and readers alike are doing online.

Gregory Donovan, senior editor, *Blackbird*

Online literary journals, readily accessible and often free of charge, actively bring new readers to fine arts writing—including thousands who might not otherwise discover it—and by expanding that audience, keep our national and international literary scene not only alive, but lively. Digital publishing surges forward with problems and developments familiar to lovers of music, yet it can, if handled intelligently with expert curatorship, be very good for lovers of artful writing. In 2006, *Blackbird* offered a previously unpublished sonnet by the young Sylvia Plath, including her typescripts and the annotated page from her own copy of *The Great Gatsby* which inspired the poem, and not only made international news, but told an important story about how a poet is made, not born. That event helped announce the online journal's arrival as a force to be taken seriously. *Blackbird* not only publishes striking fiction, poetry, creative nonfiction, and drama, along with process presentations in the visual arts, but also audio, video, digital photography, and new "hybrid" forms such as the video essay. Our first issue included an essay with illustrations that *moved*, and now *Blackbird* enjoys an international readership of hundreds of thousands—neither achievement quite feasible in print.

Thom Didato, editor, *failbetter.com*

Getting readers by the tens or hundreds of thousands as opposed to just ten to a thousand! Online publishers also utilize the medium in ways that traditional print cannot (audio, visuals, etc). Even a fairly Luddite site like *failbetter* uses the technology behind the scenes (determining which works get read, php database prompting of similar stories/poems from past issues). But let's put all that gizmo stuff aside. Online publication offers a new and much larger audience, for an art form (literature) that can surely use one. Listen, I didn't give up on music because the industry moved on from eight-tracks and cassettes. So why in hell should the publishing industry cling to the printed word when it can offer the same product (or newer products when it comes to matters of style and form) in a new way? And let's face it, what is "new" changes rather quickly. In many ways, online publishers are quickly becoming "ye olde publishers" in an age where folks are freeing themselves from the desk computer screen and jumping on the Kindle/iPad/e-reader bandwagon. For traditional literary print magazine editors to claim some sort of moral/artistic superiority via the medium of paper over all else is insane. To use the music metaphor again: sure, I still own LPs, but I do not refuse to own/use an iPod! It is as my *failbetter* colleague, Andrew Day, likes to construe this outdated debate between print and online: "Person sees future, person sticks head in sand, future comes anyway."

Marc Watkins, books editor, *Front Porch Journal*

Online journals will never replace the joy of picking up a physical print copy of a journal, but they can certainly augment print journals with wonderful content such as live readings, blogs, and book trailers, features the print-only medium cannot match. Readers can find this in online-only magazines such as *Front Porch Journal*, which offers its readers splendid literary content on a free basis with the unique bonus of having the option of viewing a full archive of over a decade of live readings from authors visiting Texas State University. However, I believe the true future of small magazine and journal publishing lies in the combination of both a strong online and print presence. Online-only journals will truly come of age when they adopt a quarterly or yearly print run. One can already see this in Rutgers's *StoryQuarterly* model, and the really fantastic web/print editions of *Dark Sky Magazine*. The days of the fly-by-night web journal are quickly becoming eclipsed by passionate editors who actually care about making a name for their journals rather than indulging their friends by publishing a seemingly endless supply of whimsical fuckery offered to them.

Steve Himmer, editor, *Necessary Fiction*

As much as I love print, I want people to read my work and I want to develop an audience. That's a whole lot easier when readers can find a story online instead of tracking down old journal issues. The emphasis on short forms gives online journals an identity apart from print, but it's also limiting and I'm glad longer work is becoming more common. Equally limiting is thinking of the web as a proving ground for print. Shaking off that anxiety might allow an embrace of the web as its own medium—I'm shocked there hasn't been more interest in web-native forms, and more synergy between "online literature" and "electronic literature." The web is most exciting when it does things print can't. Web journals can publish faster, adding new content daily in a conversation with readers (though the noise of that conversation, with so many journals and writers, can be its own problem). It's easier to present an ongoing project quickly enough to keep readers interested, but slowly enough to digest it piece by piece. I think of print as more meditative than conversational, and see the two having a complementary rather than competitive relationship.

Anmarie Trimble, editor, *Born*

Because a project such as *Born* could never exist in print (we focus on multimedia collaborations between literature and art), I rather disagree with the question. I don't see it as a matter of print journals failing, but rather online literary journals having exposed the potential to reach broader audiences in new ways. The internet has revealed there's a readership for poetry outside the world of traditional literary journals—indeed, a significant portion of our audience would likely never pick up a traditional journal. I find most exciting the literary projects that take advantage of multimedia's unique publishing characteristics. For example, Fish House's use of audio (http://www.fishhousepoems.org) brings poetry back to its oral roots, brings back the music of the speaking voice. Print can't do that. Some of *Born*'s cinematic work joins voice and image, blurring the boundaries between literary arts and film, perhaps even challenging our ideas about poetry. After all, what we think of as poetry today is a reflection of the technology of writing. Originally poetry was spoken, so there were no stanzas or line breaks. But with multimedia, what happens when a poem can *move*? Because we're still asking these kinds of questions, I don't think we can say online journals have come of age. We're just now learning to fly.

Steven Seighman, editor, *Monkeybicycle*

I think online literary journals are enabling more dialogue between author and reader through comment sections, message boards, and the like. Print just can't do that. I'm not sure if it's good or bad, but there's definitely more interaction happening. Online journals are also probably inspiring more writing overall. With new content going up in a lot of places on a weekly or sometimes even daily basis, it's creating more opportunities for authors to get their work published. Print journals take a lot of effort and a lot of money to put into production, so you'll see those maybe once or twice per year. Online journals are definitely coming of age. New ones are created every day and with print journals becoming closer and closer to extinction as each year passes, online publication isn't exactly the only option yet, but it does seem to be the one that is gaining momentum. Another thing online journals do that print journals obviously can't is incorporate multimedia. Sure, you can get a CD or DVD attached to your book, but those kinds of options are limitless online. They cost very little to produce and can be done frequently. It's adding another, constantly evolving, dimension to the reading experience—something that just can't be matched in print.

Andy Hunter, editor, *Electric Literature*

The obvious answer to "What are online literary journals doing that print journals are failing to do?" is: reaching thousands of readers. A reasonably successful literary website has a readership of over ten thousand; fewer than five print journals in the world have that many readers. And they're creative, because they're not bound by the physical limitations of print. Online, a literary journal can be a map, like http://mrbellersneighborhood.com/, or a Twitter account, like http://twitter.com/nanoism. *Failbetter, Anderbo, Guernica*, and *Smith* have all published outstanding work, and great print magazines like *Rattapallax* are making the transition to online publishing. There's every reason to be optimistic about online literary journals, especially as e-readers make it easier to read online work (I've always found it hard to read meditatively on a computer, but you can subscribe to an online journal's RSS feed on a Kindle or iPad, where the reading experience is superior). The only reason online journals are not a panacea is their inability to pay their writers (*Narrative* magazine does, but only by charging other writers a submission fee). I want writing to remain a paid profession, so I hope online publishers will try to find innovative ways to compensate their authors.

Jason Jordan, editor, *decomP magazinE*

Online journals can do a lot that print journals can't—host audio and video, contain interactive design, allow commenting and link clicking, provide twenty-four/seven publishing opportunities, permit instant editing, etc. I think web journals have come of age in the sense that they're continuing to gain respect. They're also more widely accessible than print—especially if archives are taken into consideration—and almost always free. In fact, it's more difficult to find online journals that charge to read content than those that don't. As for the future, I believe we'll see even more innovation in the years to come, though I can't predict exactly what that will entail. Naturally print has the upper hand in certain respects, but rather than debate web versus print, I've found that considering the journal and its reputation is more important than considering the means by which it delivers installments. After all, there are great web journals and great print journals. And many publish in both realms. Lee K. Abbott says it best, I think, in Dzanc's *Best of the Web 2009*: "Good writing is good writing, no matter where we find it."

Rebecca Morgan Frank, editor in chief, *Memorious: A Journal of New Verse and Fiction*

Yes, online journals have "come of age": we've evolved from being the medium that people did not take seriously, and considered ephemeral, to being an enduring medium that models innovation in the important work of keeping literature relevant and accessible to readers. Print journals are following the lead of online journals by going online-only themselves (*Triquarterly, Shenandoah*), by having a companion online version with different content (*Harvard Review, AGNI*), or by offering limited content and archives online. Online and print journals are essentially doing the same work: bringing together writers and readers. The practices of readers are now closing the assumed gap between these mediums. Online journals offer a way to navigate limitations of time and space, both geographical and material, with the presence of easily accessible archives that keep issues current, and with a more effective distribution model, as well as freedom from the restrictions of the dollar-based page count. Online journals can host longer works, accommodate longer lines, and are freed from the break of the page. They also offer unique opportunities for collaboration with other art forms: *Blackbird* offers video essays and videos of dance; *Born* brings together writers and artists in multimedia projects; and here at *Memorious*, our art song contest brings together composers, chamber musicians, and poets. Such innovations ultimately expand the audience for literature.

John W. Wang, editor, *Juked*

One advantage online literary journals have over print journals is their ability to reach out to an endless audience. Outside of a few exceptions most print journals don't ever get read. Stories get published, reach a relatively small audience, then they sit on shelves and collect dust and that's that. Anyone can access online journals, from anywhere, and, assuming there's an archive in place, they will remain accessible indefinitely, or until the world ends/journal dies. It's also much easier to hunt down material by a particular author you're looking for, if they're published online. Granted, we may see a greater noise-to-signal ratio when comparing online versus print, but the same principles that allow greater noise also allow for more avant-garde material. Publishers have more room (and less cost) to take risks. Some work, some don't, but that's what you get when you push the boundaries. I don't know that online journals have "come of age" (depends on criteria), but people aren't quick to dismiss online journals like they used to, and that trend will only continue. Finally, I get the sense online journals are part of a living, organic community, more so than print. The readers and authors interact with each other and comment on the respective works, often immediately after a work is published. There's an enthusiasm and camaraderie surrounding the online literary community that the print world would find very difficult to match.

Ravi Shankar, editor, *Drunken Boat*

Online, the word, once static and paginated, has morphed into movement and sound, hyperlink and interactivity, changing the experience of reading into something richer and more intertextual. One example of this is the nascent genre of web art. A piece like Juliet Davis's "Pieces of Herself" (http://www. drunkenboat.com/db8/panlitwebart/davis/) tells an aural and visual story through our actual passage through the rooms of a house and our engagement with the animated body. Another example would be Molle Indistria's "Every Day the Same Dream," (http://www.drunkenboat.com/db12/06des/molleindustria/index.php), an interactive literary video game that enacts the life of a "Marcusean One-Dimensional Man," who goes through his quotidian life from wardrobe to wife, traffic jam to cubicle, then back again, in an endless repetition that is both hilarious and horrific. Even when we engage with more straightforward literature, as in poetry, like that of Eritrean poet laureate Reesome Haile, (http://www.drunkenboat.com/db3/haile/haile.html), we can see the script of Tigrinya, the endangered tongue he works in, and hear the guttural stops of the beautiful ancient language being voiced as we read along with the work in translation. The distribution of this work is vast, its revision constant, proving that the online journal does things about which print can only dream.

Brian Allan Carr, fiction editor, *Dark Sky Magazine*

I think the main differences between print and online journals are the results of limitations and capabilities inherent to the respective mediums. Online journals are able to publish more and promote their writers more easily, and writers are able to utilize online journals to more readily draw attention to their work; print journals afford a stronger sense of permanence. Online publishing allows for more options and more opportunities to be creative from a marketing standpoint; print journals feel better in the hands. Both mediums can be inventive with design—though it seems easier (albeit more expensive) to put together a unique/well-designed print journal. Both mediums can offer great writing. Perhaps the debate is dated. I first read Baudelaire online. Did that make *Paris Spleen* a shabbier bit of writing?

Kim Chinquee, fiction/nonficton editor, *elimae*

I don't particularly see print journals failing in any way: online journals simply have more opportunity to turn things out in a more timely manner. I've edited both print journals and online. Back in 2004-2005, as fiction editor of *Night Train* (when it was strictly print), the process was just much more in-depth (galleys, layout, actually going to print, distribution, etc.) than my experiences in editing for an online journal (*elimae*). I'm not versed in html coding and am only speaking from my experiences. Also, online journals seem to reach a wider audience, as it's easier for a reader to click a link and read than to buy a journal at the bookstore, or order it online and wait for it to arrive. Furthermore, some online journals allow comments, and include blogs, which allow readers to participate in an ongoing dialogue. On the other hand, online websites do disappear. And there's a delight in holding that print journal and seeing the work inside, and putting the journal on a shelf—indulgences that simply aren't possible with online journals—so they're just two different species. I love *elimae*'s elegance: it's classy and consistent, with an aesthetic I admire. I love *Electric Literature*'s savvy look, the quality of the work and the efficiency of the web page, the attitude and the mission (to use new media and innovative distribution to return the short story to a place of prominence in popular culture), the fact that they utilize the medium as opportunity, rather than seeing it as doom.

What Must Independent Presses Do Today to Survive and Thrive? Wings Press of San Antonio Shows the Way

Wings Press is a plucky San Antonio independent literary press that's been around since 1975, and shows an uncanny abillity to pick up major literary awards. For instance, Maria Espinoza's novel *Dying Unfinished* won the 2010 Pen Oakland Josephine Miles Award, Pamela Uschuk's *Crazy Love* won the 2010 American Book Award for poetry, and Carmen Tafolla's *The Holy Tortilla and a Pot of Beans* won the 2009 Tomas Rivera Award for Mexican-American young adult literature. Wings is in the middle of a major project to convert all of their books into e-book format. Publisher Bryce Milligan offered these thoughts:

Wings Press's durability, and its ability to win notable literary awards.

It is in the nature of small presses to appear, fill a certain need—often political or cultural in nature—and then vanish. A few gain a certain longevity simply by having more broadly based objectives, such as publishing regional authors, or titles relevant to a particular geographic region, or just good literature, whether mainstream or cutting-edge. Wings Press was the first in Texas to begin consciously to publish "multicultural" literature, which is to say, Wings will publish good literature no matter who wrote it or whether a potential audience for it exists. We've had Chicano and Chicana authors in our list for decades, simply because the writing was exciting and relevant. Eventually the country caught up. Wings is proud to have several authors who can be described as essential to the Latina canon, if there is such a thing: Lorna Dee Cervantes, Carmen Tafolla, Ana Castillo, Maria Espinosa, Cecile Pineda, Mexican novelist Cecilia Urbina, Argentinian political novelist Alicia Kozameh, Chilean poet and scholar Marjorie Agosín, among others.

Wings thrives in San Antonio now, but it has been a long haul. I can truly say that the press has been kept alive by the hard work of our authors, some of whom do dozens of appearances a year. Some rely on bookstores to stock their books for a reading, but some just pack their trunks with books and head out on tours that have included coffee shops and community centers as well as universities along the way.

San Antonio is a wonderful place to write, especially since the internet has brought the world to every writer's doorstep. But the cultural ambiance here, the interwoven linguistic environment, the curious mix of left-leaning politics and a history of activism with the city's substantial retired military population, the antiquity of the place combined with a forward-thinking city government—all of this appeals to the imagination. It also makes San Antonio a positively liberal oasis in Texas. If it's a wonderful place to write, it seems like a wonderful place to run a press.

Their digital archive project.

I'm about halfway through turning the Wings backlist into e-books. So far this year I've gotten over forty completed, and another forty are in the works. Now, that does not mean that they are all available on all formats—yet. It seems that the Kindle versions appear first, but the ePub versions (for Nook, Sony Reader, and iPad, etc.) take longer to appear. Nevertheless, they are beginning to show up, so it is just a matter of time before the entire Wings backlist will be available.

Of course, there are difficulties—turning twenty-year-old PageMaker files into contemporary PDFs can be time-consuming, for example—but there are also fascinating design issues. Designing e-books turns out to be a lot like designing a scroll, so I studied some ancient scrolls available online and I examined a number of e-books. Many cherished elements of the book simply don't make sense for e-books, or e-scrolls. White space, for example, has absolutely no appeal on a small screen. The use of the page as a dividing device, like you find in novels comprised mainly of vignettes, is not only useless, it feels clumsy. The formal index relates to fixed pages, which can still apply if a physical book has been scanned and not redesigned, but the on-board search engine is a lot faster. Of course, there is a lot more to a well-researched index than just a list of word appearances, but that will soon be a lost art. And fixed page numbers themselves don't really mean a lot anymore in an e-book, and can be confusing when they conflict with the reading device's page counter. So e-book design is an evolving field.

The big push at Wings was to turn the complete works of John Howard Griffin into e-books. These are finished and have been submitted, but none have shown up anywhere. Now, on Amazon, you can get Kindle versions of *Black Like Me, Available Light,* and *Street of the Seven Angels,* all by Griffin, all Wings editions, but currently these are versions scanned originally for the Search Inside the Book promo, not the full Wings Press e-book editions submitted over the past several months. This is quite frustrating, but I'm pretty sure that patience will win the day. Amazon Digital does pay for what they sell, but their versions do not have all the extras that the actual Wings e-books do—added reviews, extra photos, new biographical info, not to mention that the texts have been re-proofed. In the case of *Black Like Me,* the Wings e-book is the same as the forthcoming fiftieth anniversary edition, and that text has been completely re-edited from the original manuscripts, has a new afterword, and additional critical materials.

I am fairly certain that online access to the titles of independent publishers, whether as e-books or printed editions, is the only thing that will keep independent publishers alive. When a customer goes to a physical bookstore and asks for a title from an independent press, it is highly unlikely that an independent press's title will be on the shelves. Worse, it is less than a fifty-fifty proposition whether or not a specific title can even be ordered. The problem here is simple human error. It does not matter how good your distribution system is; all that matters is the competence of the bookstore clerk.

For example, I was in a large chain store in Dallas last week. One of my authors, Bryan Woolley, was a quite beloved raconteur/columnist for the *Dallas Morning News* for many years. His new memoir, *The Wonderful Room: The Making of a Texas Newspaperman,* actually appeared as a series of farewell columns in the *Dallas Morning News* when he retired a couple of years ago. The clerk at this chain bookstore, only a few blocks from the author's home, told me in no uncertain terms that the book "could not be ordered." I insisted that he look it up on Ingram, where it showed "out of stock." As has happened so many times that I have lost count (and lost a lot of hair in the process), this clerk told me that the book was out of print and that the only way he could get a copy for a persistent customer was to look on Amazon for a used copy. Of course, on Amazon we found that it was not only in stock and available both in cloth and as a Kindle e-book, it was discounted twenty-five percent in both cases. Hmmm.

This kind of error among bookstore clerks and even managers is the bane of smaller presses. I've tried to explain that "out of stock" means just that—if you order it from a distributor like Ingram, they will order it from wherever they get their books (either from a distributor like I use—Independent Publishers

Group—or directly from the press). It is not complicated, and it only takes a few days to get the book, even when the first source lists it as "out of stock." Lord, only the Library of Congress is never "out of stock" of a particular title.

But e-books already are leveling the playing field between the independents and the larger houses when it comes to sales overseas. One of my authors, Ann Fisher-Wirth (author of *Carta Marina*), has a fan base in Sweden, and over the last year or so we have sold a couple of dozen copies there. They must be dedicated fans, because a sixteen dollar paperback poetry collection goes for twice that once it has crossed the Atlantic. But once the e-book appeared, sales for the e-book eclipsed the overseas sales of the hardcopy within a few weeks of the release.

What makes for a successful small press author.

A successful small press author is one who knows upfront that a book may get great reviews, may win major awards, may be available across the country, but building a readership means making lots of personal contact with readers. Margaret Randall, whom we think is publishing her ninetieth book this year, just told me that she's got two dozen gigs lined up this spring, from Cuba to California. That's what it takes.

Even well-informed literary people have the mistaken idea that if a book doesn't get reviewed in *Publishers Weekly* or the *New York Times Book Review*, then this means the book is somehow not as good as those that do get reviewed. Not at all. You can't imagine how many books they get in their offices. And there is a natural tendency for review editors to pay more attention to authors and presses they know well. On the other hand, there are some journals that do not just suffer from a plethora of choices. It is not all about money, but too often it is. There are some highly respected journals in this country that I can guarantee will review several of my books in a row if only I will buy a fairly large ad. They would never admit to this, and are scandalized when you point it out, but if you don't buy ads every year or so, they will forget that your zip code exists.

So a successful small press author realizes that getting reviews in important places is a gamble, and that a large advertising budget is out of the question. Which leaves personal contact and word of mouth. Blogging helps a lot, as it provides interaction with readers. Connecting with Facebook or whatever your social media choice is also helps. Doing online interviews and virtual tours helps. In short, writing well is and ought to be the really hard part, but promoting comes in a close second.

Advice to a young person thinking of starting a small press today.

Curiously, when I was at the Texas Book Festival this year, several people—both young and old, by the way—asked me just that. Several were interested in the book arts aspect of small press publishing, and they wanted to talk about access to good letterpresses and letterpress printers, papermakers, etc. If that is what they want to do, that's great. Literature as a whole will sail on through the twenty-first century as a primarily digitally-accessible art form, but there will always be bibliophiles who want to actually hold a book in their hands, and the more aesthetically pleasing the physical object, the better. Other folks approached me asking about publishing as a business. The answer to that one depends entirely upon their objectives. But in general, I would advise a young person interested in starting a "traditional" small press—one that aims at publishing good literature, often poetry or commercially risky fiction—to learn a lot about online marketing, to set up a website, to develop a contact list among reviewers, all before they put out their first book. It sounds like capitalism, and it is capitalism. Selling one book funds the publication of the next book. There is no way around that except to inherit.

Design as an important element of book production.

What I am proudest of is the diversity of design you find in Wings books. On the one hand, I believe that the design must reflect the content. Holding the physical book in your hand, or viewing the cover on a screen, there must be something about the design that relates viscerally to the character of the book. That being said, I as a designer also know that an author who is not completely pleased by the final product is not going to go out and tell everyone how great his or her new baby is. So I always try to get a good deal of author input into the design process. I read a text, I think about it, I even dream about it, and then I find myself scanning leaves I gathered from beside the San Antonio River, or searching the local galleries for a print that fits a certain theme, or simply recreating the image in my head in Photoshop. I can tell you this—much to the chagrin of a few authors—that I'll postpone publishing a book if the design has not come together.

Most noteworthy successes.

A recent unusual success is going on right now. Carmen Tafolla and Ellen Riojas Clark did a small book last year entitled *Tamales, Comadres, and the Meaning of Civilization*. It is a charmer that reflects how important tamales are not only to Latino culture, but to the history of the Americas. And there are some very tasty recipes in it too! Well, last year's edition was a small one, done as a fundraiser to support the Guadalupe Cultural Arts Center. This year we put out a larger edition. By pushing here and shoving there, we got the region's largest grocery store chain interested. So this December, the authors are doing thirteen local signings, seven of them at H-E-B grocery stores. In south Texas, we don't have as many bookstores as we should, so H-E-B has started building "literacy centers" in some stores, especially in communities that don't have a bookstore. They are also carrying some of our books that have regional themes, like Jay Brandon's *Milagro Lane*, a mystery set in San Antonio. The sales have been quite good so far.

I can't really say what my biggest success has been. They don't really come all at once. It is really nice when you realize that a book is going into its third or fourth printing and shows no sign of slowing down, but that is a process that may take two years or ten years. It is a success either way.

The effects of the economic downturn and new technologies.

The economic downturn has been both troublesome and enlightening, coming as it has just as e-books began to enter the market in a serious way. A whole lot of people got e-reading devices over the last couple of years simply because they were the new gadget to have. And hey, a lot of them discovered books. Or at least that is what the sales figures seem to indicate. But part of that has to be that e-books are so much less expensive than paper ones. And any fourth-grader with a forty-pound backpack will tell you that they are easier to cart around. This generation relates to text differently than does every generation before it. There will always be people who want to hold a physical book on their lap, who appreciate fine bindings and gilt edges, but I guarantee they will be a smaller and smaller proportion of readers.

Paul Ruffin on the Role of Texas Review Press on the Southern Literary Scene

Yale, Harvard, Oxford, Princeton—these are the names that roll off the tongue when university presses are mentioned. But hold on—there's something brewing in Huntsville, Texas, too.

Huntsville, you say? The execution capital of the world? That may be true, but they also have Sam Houston State University, which hosts Texas Review Press, a member of the Texas A&M University Press Consortium. With some other university presses in the region recently curtailing operations, the burden is all the heavier on Texas Review Press to publish important writing that might otherwise get overlooked by the commercial presses. Paul Ruffin—poet laureate of Texas in 2009, and author of many books of fiction, essays, and poetry—runs this dynamic press.

You are the founder/director of Texas Review Press, a member of the Texas A&M University Press Consortium. How has the press evolved over the years, and what are its current priorities? What is distinctive about Texas Review Press? Have you accomplished everything you wanted to when you founded the press?

When I arrived at SHSU back in 1975, my dean gave me five hundred dollars to develop a literary journal, and the next year I came out with the *Sam Houston Literary Review*, a sixty-four-page stapled publication. It was a modest beginning, but by 1978, when *The Texas Quarterly* folded at UT-Austin, our regional reputation had grown to the point at which I felt comfortable assuming a little more impressive-sounding name, so I renamed the journal *The Texas Review* and published the first issue under that title in 1979.

That same year I had enough money in my budget to publish our first book under the imprint Texas Review Press. It was a collection of Texas poetry and photographs appropriately called *The Texas Anthology*. Then I discovered a much cheaper way of producing books: I'd accept a poetry chapbook and imbed it in an issue of *The Texas Review*, then have the printer run an extra three hundred signatures (typically thirty-two pages, two sigs) and print a cover for the chapbook. All I was paying for the interior pages was the cost of ink and paper, and the covers were all in black ink, so the cost per unit was quite low. I did this for six or seven years, until I finally had a budget large enough to publish full-length books. By this time the administration was giving me enough money to manage at least a book a year in addition to two issues of the journal.

Before Bobby K. Marks stepped down as president of SHSU—along about 1996, I would guess—he called me to his office one day and said that he wanted to do a little something to help out my operation: he set up a line-item budget allowance that would permit me to gear up production to the point where I could publish three or four books a year, allowing me to seriously apply for admission to the Texas A&M University Consortium.

The first time I appealed to them, the Consortium turned me down: I just didn't have enough books to prove that TRP was a viable enterprise. Without the Consortium, we simply didn't have any way to promote our books, so I applied again, and in 1997 we joined the University of North Texas, SMU, TCU, A&M, and the Texas State Historical Society as part of the Texas A&M University Press Consortium. From that point on we started producing four to six books a year, and our books were being represented and sold all over the world. By 2009 we were publishing a dozen books a year.

For 2012 I have twenty-three books scheduled for publication, thanks to the generosity of the SHSU administration in maintaining my budget, providing adequate facilities and equipment, and allowing me to use three graduate interns each semester from the English Department.

One thing that is distinctive about TRP is that for many years now we have had our four international book competitions—X.J. Kennedy Poetry Prize (best full-length collection), George Garrett Fiction Prize (best novel or collection of short stories), Clay Reynolds Novella Prize, and Robert Phillips Poetry Chapbook Prize—and we've had winners from all over: Japan, the Czech Republic, Africa, and probably at least half the states in the Union.

We have also initiated a new breakthrough award for the best collection of Southern poetry by a poet who has never published a full-length book, and we are doing this state by state. The winner from Mississippi, Noel Polk, is our first. Each year we will publish a breakthrough book from another state until all the Southern states are represented in the series. We've also started a *Southern*

Poetry Anthology series in which each year we publish a collection of the best poetry from a Southern state or region. Our first was South Carolina, followed by Mississippi and Contemporary Appalachia; we are bringing out Louisiana this year. Some of these are being used as classroom texts. What we'll do beyond all this to promote Southern literature is uncertain, but I'm thinking about a breakthrough series in Southern fiction (novel or short stories) and fiction anthologies featuring the best short fiction from each of the states.

I try very hard to work three or four Texas writers into our lineup each year, since I feel that one of our highest callings is to promote the literature of our state, and we average, I'd say, at least one book a year that focuses on Huntsville.

So we are a university press dedicated to promoting literature at the local, state, regional, national, and international levels.

If I had to cite the most distinctive feature of Texas Review Press, I would have to say that it is our internship program, through which our graduate students in creative writing are permitted to work as the staff of a university press and an international literary journal. We typically have three to four grad students on staff, along with student interns from our graduate Editing/Publishing Practicum.

That class itself is, I think, one of the strongest attractions to our graduate creative writing program. Each semester that I teach it, the students do research for a book of their own, organize the materials, write and edit the book, and design the cover. It is their book, and they are listed as the editors. The book then becomes just another in our lineup for the year and TRP runs it in the Consortium catalog and publishes it. It's quite exciting for these students to see their books all over the internet and in bookstores. We've had quite a lot of success with these books too. *Mascot Mania*, a book featuring and cataloging all the Texas high-school mascots, was picked up by the Associated Press and reviewed by most major newspapers in the state and featured on several television and radio shows. Likewise we had great success with a collection of nonfiction and art from Texas Death Row. *Upon This Chessboard of Nights and Days: Voices from Texas Death Row* was the subject of a Voice of America story and showed up on television and radio stations and on internet sites all over the world. One of the finest moments for me, though, is sending out royalty checks to those graduate students—those checks might not seem like much to most people, but the students get a real kick out of them.

We have just instituted an MFA program in creative writing at SHSU, and I am hoping that TRP will be attractive to prospective students. They will be hard-pressed to find anything in the country comparable to our internship program and the Editing/Publishing Practicum, which guarantees them a book of their own. I think that we have a very bright future ahead of us.

What is your relationship with the university? Is it a loose relationship or a tight one? Does the university's financial situation affect you?

I am totally devoted to SHSU, which has been my home for a very long time. I cannot imagine having done better anywhere else. The administration has supported me all the way in every way that it could, and even in these financially troubling times I feel secure that they will go right on supporting the press and journal. They seem to recognize the ambassadorial role we play for Sam Houston State University: where our journal and books go—and they go all over the globe—the name Sam Houston State goes.

We've had some difficult economic times. Have you been affected by state budget cuts? What steps have you taken to alleviate the situation, and what other things would help to keep the press on a sustainable financial footing?

We are able to grow as a university press because we keep our expenses at a minimum. To this point our budget has not been touched. We derive around sixty percent of our operating budget from sales, and, though we had a couple of tough years, our increased production has resulted in more total revenues. Face it: university presses are high-profile targets when administrations start looking for places to cut, and many such presses have large, expensive facilities and state-of-the-art equipment, and most of them have several full-time employees plus interns.

I have six hours' reassigned time as editor of *The Texas Review* and director of Texas Review Press, plus a summer stipend equal to two classes, and I have one half-time assistant, plus three interns each semester, and we are housed in part of the bottom floor of the English building. I am not whining here: I have not asked for more. I believe that my administration recognizes the role we play in ensuring the survival of literature in the state, region, country, and world, and I am confident that they will go on supporting us as long as we represent the university the way we have in the past and as long as we demonstrate our ability to fulfill our role without requiring increased annual budgets.

How has the press responded to the advent of new technologies? What more would you like to do in this direction?

New technology has made it much easier for us to increase our production year by year. There was a time when we had to type up manuscripts, often from handwritten submissions, and I laid out the journal and our books on a light table, cutting out paragraphs, lines, words, and even letters with an X-Acto knife from a waxed galley sheet, and then the layout boards were photographed with an enormous camera, negatives made, and plates burned. It took forever to get something done. Now, after working things up on the computer, I send PDF files of our text and covers to the printer. Corresponding with authors through email just streamlines everything. I sometimes marvel at how far we have come in so short a length of time.

What books have been some of your most important recent successes?

Well, you have to remember that a "success" for a small university press is to earn back more revenues than you put into a project. So defined, we've had a great many successes. Recently, though, I would mention *Mascot Mania* and *Upon This Chessboard of Nights and Days: Voices from Texas Death Row* as resounding successes, not because they earned us much more than we put into them but because they were media darlings for a while. As I mentioned earlier, *Mascot Mania* was picked up by the Associated Press and paraded all over the state, and the Death Row book was featured all over the world through Voice of America. And both these were books that my editing/publishing class produced. Those two books probably brought us more attention than all the others combined over the past decade.

I would certainly mention Richard Burgin's *Rivers Last Longer,* a novel that has received fine reviews from all over, and Eric Miles Williamson's novel *Two-Up*, already translated into French and recently accepted by a UK publisher. I have high hopes for Williamson's *Say It Hot*, which, if taken for what it is and not simply as some sort of personal rant, will force people to reconsider their opinions of some of American literature's presumed icons. Our fairly new *Southern Poetry Anthology* (collections on Contemporary Appalachia, Mississippi, and Carolina already out, with Louisiana close) is making its way into classrooms across the South, so I have high hopes for it.

What titles are you most looking forward to in the near future?

I'm eager to continue with that *Southern Poetry Anthology* series and also with a new series I've introduced: the Southern Poetry Breakthrough prize. We are publishing the best book of poetry from each Southern state by poets who have never had a first book. One of the finest roles of the university press is to discover and promote exceptional new talent. I believe that these books will result in even more regional recognition. I'm always eager to see what our international competitions will bring each year. I like to get our Editing/Publishing Practicum books out, since they are usually of local interest. The class is working on a book on Dan Phillips right now that we'll bring out next year. Dan, who has an operation called Phoenix Commotion, builds both spec houses and houses for indigent families in the Huntsville area, and he uses mostly recycled materials: he has built home after home using almost nothing but materials he has salvaged from the county dump and that people have donated to the cause. It will be, I think, a fine book.

Recently, some other Texas independent presses have either ceased to exist or cut back on publishing literary work. This should have enhanced your position as almost the lone standard-bearer (shall we say the lone star?) in Texas. Has this unfortunate situation worked to your benefit?

The collapse of SMU Press—though it may be resurrected as an all-electronic press—was especially significant, since they were known for their excellent fiction offerings. The fact is that poetry and literary fiction just do not pay the bills anymore, if they ever did, so more and more independent and university presses are declining to consider manuscripts in those genres. A number of them are still doing a book of poetry or fiction a year, usually through some prize they established long ago and wish to retain. The university press, from the first in America at Cornell in 1869, was never expected to be commercially successful: it is a part of academe, and its highest calling is the dissemination of every sort of art and literature, not the generation of revenues. Far too many university administrations are training their sights on their presses, simply because they are an easy target these days. You don't see many athletic programs being cut significantly or shut down, do you? Whether all this economic turmoil has benefited us or not, I cannot say, though I suspect we'll begin to pick up better and better manuscripts as the years progress. We intend to go on producing the best books that we can as long as we can. Many of those books will end up in electronic editions, but they will be printed books first.

What is your opinion of the recent closing of Borders? How does the paucity of bricks-and-mortar stores affect you—or does it? If you could wave a magic wand, what changes would you like to see in the distribution system for the benefit of independent presses emphasizing quality literary work?

The most immediate impact of the closing of Borders on us was to generate some concern about whether the Consortium would ever be able to recover some of the money they owe us. It would be nice if more stores carried the books being produced by small independents and university presses, but they are all swept up in the same commercial frenzy to provide what they think the average American reader is likely to fall for, and that is self-help books, books by and about the rich and famous, etc. I wonder sometimes how Hemingway and Faulkner would fare. Chances are that some university press would have ended up publishing their books. I also wonder who will represent the world of American literature in the textbooks of tomorrow.

What are some misconceptions people might have about a press located in Huntsville that you would like to remove?

It does not matter where a press is located as long as it does its job. Whether you're working on the bottom floor of the English building at Sam Houston State University in Huntsville, or in some spacious modern complex high above the streets of Manhattan, you are measured by the work you produce. I'll guarantee you that all those throngs of people lugging around manuscripts out there are not concerned about the location of a potential publisher.

You've recently published a novel by Richard Burgin, a major American short story writer, and winner of multiple Pushcart prizes. Does it seem amazing to you that such a novel was not published by a major New York house? Do the New York publishers know what they're doing?

I am both amazed and grateful to be able to lay my hands on these manuscripts. Quite a number of our books would have made it in New York two or three decades ago. Sure, they know what they are doing: they are playing it safe and avoiding economic collapse. They used to be willing to take on promising writers and cultivate them through an initial commercially unsuccessful book or two, realizing that eventually their work might result in a tremendous payoff. Not now: the bean counters are in charge of the temple up there, and they are far more interested in lucre than in literature.

You just published a book of familiar essays—your fourth one—called Travels With George in Search of Ben Hur and Other Meanderings *(University of South Carolina Press). Tell us what appeals to you about this form, and how it's different from the more popular "creative nonfiction" genre promoted by MFA programs?*

I don't even know what they're doing in the area of creative nonfiction in the workshops these days, so I don't know whether the form as I practice it is very different or not different at all. I have published poetry and fiction (novels and collections of short stories), and I have to say that familiar essays are presently my favorite form. For one thing, the ideas for these pieces clutter my mental attic: they are everywhere I step. I have written a weekly newspaper column for over twenty-five years, and I don't recall a time when I didn't have in mind something to write about. Day-to-day living provides me with a wealth of material. For instance, right now, because of the terrible drought we're enduring, I've been writing about wells I've known: the one my father dug over in Mississippi, the one I once cleaned out for my grandfather, the one in my backyard. Sometimes I'll pull some of my fictitious characters in to help me, as I did this week. I have a guy by the name of Grady Johnson over in Mississippi whom I pull into these pieces strictly for entertainment purposes. He talks just like any of the redneck characters in my stories, and the situations are made up. If I'm writing about West Texas, I'll enlist the help of Mr. and Mrs. Pate: I've learned an awful lot about the world just sitting on their imaginary porch listening to their stories. These things read like familiar essays, but they are in fact fiction. Almost everything in *Travels with George* is autobiographical.

What was your relationship with legendary Southern writer George Garrett?

George and I had a long, wonderful history. I first met him when he visited the Center for Writers at the University of Southern Mississippi, and we were close friends from that point on. We joined forces on several literary projects, mostly anthologies, and he served as my fiction editor at *The Texas Review* for many years. We traveled together on reading tours a few times—as a matter of fact, the title piece in *Travels with George* is a chronicle of a road trip we took in Texas back in the mid-1990s—and I gotta tell you that he entertained every mile of the way. On a New England tour once he put me and my wife up for a couple of days in their house in York Harbor, Maine, and he prepared two big lobsters for me for dinner one night. Not many people would do that. George has probably been the single most important influence on my writing life. He was a man who excelled in every discipline he put his pen to—poetry, short story, novel, essay, screenplay—and that became my aspiration. I've done OK, I think, in everything but the screenplay. One final statement on George Garrett: he never got the kind of recognition he deserved for his writing. Never won a Pulitzer, though many of his books were vastly superior to books that did. Southern white male writers seldom do, you will note. George Garrett should be ranked among the eternal Greats in American literature—and maybe eventually he will be.

You were the poet laureate of Texas in 2009. How was the experience?

It was a wonderful experience and a great surprise. I've lived in literary obscurity for so damned long, I figured that I was destined to remain there. It was recognition by my adopted state, and it felt good. I've had lots of invitations since then to do readings and workshops and to submit poetry for publication, and I got a book out of it in TCU Press's Poet Laureate series. The high doesn't last long though—soon enough you are living in literary obscurity again.

You've written a memoir called **Growing up in Mississippi Poor and White but Not Quite Trash.**

I've published big chunks of that thing here and there—the last section of *Travels with George* is about my coming to sexual awareness, and *Boulevard* has published two large sections of it—but I still haven't wrestled the thing into shape. Every time I think it's ready to go, I write another little section. It's the story of my growing up in poverty on aptly named Sand Road, about five miles from Columbus, Mississippi. I focus on four areas of my evolution: family life, religion, racial issues, and my very slow awakening to sexual knowledge. The problem with writing a memoir is that the more you dredge around in the pit of your mind for memories, the more you find. One thing leads to another…

While we're talking about poverty, there's very little American fiction dealing with the realities of the working class. Why is this the case? Who do literary writers really write for?

Oh, there are plenty of writers out there who deal with the working-class world, but nobody's paying a whole lot of attention to them. Everybody wants to read about being poor and black or poor and Hispanic, but it seems to me that there's not a whole lot of interest among the general public in reading about being poor and white. I don't really care: I'm going to go on writing about that world whether anyone reads my work or not. Literary writers apparently write for each other.

You are the rare writer who publishes in multiple genres—fiction, poetry, and essays. Why is it that most writers these days stick to a single niche?

I fear that most people get too comfortable with a particular genre and feel that they might jinx themselves by trying something new. The movement for me from lyrical poetry to dramatic poetry to familiar essays and fiction was so seamless that I wonder why I didn't make it sooner. I started writing both poetry and fiction in church when I was a kid to keep from going crazy with boredom, and I've always felt comfortable writing either. I wrote essays in school as "punishment" for getting into trouble—I wrote my way out of many a paddling.

Do you think an American writer deserves the Nobel Prize? Who? Which recent Nobel literature choice has been particularly apt, in your opinion?

To my way of thinking, John Steinbeck was the last American to win the Nobel Prize for Literature (1962) whose work was truly worthy of such recognition. When you examine the winners of that prize since then, you see agendas at work that you know will never permit another American of genuine lasting literary quality to win as long as those agendas are in place. Could Hemingway or Faulkner win today? It is doubtful. As for prospects for Americans right now, I don't know. You see names like Roth, Pynchon, and Oates tossed around, but the only American writer I know who rises in literary excellence to what I regard as the essential level is Cormac McCarthy, but he's a Southern (more or less) white male who doesn't socialize well. I figure that he's a long shot, but he is certainly deserving of the honor.

You've built yourself as an influential writer, editor, and teacher from what is proverbially known as a hardscrabble background. What advice do you have for writers coming from similar experiences?

Get up every morning with one realization in mind: If you don't like your life, you can change it. You can do that in this country, in spite of all the petty forces arrayed against you. If you want to write, then write—if you're good enough, someone will publish you. If you are not good enough, then work at it until you are. If you fall short of your dreams in this country—assuming that they are reasonable—it is because you didn't try hard enough to realize them. Take pride in what you do but remain humble in knowing that you can do better.

A Fabled Indie Press Reaches Maturity:
What Can We Learn from Coffee House Press?

Coffee House Press (CHP) of Minnesota is a national treasure. Few independent literary presses can match its long record of publishing some of the finest fiction and poetry in America. I talked to publisher Allan Kornblum,[1] associate publisher Chris Fishbach,[2] and managing editor Anitra Budd about the press's history and prospects, and about the challenges and rewards of independent publishing in general. Perhaps some budding literary entrepreneurs out there will be inspired by this great success story!

Coffee House Press is one of the more established and prominent of the independent literary presses in this country. Could you talk about the evolution of the press in its very early days and its maturity?

Allan Kornblum: In December 1969, I was working the midnight-to-eight-thirty shift at the Grand Central Station post office in NYC, and attending poetry workshops at the St. Mark's Church Poetry Project. One evening, the workshop leader told us that we had been asked to help collate the pages of a mimeographed magazine. In one of the back rooms of the old church, we were greeted by a group of two by six foot tables, each with five stacks of two hundred and fifty pages. When I completed my assigned portion, I sidled up to the editor, told him how much I liked his magazine, asked if he'd like to see some of my work. He looked off in the distance, sighed, and said, "I've always thought poetry should be as hard to break into as the Longshoreman's Union." To hell with him, I thought—I'll start my own. I've always been grateful for that kick in the pants, which can sometimes be far more productive than well-intended encouragement.

---

1. Allan Kornblum died November 23, 2014 at the age of sixty-five.

2. Chris Fischbach has ascended to publisher of Coffee House Press.

I had already planned to attend the University of Iowa next year, so I told all my NYC friends that I was going to start a magazine following my relocation. And when I arrived in Iowa City in July 1970, I started looking for poets as lively as the ones I'd met in New York. By the end of August, I had produced the first issue of *Toothpaste* magazine. In September, I signed up for a class called Intro to Typography, hoping it would help me understand the publishing process when, in the future, some NYC publishing house accepted my first book. Instead, I discovered the class was an introduction to letterpress printing. I was a bit put off at first—until I handset some type and pulled my first proof.

It was as if I had been struck by lightning and been reborn. For my class project I printed a little pamphlet of my own poems, which showed no signs of typographic talent or taste. But I had fallen in love with the craft, and was determined to learn. Over the next few years, I published seven mimeographed issues of *Toothpaste*, and three mimeographed books, while beginning to learn the craft and history of letterpress printing and small press publishing. During that time, I began to realize I would be able to *continue* learning about publishing for the rest of my life—a revelation with tremendous appeal to an idealistic young person. Today, I only wish I had a second lifetime to continue my studies.

I moved from New York, hoping that poetry would turn out to be my life's work, and hoping, as the song of the day put it, "to find somebody to love." By 1973 I was married, had purchased a printing press and (with family help) a house, and was starting to publish books under the Toothpaste Press imprint. During the next ten years I continued learning the craft of letterpress printing, while publishing approximately seventy books and pamphlets, printing another dozen books on commission, and knocking off well over a hundred broadsides, and countless posters for poetry readings.

By 1983 I had learned about editing, book design, marketing, publicity, sales, and bookkeeping. But when I finally sat down to do the math, I realized that if I were to continue as a letterpress printer, I had to move into the three hundred-dollar per copy range, and cultivate rare book collectors instead of contemporary writers and readers who wanted a challenge. I know some great people who went the "rare book" route, and they have produced works of surpassing imagination and inspiration. It just wasn't the right road for me.

In May 1984, we closed out the Toothpaste Press imprint, and incorporated Coffee House Press as a Minnesota nonprofit, and later that month, over Memorial Day weekend, we exhibited our first fall list at the ABA convention at Moscone Center in San Francisco, with galleys of the new titles, and the last letterpress titles from Toothpaste. By fall 1985 my wife and I had sold our Iowa home and moved to the Twin Cities, where Coffee House served as the first "visiting press in residence" at the new Minnesota Center for Book Arts in downtown Minneapolis. Three years later, we moved into our own quarters, a block away. We began establishing our new identity with a continuing string of trade books, while holding onto the past for a while, with a secondary list of letterpress pamphlets published under the Morning Coffee Chapbook Series imprint. During our first ten years as Coffee House, we published thirty letterpress chapbooks, and three deluxe letterpress titles in the three hundred to five hundred-dollar range, just to see if we could do it. The deluxe books each won citations from the American Institute of Graphic Arts, including a Fifty Best Designed Books of the Year award.

But combining letterpress printing with a small, rapidly growing literary publishing house became complicated and counterproductive. Although no press release was ever produced to announce the change, by the end of 1994 we had completed our last letterpress title. Our identity was continuing to evolve, as it has ever since, but we had established our reputation in the literary and publishing communities as one of the top small literary presses with a strong multicultural list, and as one of the presses that might prove to be a survivor.

And survive we did. Today, we have an outstanding staff, and we're in the middle of a carefully planned leadership transition. Chris Fischbach will become publisher in July, and I'll continue at the press as founder/senior editor, gradually reducing my hours over the next decade, while doing some writing and consulting. Meanwhile Coffee House Press is poised for continued growth, with a new website, a redesigned database, and a backlist that provides half our annual book sales income. I look forward to watching Coffee House grow under a new generation of leadership. Nothing is given, but if my health holds out, I'll be celebrating the press's thirty-fifth anniversary in 2019, my fiftieth year in publishing in 2020, and my wife and I will celebrate our fiftieth anniversary in 2022. I look forward to popping a lot of champagne corks.

What were some of the most difficult challenges you had to overcome before CHP hit its stride?

Kornblum: I was an English major, who in turn hired other English majors, and invited yet other English majors to join our board. And there we were, running a small arts organization that grew tenfold in ten years. Although I had already served my own kind of apprenticeship during the Toothpaste Press period, I still had a lot to learn about the publishing business, about scheduling, staff development and supervision, business management, and fundraising, all while the press was growing by leaps and bounds. Realizing I was in a growing business and developing all the skills I needed on the fly—that was quite the challenge.

Is it fair to say that most of the important/innovative poetry in this country is being published by independent presses?

Chris Fishbach: Yes, this is a fair assessment, if only because probably ninety-nine percent of the poetry actually published in this country is by independent presses. But "important" and "innovative" are very different terms. I'd say that all or most of the big houses are publishing some important work, since what they publish is work that is respected and read by many people in the poetry world who are respected by other poetry readers (how is that for circular logic?). But innovative? It depends on whom you ask, I suppose. But since you are asking me, let's just say that I tend to not look to the big houses to find out what is innovative these days. Sometimes I wonder if "important" and "innovative" are even what I care about when I read poetry.

Kornblum: I think it's fair to say that the major publishing houses are staffed with gifted professionals who would love to publish more poetry. But to the people who pay their salaries, thinking a year ahead is long-range planning—building a backlist of poetry that might take five to ten years to start making money seems ridiculous. So a few senior editors might get to pick a few poetry books, but they would love to do more if they could. However, the money-people do have a point—poetry books *don't* sell the kind of numbers needed to pay the rent and make the payroll. As a result most poetry books *are* published by nonprofit literary presses that receive donated income to cover a portion of their costs; they're published by university presses, which are also subsidized; and they're published by very small presses that publish one or two books a year, and don't know how to reach the review media or get their books into the stores. Of course when I began publishing, back in the 1970s, we were all in the same "micro-press" boat; now there's a top tier of small indie presses that are routinely reviewed in *PW, LJ,* and on the best of the internet sites, and have national distribution to indie booksellers, to the chains, and to Amazon. Coffee House was among the presses that contributed to the development of that tier, and we work hard to remain worthy of our reputation. But we respect our colleagues at the major houses, and are not arrogant enough to believe that true editorial wisdom is the special province of the small indies.

Let's talk about some recent books that have especially struck me. **Dear Sandy: Letters from Ted to Sandy Berrigan** *is a new book of Ted Berrigan's letters to his wife Sandy. It seems to me one of the year's landmark literary events.*

Kornblum: Coffee House has been associated with New York School poetry from its inception. Personally, I actually had a class with Ted Berrigan in the spring of 1970, just before I moved to Iowa. Ted had just moved back to New York from Iowa, and as I later learned, the woman I wound up marrying did some babysitting for Ted and Sandy in Iowa City. When Ted died shortly after we made the transition from Toothpaste to Coffee House, we published *Nice To See You: Homage to Ted Berrigan*, edited by Anne Waldman, which included poems, stories, essays, and drawings by Ted's many friends and students. Later on, we wound up becoming the primary publisher for Ron Padgett's poetry, and so when Sandy Berrigan talked to Ron about turning these letters into a book, Ron turned to Coffee House.

Editing these letters brought up a lot of very interesting issues. Do you reproduce every typo the author made in a love letter written in the heat of the moment, or do you fix the typos as the author would have, if he were there to supervise the book? I'll let Chris talk about those discussions, and the extremes he went to, including a trip to New York to look at some of Ted's other letters at Columbia University Library. Chris and Ron worked hard to earn the starred review the book received from *PW*.

Karen Tei Yamashita's **I Hotel** *was a finalist for the 2010 National Book Award. What is your history with Karen? Can there be broader readership for works of this experimental nature?*

Anitra Budd: One of our authors said something I found very enlightening about so-called "experimental" literature (as an aside, I worry that the term "experimental" has too much baggage to be truly useful in discussing literature, but that's another story). A reporter, after hearing the description of this author's admittedly complex novel, said "Wow, that sounds really complicated." The author immediately responded "No! It's not really complicated. If you like *Lost*, you'll like this book." What struck me about her answer was the idea that while people routinely bemoan the lack of readers for innovative literature, millions of viewers religiously tuned in to a television show that was *incredibly* complicated, and, dare I say, experimental in its storytelling. I'm sure that many of these people didn't consider themselves consumers of experimental media; they were just drawn to a well-told, well-paced mystery with complex characters. Could these viewers apply the same fervent attention to experimental literature? I'd like to think so. I think part of the challenge we face as a publisher is convincing readers that words like "experimental" and "innovative" can encompass a wide range of artistic expression, and shouldn't automatically signal "too intellectual" or "unrelatable."

Kornblum: History: In January 1989, Karen sent me a query letter along with a first chapter of a book she called *O Matacao*. That sample chapter introduced a Japanese man who promptly fell off a cliff. When the man awoke, a little ball was floating six inches in front of his head. And it turned out that the ball was going to be the narrator for much of the book. I was captivated immediately, and asked for the entire manuscript. I didn't hear from her. After a while, I actually dug out her query, and sent another letter asking for the complete manuscript again—that's how much that sample chapter had impressed me. It finally arrived later that fall, and I brought it with me when we drove down to Iowa to visit my in-laws for Thanksgiving. On the way back to the Twin Cities, my wife took a turn at the wheel, and I started reading the manuscript. With every page, my excitement grew. I wanted to share the energy, and started reading aloud to my wife. I kept thinking about how much I had loved *V.* by Thomas Pynchon, when I read it in high school, and I wondered how I had gotten so lucky to have a manuscript that great, sitting in my lap. After some editing and a title change, *Through the Arc of the Rain Forest* came out on our fall 1990 list, and we sold out of the first printing of three thousand copies in the first three weeks. *I Hotel* was Karen's fifth book, and that sense of excitement I had back in 1989 has never gone away. Karen and I are only two years apart; and all four of my grandparents immigrated from Eastern Europe, while all four of hers immigrated from Japan. So, to some extent, I think of her as a favorite, distantly-related cousin, as well as a gifted author with an international vision, who has honored us by giving us the opportunity to present her work to the world.

Readership: Your question begs a return question—how broad is broad? Karen's third book, *Tropic of Orange*, was published in 1997, and since then, we have sold twenty thousand seven hundred copies. *I Hotel* has sold more than ten thousand copies in its first year, helped along with that boost from the National Book Award recognition. Had the book won, we would definitely have doubled that number quickly. No, those aren't best-seller numbers, but there isn't a publisher in New York that would sniff at those sales—and for experimental fiction, those are eye-opening numbers. The major publishers have a little secret that most people don't know—other than brand-name authors, most books don't sell more than five thousand copies, and that's at Random House as well as at Coffee House. I'm not going to moan about living in a world that doesn't value experimental fiction, when people are still being evicted from their homes every day. I have no complaints about our audience. Readers are out there—it's part of our job to reach them.

Among your best recent poetry books are Steve Healey's 10 Mississippi *and Julie Carr's* Sarah—Of Fragments and Lines. *Very different aesthetics. How do you come to consensus at the house over which books to publish?*

Fishbach: We don't always come to a consensus. However, when Allan hired me, fifteen years ago, part of the interview process was a discussion of which poets I admired and why, so he knew that there was a certain shared aesthetic between us. However, we do have differing opinions, and there are poets on our list that would not have been Allan's first choice, and vice versa. But for the vast majority of our poets, we agree. I'm lucky that for the past ten years or so Allan has more or less trusted me to acquire whichever poets I wanted.

As for the titles you mention, the answer is not that easy since Julie's book came to us through the National Poetry Series. We chose the judge, Eileen Myles, because we admire her work, but she chose the book. We think it's a great book, but it might not even have been submitted to us, had it not won that contest. Maybe it would have.

A large portion of Steve's book engages in documentary poetics, and if you look carefully at our list, there is a strong strain of that here. Ed Sanders, of course, but also Brenda Coultas, Mark Nowak, Paul Metcalf, Anne Waldman, and so on. That, and you can also trace Steve back to the New York School if you take a slight detour through Northampton.

Budd: Some of our greatest strength stems from having editors who have been associated with the press for a long time: Allan, our founder, still acquires and edits books; Chris has been with the press since 1994; and I've worked with the press in different capacities for nearly a decade. Because of all this experience, we each have a very strong and intuitive sense of what a Coffee House Press book is. We also trust each other implicitly—because of that trust, I always understand why we make the publishing decisions we do, even when, as Chris says, a title isn't necessarily my first choice.

Kornblum: Answer 1: Chris and I agreed on most of the books we selected over the years. But Chris and I had a spoken agreement that we could each pick at least one book a year that the other didn't like. That way we avoided "committee think." And now Chris is developing a similar working relationship with Anitra. At Coffee House we have fostered a culture of mutual respect, and given our staff room to work and grow. That was always a priority for me, and I can tell that Chris feels the same way, as I watch him conduct staff meetings.

Answer 2: Chris once told me that he sometimes envisioned Coffee House as an ever-expanding table, with all our authors seated, reading their work to each other in an ongoing conversation. Well, if all our authors represented one aesthetic, what would they have to talk about? We believe there's room for an endless variety of writers and writing styles at our table, along with endless refills made from freshly ground French roast.

Andrew Ervin's **Extraordinary Renditions,** *a collection of loosely linked novellas, was one of the year's most memorable books of fiction for me. Did you work closely with Andrew on editing the book? How did the book come to your attention?*

Fishbach: I worked very closely with Andrew on this book. However, I have a policy of not being public about the extent of the editorial process between author and editor. It's like the doctor-patient privilege. If he wants to discuss that, he should feel free to.

The book came to my attention in a very old-fashioned way. Andrew approached me at a bar during AWP and asked me if I would consider his book. I asked him to tell me about it, he did, and I said yes, please send it. I read it, and then I called his agent and told him we'd love to publish it. Not a very exciting story, really, but I guess it's important because as an editor I want to be known as being approachable, not hidden away in my office, protected by assistants and interns. Everyone at Coffee House feels it's important for us to be out in the world.

Budd: Without revealing too much about the editing of *Extraordinary Renditions*, I can say that throughout the process Andrew exhibited one of the traits that is most common among our authors: he sweated the small stuff. I've heard horror stories from industry colleagues about authors who feel that copyediting and proofreading are somehow beneath their concern. This couldn't be further from the truth when it comes to Andrew, and to our authors in general. He gave just as much attention to the placement of a comma, or the choice of one word over another, as he did to every other part of the editorial process. It's this level of professionalism and attentiveness among our authors that makes it really easy to love my job.

Two important veteran poets you have recently brought again to prominence are Ed Sanders and Bill Berkson, the former generally classifiable under the Beat category and the latter under the New York School. I cannot think of two poets more worthy of broader acclaim.

Kornblum: Well, of course we're pleased that you feel that way, as we do. But since you didn't supply a question, allow me to ask one, and then answer it. Why is a small indie press taking the financial risks involved in publishing major selecteds and collecteds, the kind of book that used to come from Knopf and Harcourt?

First of all, Knopf still does publish major poetry books, as do Penguin and HarperCollins through Ecco Press, among others. And small presses aren't new to major titles—New Directions published *Paterson* by Williams, and *The Cantos* by Pound. And of course Shakespeare and Company published the first edition of Joyce's *Ulysses*. We have examples to draw on.

As to Coffee House: We have told a number of our authors that we believe in them and their work, and will be there for them throughout their entire career—if they want us. But if we want them to make such a commitment to us, we need to be able to meet their publishing needs as their careers advance. Taking on titles like the Sanders and Berkson books is simply the fulfillment of part of our mission. And we're by no means the only indie press capable of publishing major collections in addition to the more typical ninety-page poetry book. Good indie presses can now provide career-long support to writers.

But beyond the internal capacity to print such books, indie presses are taking the necessary steps to assure their long-term survival. Copper Canyon Press, Graywolf Press, BOA Editions, and Milkweed Editions are all in their second generation of leadership, and Coffee House Press is in the process of completing a leadership transition right now. This development, in part, is a reflection of the maturation of these publishers' boards. They have realized the responsibility publishing important books entails, and by seeing their organizations through leadership transition, they have secured a portion of our literary patrimony for future generations. At Coffee House, we're pleased to be participating in this process.

A young African-American poet with great technical verve is Akilah Oliver,[3] whose A Toast in the House of Friends *you recently published. What is unique about this collection?*

Fishbach: I love how Akilah transforms her grief about her son into a gathering of language that feels new, that walks the line between spoken and written traditions, that combines memory and anger using various cultural and artistic traditions to make something new. I love the way her language interacts with the visuals. I love how it's a book of the city that feels authentic. I love that it's a book that feels like it can do something, that it can both be read as a wonderful work of art and as a tool for change. I love how she fits into the Coffee House list that triangulates around Anne Waldman, Brenda Coultas, and Quincy Troupe.

Perhaps your best-known recent book is Patricia Smith's Blood Dazzler, *which was a finalist for the National Book Award. Along with* Blood Dazzler, *you also published, at the same time, Andrei Codrescu's* Jealous Witness *and Raymond McDaniel's* Saltwater Empire.[4] *Again, three distinct styles, the last belonging to language poetry, yet unified by the theme of Hurricane Katrina. These three seem to me to be the most important poetry books dedicated to the disaster.*

Kornblum: It was a responsibility to publish those responses, and a pleasure to hear such distinctly different voices and perspectives. At times, Andrei Codrescu seemed shocked that he *could* be shocked by a government, after growing up in Stalinist Romania. He almost wanted to go back to being jaded, to being bemused by inaction and corruption wreaking havoc with people's lives. But the scale was so large, that Katrina just blew away his Eastern European cynicism.

Patricia Smith grew up in Chicago, another city defined in part by water, and in part by political corruption, just like New Orleans. But Patricia didn't *react* to Katrina's victims—rather, they *inhabited* her, they spoke through her, they screamed through her. Each time she reads those poems, those people live again.

Ray McDaniel was the only Gulf Coast native of the three, the only one who had the smell of that sea in his nostrils from birth. I heard such a deep, resigned pain and sadness in his voice, as he went back to the place he once called home…but this time it wasn't just difficult to recognize because "you can't step into the same river twice" or "you can't go home again"—this time *home*, in all its complexity, simply wasn't there.

---

3. Akilah Oliver died in February 2011.

4. My collective review of these three Hurricane Katrina-related books appeared in *Michigan Quarterly Review* in 2009.

In light of these and other successes, what can you say about the abilities required in the current economic and cultural environment to make a success of an independent press?

Kornblum: The e-book represents evolution, not revolution. But it does present a new set of challenges, which are certainly compounded by the current economic and cultural environment. I mentioned my love of the history of the book—I believe it might prove helpful to consider the values and innovations the Renaissance publishers introduced when they *created* the *printed* book, as we know it, between 1450-1600.

SPEED: Handset type may seem slow and clunky today, but it was the internet of the time, producing multiple copies of books at what seemed like lightning speed. This is the only value that the printed book has, in fact, lost forever to the new media.

ADVOCACY: The Renaissance publishers believed fiercely in the importance of the books they published, and their capacity to change the world. Today, major houses only publish books if they believe they can make money from them. Not quite the same thing.

ACCURACY: Suddenly it was possible to proofread a text, make corrections, pull a second proof, and make a final round of corrections before printing. Today we have not only taken this advantage for granted, major houses have practically abandoned editing and proofreading to save a dime and increase their profit margin.

ARCHIVABILITY: Print a thousand copies of a printed book, and odds are, even through fire, flood, or the ravages of war, a copy will survive somewhere, somehow. How much confidence can we have that books published in e-book format only will be readable in twenty-five years, fifty years, a hundred years? I own books that old, and I don't need an upgrade to read them.

ACCESSIBILITY: Computer access, internet access, or a reliable source of electricity—none of these are required to read a printed book. In a secondhand bookstore, all of history and literature are available very inexpensively—and in a library, books are free. We are in danger of recreating the world of haves and have-nots in this exciting information age. The printed book continues to remain more accessible on any income level than any other form of information.

BEAUTY: A mass-market paperback may not be a thing of beauty, but a well-printed book can lift the spirit at a glance, like the best works of art. Goodness knows our spirits need lifting these days.

The printed book cannot compete with the internet for *speed*, but publishers can and should *own all* those other values. We should believe in the books we publish, and publish books we can believe in; those books should be carefully and responsibly edited and proofed; printed with materials that are made to last; available as possible to readers; and designed with the same care their authors take, on every single page. Those are the values that should drive every publisher, corporate-owned or indie.

Are indies better positioned to take advantage of the rapid changes going on in publishing and bookselling? Maybe—new ideas reach decision-making levels at an indie press when someone walks across a room and knocks on a door; at the major houses, new ideas have to make their way through several levels of management, and major initiatives need approval from the money-people, and the legal department. Advantage indies.

But if a new initiative falls through, the major houses have backlists that provide more than fifty percent of their annual income in sales and subsidiary rights. And those same money-people who can slow things down can provide the resources to cover the cost of failed initiatives without putting the entire house at risk. Advantage majors.

Publishing is one of those places where art and commerce meet and a press that forgets to mind the store in the excitement of the moment can lose the store and hurt its authors and its readers in the process. Indies need to take advantage of their ability to be nimble, control the costs of new initiatives, and live up to the values that made the publishing industry the heart of the marketplace of ideas, and the expression of the yearnings of the heart.

Can you propose structural reforms in the publishing and bookselling industries to make independent presses more viable?

Kornblum: I have heard this question from many small press publishers over the years. "Why can't we," they ask, "demand that Amazon, or Barnes & Noble, or Baker & Taylor, or R. R. Bowker change their way of doing business in order to help indie presses?"

This year [2011] six of the twenty finalists for the National Book Awards came from indie presses; the Pulitzer Prize for fiction went to an indie press; indies have never been more visible in the publishing world. But we still don't have enough financial clout to insist that the industry be remade for our viability. Rather than imagine telling the major publishers and chain booksellers how they should change for our convenience, we need to know the industry inside out and find allies to help us face the challenges that we are actually all facing together.

What is the future of reading in America? Is there a danger that technology is becoming an aid to closure of thought rather than its expansion?

Budd: Suppositions about the future of anything are usually pure fantasy, so I won't add mine to the pile. Let's just say that I'm excited about the future of reading, whatever it may hold. No matter how many predictions I read about the coming extinction of the American reader, I still see people glued to books and newspapers and Kindles whenever I'm out and about. Maybe I'm biased because we're based in Minneapolis, which has a reputation for being a very literate city.

When it comes to the question of technology and reading, I do have one big concern: a potential gulf between the digital haves and have-nots. I don't want to live in a world where the information in books is only accessible to people who can afford (and are comfortable using) an e-reader or a computer. I also worry about the increasingly pervasive attitude I sense in our industry that technology, in and of itself, is automatically a good thing (and I say this as a person who loves technology). Without an initial focus on finding, acquiring, and shaping the best possible work, worrying about whether that work is simultaneously released as a e-book or paired with a custom app feels like putting the cart firmly before the horse.

Fishbach: The future of reading in America is up to readers and writers. It's not up to Amazon, Barnes & Noble, Apple, or Google. It's not up to panelists at BEA or Frankfurt. Anyone who tells you they know what the future will be like is trying to sell you something.

Kornblum: I believe that anyone who lasts longer than a few years in publishing has to have an optimism gene that overrides cynicism, regardless of evidence. I believe that as soon as humans began using language, one person turned to another and said, I have a story to tell. The desire to tell a story, and the desire to hear it, is imprinted in our genes. I believe the pleasure of experiencing that story on a printed page has also been imprinted in our genes, and it's not going away soon.

I also believe the words ascribed to Mark Twain and William Gladstone: There are lies, there are damned lies, and there are statistics. Finally I believe one should always be wary when declaring that the younger generation is going to the dogs.

In other words, there will always be new readers in America. But I am equally confident that there will always be people who will use whatever media might be available, to oversimplify complex ideas for money, power, and the glorification of their ego. In every generation there have been moments when it seemed as if such voices would drown out all reasonable discourse—but they never do. That doesn't mean such people can't do serious damage—they can. But don't blame technology.

And do be aware of how the professional researchers in many fields are using internet-supplied input from amateurs for many kinds of research, ranging from biology to cosmography. Think about how many people have contributed to Wikipedia, and the Internet Movie Database. We're just beginning to discover what might come of linking the world electronically. I can't wait to see what comes next. But then, I always liked a good story.

How Can Independent Bookstores Succeed in the New Economy? San Antonio's Twig Book Shop as a Case Study

The Twig Book Shop has long been a fixture in San Antonio's literary community. It recently moved to a more spacious location in the historic Pearl Brewery building at 200 East Grayson Street. I asked manager Claudia Maceo about what makes The Twig unique, the economics and daily operation of independent bookstores, how independent bookstores can do well in the changing economic climate, the challenges posed by technology, and the innovative means available to make independent bookstores more vital than ever to literary culture.

What is the history of The Twig Book Shop in San Antonio? What role has The Twig played in the local literary community?

The Twig budded from L&M bookstore back when Harris Smithson owned the two. As best as we can figure, based on those who can still remember, The Twig came about in 1972. Local lore has it that Harris and others were at a cocktail party when one quoted Alexander Pope, "'Tis education forms the common mind: just as the twig is bent, the tree's inclined," and the other responded that The Twig would make a fine name for the new bookstore.

Most notably, The Twig has evolved as a destination for its children's books, local authors, and Texana—Texas geography, history, and biographies, and a showcase for local publishers. We also have many off-site sales for schools, literary organizations, and nonprofits.

You moved recently to the new location in the historic Pearl Brewery building. What was the reason for the move, and what are your feelings about the new location?

The Pearl development team invited John Douglas, the owner of The Twig for the past eleven years, to consider opening a bookstore at Pearl. He and his wife Frannie have owned Viva Bookstore for about thirty-five years. At first he was not interested, but about six months after the initial contact, they approached him again. By then I had begun to move to The Twig from Viva so I could take over the manager position from Susanna who was interested in becoming semi-retired. It seems that there were concerns about the previous location and a sense of possibility offered by Pearl. We decided to listen to what Pearl had to say. The Twig had been in its location for many years; it had evolved several times by moving and branching out (no pun intended). After many conversations with Pearl representatives and bookstore consultants, John and Frannie finally chose to take that leap to share the vision at Pearl, a vision of partnerships and being a place where people from all over San Antonio can gather.

You come from a background in teaching. What made you take on the job of managing The Twig, and what are the things about the bookselling business that have most surprised you as a newcomer?

That is one of my favorite questions to ponder because it is a never-ending marvel to me. I am sure in my past I have vowed never to work in retail because here I am. You really have to watch out for such vows.

I decided to retire at age fifty-two when I became eligible after thirty years of teaching. I had had a rich career that included all elementary levels and college teaching. After a wonderful year with a dear class of fourth-graders and a fabulous team of teachers, I knew I was standing at a threshold. I had thought I might join the Peace Corps. I thought I might teach at the Defense Language Institute. I was not going to retire to eat bonbons and watch soap operas. I knew there would be a new chapter of my life to launch. I even fantasized I'd have time to write for once (me, chuckles). I was also teaching at UTSA as an adjunct, so I finished that summer semester and became officially retired. That September, I opened an email one Sunday afternoon that announced a part-time job opening at Viva Books. I thought that might be fun for the interim. I sent off my resume, interviewed with the manager there, and was hired. What a blessed place that was. What a gentle birthing into retail! As I stated above, John and Frannie own Viva and The Twig. One thing led to another and here I am. I had been a longtime customer at The Twig too.

How are independent bookstores different from the chain bookstores?

Over and over customers share that they feel the charm of the store, appreciate the personal service they receive, and value our knowledge of the books in the store. We are willing to do out-of-print searches and order straight from the publishers. We carry self-published books too.

What are the economics independent bookstores have to operate under?

Uhhh, supply and demand? Seriously, it is very hard. There are many independent bookstores pulling up stakes every year. At best, turning the bookstore inventory as many as four times a year and minimizing costs, a successful bookstore can expect a two to three percent profit margin. We try to be conscientious of what our customers want by maintaining a high literary standard and knowing what is available. Beyond that, we try to educate our customers how important it is to buy locally. I think San Antonio has shown an increased awareness of the importance of buying locally, keeping their money here and therefore investing in our community.

Is it very hard to make independent bookstores successful?

Yes. I try to stay focused on what we do well, like customer service and book knowledge, and not on what we cannot provide. We cannot compete against electronic books and deep discounts, so we won't compete in that arena.

What are the most difficult obstacles to making independent bookstores profitable that you have encountered so far?

The low profit margin if one only sells books, and the challenge of providing customers an experience they cannot get online or at a chain store. We small stores have all the same demands on our personnel as a large store with far fewer employees—the same number of hats with fewer heads.

What does the book-buying public understand least about independent bookstores? Are there some misunderstandings you'd like to remove?

When I first began to work at Viva and found the tasks to be so complicated, my colleagues would chide me, albeit lovingly, by saying, "And you thought we were just a bookstore." It is a fantasy to think that you can sit behind a counter and read until a customer comes up to pay for a book. Bookselling requires physical and mental stamina. Ordering books requires poring over catalogs with publishing representatives, vendors, and authors. These days a bookseller must have a comfort level with various computer programs from point-of-sale programs to search engines and publication designs. Boxes of books come daily that must be unboxed, received, and shelved. Organizational skills go beyond alphabetizing. Marketing books once they are in takes retail and design sense. Shelves must be culled of books that are not selling and returned to the publishers or authors. And there is always dusting and sweeping to be done. Oh yeah, and then read, read, read. I used to feel like all I had time to read was the back of a book. After a year as manager that has improved somewhat.

I have found booksellers to share a common ideal about the world. We care deeply about our communities, about the power of the written word throughout the centuries, the importance of sharing the stories of our human condition. We are finding and even creating new ways to connect with each other, between various organizations and businesses, in partnerships and special projects.

In the current economic climate, specifically as it relates to books, what do independent bookstores have to do to survive and even thrive?

Be all the more attuned to customer needs and interests to sell more books, sell book-related items, provide services, and use space in avant-garde ways. In addition to books, we also sell some locally-made cards and art. We sell related stuffed animals and puppets, bookmarks, booklights, magnifiers, puzzles, hats, cards, and stationery. We have used our space to host the Shakespeare and the ballet companies, promote plays, support local authors in readings and book launchings, and we have joined in organizational purchasing promotions.

On a day-to-day operational basis, how does the independent bookstore differ from the large chains?

As I said above, the plethora of hats on fewer heads seems to be the biggest operational difference. I do not have a different book buyer for children's books and adult books, much less the different genres. I do not have floor managers or personnel directors. No marketing director, etc.

Do you make book buying and promoting decisions differently than the large bookstores?

Not having worked in a large bookstore, I cannot be certain, but my impression of an obvious area in which we differ is that we forego the large bulk purchases of mass-market releases. Instead of the *New York Times* best-sellers we display our best-sellers based on independent booksellers data. The results often overlap but include more literary works in general.

What should the book-buying public do differently?

Think of your local independent bookstores as community gathering places. Look for events there, subscribe to their email lists, check out the websites. Browse the shelves for autographed copies of books by local authors; they make unique gifts. For those people who do not think of themselves as readers, I believe that they just have not found the right book yet. A bookseller at your local bookstore may know of just the right one to get them started. We often carry books that someone might not buy for themselves but would love to have as a gift. So many people find that the books they purchase reflect who they are.

Tell us how recent technological innovations affect your business—both negatively and positively.

Our website has become more significant. A person can now order a book from us online. We post our events there and news about us. We also are learning to use Facebook and other social networking sites effectively.

OK, I know you are referring to the Web Retail Empire That Must Not Be Named. It has had a very painful impact. I do not believe that books will disappear for a very long time, if ever, but we must be attentive to what our customers want more than ever. Research shows that many electronic book buyers are still buying hardcopies. There are still gratifying and useful reasons to do so. I have a feeling that there will always be something endearing about a smear of banana on *Goodnight Moon* that you shared with your one-year-old whose sentimental value cannot be replicated even when those electronic devices can display children's books. Billy Collins recently shared that poetry is often reformatted on some electronic devices so that the lines fit into its dimensions, thereby changing the intent of the author's very intentional shaping of the poem. Perhaps books will become collectors' items, displayed as art, souvenirs, or in display cases like spoons, thimbles, or shot glasses. We must be willing to compensate by providing what our patrons want and expand our inventory and services to include items that can still reflect our unique, community-minded philosophy.

Do independent bookstores need more help from the publishing industry?

They are hurting too but also compensating. The bulk of our revenue is made during the last quarter of the year. But we must order year-round and have ordering peaks throughout the year. Visited by publishing reps seasonally, we want to provide the most recent releases and also provide for store events. Publishers' patience with the cash flow has shortened considerably from what I've been told. It does not take long to be put on credit hold in which case books are not shipped. Books not shipped mean books not sold which means no cash to pay for those already ordered. We really really want to be able to pay our local authors and publishers in a timely way, but often I feel like I must say, take a number. Taxes, salaries, the big publishers, our main distributor! Take a number. It is not uncommon to hear booksellers utter prayers of thanksgiving, see them cross themselves, genuflect, make some grateful gesture to owners with deep pockets or a strong local economy with long-standing, positive relationships with their banks.

What's it like at the booksellers associations and other meetings you've recently attended? What is the mood, what are business insiders excited (or worried) about?

Many have referred to the recent past with a dark look of fear remembered. However, this year at the American Booksellers Association Winter Institute and at BookExpo America, I heard members with many more years than my own remark that the tone was encouraging. Fewer bookstores are closing, the sessions are geared toward making modifications to what we are doing in ways that can be competitive and emphasizing our charming and delightful relationships. It was a lovefest. Many authors are also taking stands, becoming vocal advocates for the independent local bookstores.

What are your plans and visions for The Twig?

The partnerships within San Antonio—and beyond! I mentioned earlier the Shakespeare Company, the ballet company, playwrights, poets. We can be a gathering place for so much more that has any sort of literary connection. Literacy is not only reading, but writing, listening, and speaking. Right now, in the works, is a multifaceted project with the San Antonio Museum of Art in which we hope to provide family-oriented activities and related books while they host a visiting exhibit from the Brooklyn Museum of Art on Egypt. We hope to plug their monthly thematic family events that are coordinated with the Bureau of Cultural Affairs and the Chamber of Commerce. We currently participate with a literacy program where we are a donation site for new and gently used books that will be distributed to children identified as needing books by their schools this fall. These are just a couple of examples of how we hope to forge our future at The Twig.

What's the most pleasant surprise you've had since you started managing the bookstore?

Without a doubt, the experiences I have had day after day of someone coming into the store with one intention but having an almost magical mystical creative experience—a connection, an idea, a possibility forming beyond anything either of us may have predicted. We are truly realizing that we are greater than the sum of our parts. We must live into those experiences and live with the awareness that the possibilities come in unsuspecting packages.

How Can Poetry Become Eclectic and Diverse? Interview with Raymond Hammond

Raymond Hammond is editor of the poetry journal the *New York Quarterly* and the related book imprint NYQ Books, as well as being an esteemed poet in his own right and the author of a lively polemic, *Poetic Amusement* (2010). Here he offers a picture of the state of affairs in the poetry world, describing the conditions working for and against a broadening of the poetic sphere to include more diverse concerns and thematics than presently seen in contemporary American poetry.[1]

How was your relationship with William Packard, the founding editor of NYQ? What kind of an editor was he, and what did you learn from him?

Bill was an amazing mentor. He took me under his wing and taught me everything that he knew. He was very giving with his knowledge and experience. I first studied with Bill in his workshop at NYU, but by the end of that semester I knew that I wanted to study with him full-time so I enrolled at NYU in the Masters program at the Gallatin School in order to do that. One thing that solidified our relationship early on was my serving a warrant that he asked me to serve against his ex-student who was harassing and stalking him. When he handed me the warrant one night in class, he said that NYPD couldn't find her. I went out and found her that first night—that impressed him about my character, he would later tell me. Bill was a tough editor. He always called it like he saw it, never shied away from the truth—no matter how many tears that would bring. He knew the aesthetic that he had for the editorial voice of the magazine and

---

1. I have had to abridge this interview here, but the complete interview, where publisher Raymond Hammond talks about the qualities of *New York Quarterly* as a journal of distinction, the interplay between the journal and the press, details about the publishing model he thinks can work in the midst of new technologies, and his ideal private poetry workshop curriculum, can be found at http://www.huffingtonpost.com/anis-shivani/a-great-contemporary-poet_b_1142497.html.

constantly monitored that voice. After he had a stroke, the first thing he said when I went to see him in the hospital was that he was secretly concerned he would lose that aesthetic because of the stroke. I soon would bring him some poems to work on, and I never will forget the look on his face when he had finished reading them and looked up and said to me, "I still have it, the aesthetic is still there, it survived the stroke." He used to talk about how strong the aesthetic must be—in anyone—to survive something like a stroke. He also used to say all the time how people were scared of his bark. Bill was an imposing man, easily six feet and built like a linebacker. I witnessed people become demure in front of him all the time, but it wasn't his size they were shrinking from, but rather his personality which was demanding and demonstrative and sure, which was how he edited as well. But he was most proud that despite what people thought about his bark, when they got to know him, he was a big pussycat. The most important thing about writing and editing that I learned from Bill was intuition. How to develop and maintain one's intuition—that aesthetic—because he took me through the process from day one and continued to teach this to me every day until he passed and even then some from the grave. The greatest thing, however, that I learned from Bill was humility. No matter where we would go, no matter whom we met, he would always introduce me as his friend. Not once did he call me his student, his mentee, his intern—nothing other than friend. He taught me to keep the ego trip out of the poetry, because it did not belong.

In 2009 you started publishing books. What vacuum in poetry is NYQ Books trying to fill? How do you make a press like yours financially successful in an age when a successful poetry book sells a few hundred copies?

NYQ Books was always a dream of William Packard's. Not only did he tell me this on numerous occasions, but also after his death we found papers and proposals planning the creation of NYQ Books. In addition to wanting to fulfill this commission laid down by the founding editor, I wanted to begin NYQ Books to help stem the tide of the acceptance of contests as the arbiters of taste and talent. There is a vacuum of book publishers that do not run contests. At NYQ Books we select books for publication by invitation only. The poets are already known to us. We just want to publish more of their work than the magazine will allow. Despite the plans Bill had drafted many years ago for what is now a traditional print model, the press became possible for us and financially viable through print-on-demand technology and internet marketing. This model will only become more viable as we move into e-books. The old days of printing hundreds of copies of a book to sit in someone's living room waiting to be sold are over. Now with the new technologies not only do we only print what we need, but there are no storage or distribution problems and most importantly no waste; the new printing paradigm is not only easy on the wallet but easy on the environment as well.

For at least thirty years now—going back to the 1980s with Donald Hall, Greg Kuzma, etc.—there has been a sustained polemic against the McPoem (Donald Hall's term), i.e., the poetry produced in writing workshops. In the 1990s, Joseph Epstein, Dana Gioia, J. D. McClatchy, Thomas Disch, and others picked up on the polemic. From your position as an influential editor, what is your take on this controversy? Does the workshop in fact produce a uniform, unambitious, minor product most of the time?

I have come to believe that workshops are only in part responsible for the uniform, unambitious, minor products of poetry that we see over and over again. There are other elements, an entire paradigm that includes workshops, MFA programs, and contests that contribute to this. And the key in your question is the word minor. Although these works are uniform, unambitious, and minor, it is the paradigm that is elevating these drab works of banality to the level of major—and this, the entire paradigm, is the problem. The problem with the current paradigm is that it is simply based on credentials and apparently has little or nothing to do with quality of product whatsoever. When a very good, mature poet cannot get a job teaching other poets simply because they don't possess the "club card" of an MFA degree, but a twentysomething with little or no experience is able to get that same job because they do possess an MFA, then there cannot but be a deterioration in the quality of the writing. Another major aspect of this contemporary model is the acceptance of contests as being the only possible means by which to publish a book. I know people who have recently been in classes in MFA programs whose teachers stated very bluntly, "You must enter contests in order to publish." This is unacceptable and writers as a whole should not accept this as fact. If the writers did not affirm contests by entering them, then the whole problem would go away on its own accord. Contests do nothing but two things. First, they impose a fee where there never used to be a fee, and second they force the publisher to publish a book no matter how bad it is as long as it is better than the others in the contest. No one wins in the contest model. All of these fees, contest fees, reading fees, MFA fees, and the acceptance of these as the only framework in which writers may be assessed put money at the heart of the art. By putting money at the heart of the art we as a society have completely given the art over to capitalism and greed and ladder-climbing and survival of the fittest, not survival of the art. The current model is allowing money to become the arbiter of taste; those with the money to obtain the MFA and pay to submit both to magazines and to book contests will be deemed poets. Those without these means will be left behind in the dust even though much of their work is equally as good if not better. The whole structure is setting itself up to discriminate along socioeconomic lines, and this is something that everyone should be working against in this day and time. It was bad enough when the publishing community made poetry a commodity, but the current template ignores the poetry altogether and has established the poets themselves as the commodities.

Are there better ways for poets to learn their art—I purposely don't use the word craft here—than through the method of the MFA workshop, which involves mostly peer critique from others at one's own level of accomplishment?

At the feet of the masters. Now this could be taken a number of different ways, and I mean all of them. First, by reading across history, literally learning at the feet of the masters by reading those masters over and over again. Go to any library or bookstore and there they are—and relatively inexpensive (or free at the library) compared to the cost of an MFA. Second, I was fortunate to have learned under the mentor model of instruction. This goes back to the ancient days of Greece and probably beyond, mentors taking students under their wings and teaching them over years not just one semester. When I worked with Bill, I was fortunate to work with him from 1994 until his death in 2002. That is over eight years of instruction—there is no way you can pack that into the three or four months of a semester, or even the two or three years of a program. We are too quick to become poets in this society—no one is patient. Poets must graduate from undergrad, go into an MFA program, and have their first book of poems published by the time they are twenty-four or twenty-five years of age. That is way too young to know what is up and what is down, much less to contemplate the ways of the universe or even society. Now it doesn't mean they can't be on their way to becoming a poet at that age, but the pattern we are presently given in American society says that someone who has earned an MFA, won a contest, and had a book published is a "poet," and is in fact more of a poet than the person who has undergone years of life lessons and reading of the masters and patiently writing, but doesn't have a contest win or book or MFA. Two of my favorite books that we have published came from two women who did not earn an MFA or win a contest. They just simply wrote their entire lives and produced work for the sake of the work and are just now publishing their first books of poems: Eileen Hennessy and Grace Zabriskie. Third, students who do take workshops need to pay close attention to who is giving the feedback in the class—is it the teacher they signed up to learn from or the other students who are at the same level of accomplishment as they are? I heard about such a problem within the last year or so from an intern that we had about a well-respected poet who has an MFA, has won contest after contest, and has several books published by renowned presses and now teaches at a school in New York. This intern reported to me that the instructor workshopped poems by projecting the poem onto a screen from a computer, and everyone *except* for the instructor and the writer gave their opinions as to what would make the poem better. That is unacceptable and that instructor *does not* belong in a classroom. It doesn't mean that others in the class cannot have their opinions; after all, it is a workshop. But the instructor should not be a lead voice of opinion; they should be a master of the art. Think about it this way: would you be operated on by a surgeon who learned how to perform surgery not from the instructor, but from a classroom full of students who only had opinions and guesses as to how it should be done?

Your own book, **Poetic Amusement,** *is one of the better polemics in the genre I've read—and I've read them all. It's a work of synthesis and accumulation, but also provocation and originality. Do you think a book like this should be part of the MFA "curriculum"? What do you think are some of your most original ideas in this book?*

I am not sure I have too many original ideas in *Poetic Amusement.* In writing the book, I initially set out to investigate why the poems that we saw coming in as submissions were so mind-numbingly the same. What I wound up doing was conducting my own investigation of what poetry is and how it is created. I read dozens upon dozens of literary critics over history to the present, and what is contained in my book is a triptych of that journey, a reporting, if you will, of what I found. I just culled it all into one place and organized it around one topic. When I was writing the book there was—as there still is—much argument against MFA programs. There are basically the two camps: those that are for and those that are against MFA programs. William Packard at the time wanted me to decry MFA programs altogether. What I found, though, in writing the book is that the programs themselves can have a place in the literary community if they accept the fact that they need to also teach the muse. And in the book I offer several remedies to this problem. I see my book as being neither pro nor con MFA programs but rather focusing on what would best support the poetry for the sake of poetry itself. And the revelation that I have found that I don't stress enough in this book is that it is not the MFA programs themselves that cause the problems in contemporary American poetry, it is the strucure that has come to exist surrounding them. Rather than using them as a beginning, a tool for poets to learn and then go off and accomplish, the model uses the programs as an ordination, a completion: now you know everything, go off and teach it to others who will be similarly ordained as poets. And this ordination is used to exclude and discriminate, as we all know—you either have an MFA or you do not, which only serves to further the gulf between those who do and those who don't, which in turn only serves to perpetuate the vicious pro/con MFA diatribes.

You write in **Poetic Amusement** *that "the absence of passion in contemporary American poetry stems, in part, from a basic absence of investment." What do you mean by this? Elsewhere, you talk about the necessity of sincerity. Also, what is your concept of literary stewardship?*

What do you think makes all of these poems bland, ambivalent, and mediocre? That is the definition of "lack of passion." Passion, investment. and sincerity are all tied very neatly together with a little something called the muse. The muse, as I discuss it in my book, is that creative process within a poet, intuition as Bill called it, versus the craft of poetry which is the exterior, the writing of the language on the paper. It is a pretty rare treat when a poem comes into one of our screening sessions and is passionate. It does not mean it will necessarily make it into the magazine because the craft might be lacking, as many of the passionate poems we see come in from people who have to write something down but don't exactly have the training or experience to accomplish it success-fully. Unfortunately when you teach only the craft side of writing the poem, the passion gets thrown out with the muse. When poets sit down to write poems without much, if any, inspiration other than to hold onto or seek a job where that job is the extent of the investment, there is not an investment of self. The investment of the whole being of the poet into the poem is lost just as much as if one were filling in a job application. And when one is doing one thing and saying another, there is a lack of sincerity. Sincerity in a poem is a must, but, again, it takes an investment to be sincere, and poets have no incentive in this current model to invest anything, not even time. Basically, very basically, liter-ary stewardship is accepting the fact that we are stewards of literature and that stewardship is an important responsibility to know and understand each time we write. This calls for the writer to accept that there are two infinite timelines: one which extends from the past to the future and the other from the future to the past. The past influences the present which in turn influences the future, and at the same time the future influences the present which redefines the past. Where these two lines converge in the present moment is the moment in which a work may be created, and if that work is created at any other moment in time, it will follow that it is a different work. The creative principle operates in the eternal now, a timelessness/spacelessness, the present, but the poets, the writers must take time to prepare themselves to be those stewards.

Do you have suggestions for making criticism lively and relevant and influential again? What noteworthy critics do you think are writing today?

Criticism has been thrown out with the bathwater. Once creative writing became its own pedagogy apart from the rest of the English department, the critical eye that writers used to develop by reading and studying criticism became non-existent. You are not required to have any degree in English to apply to MFA programs, and most MFA programs do not require you to read much criticism; therefore, both the knowledge of good criticism and the application of that criticism is non-existent. I think that it is important to the development of the writer to develop a critical eye so that they can spy taste not only in others' work but also their own. So we are right back to the workshop education and the fact of mass student opinion being more formative to the young poet than the opinion of an individual mentor. If criticism is not read, and the only criticism observed is that of other students not wanting anyone to bash their own poems, coupled with the fact that most reviews nowadays are positive or at least "nice," then you find that criticism becomes flat and ordinary. Teach criticism and critical thinking in the MFA programs, or at least read critics from all ages, or at the very minimum study under a mentor who knows criticism. Any one of these three suggestions is important to getting criticism lively and relevant again, but most importantly, and this is where it is most lacking, return the critical eye to the creative process of writing.

What is the future of NYQ Books? Do you see a growth of other presses operating according to your model in the near future? What is worthy of imitation about your model?

I hope we have a bright future ahead of us. I would like to keep these books in print absolutely as long as possible. I, of course, want to branch out into e-books, etc., but that is down the road for us. Let me give you an overview of our model so you can see how simple it really is. First, we are nonprofit, so we let our foundation pay the base cost of the operation—thus overhead is almost nil. Second, we keep the production costs as cheap as possible via print-on-demand technology and online distribution models that are now available—this aspect of our model would not have even been dreamt of in Bill's day. Keeping production and print costs at a minimum and only ordering what we absolutely need, which leads to no storage or fulfillment costs, allows us to roll any profits right over into the production of other books. As print-on-demand and e-books become more prevalent, I definitely see other presses following this model—it only makes sense. The best thing about our model is that we can choose books to publish based upon the poetry and what we want to present to the public, not solely what we think we can recoup from sales. This also allows for a book that is selling close to a thousand copies to help prop up a book that is selling in the dozens of copies at best, so they all stay in print and remain available.

Symposium: What Goes into the Making of an Outstanding Book Cover?

Discussion of General Design Philosophy

Linda S. Koutsky, graphic designer and production manager at Coffee House Press

A cover is like a billboard and my goal is to create something eye-catching or to create an emotion so that a potential buyer sees the cover and wants to know more. It's my job to take authors' thoughts and ideas and bring them into a commercially viable cover. Because of computers, and the availability of images and fonts, these days a lot of people think they can be designers. But there's a lot more than simply putting type over a photo to make a good cover. My best covers happen when an author tells me about the spirit of their book, then leaves the visuals to me. We ask authors in our design questionnaire: (a) Describe the book's characters (if applicable) and your approach or style; (b) What colors do you associate with this book?; (c) What historical, or cultural backgrounds are associated with this book?; and(d) What adjectives describe the energy and feeling of this book? The answers from the design questionnaire and the input I get from the acquiring editor are how I begin design. Usually I'll route a bunch of layouts around the office and all our staff gets involved. Then I'll rework the covers and send them to the authors. Sometimes I'll get it right on the first or second try, but for a few books I've designed dozens of covers.

Fiona McCrae, publisher of Graywolf Press

One of our "secrets" is the degree of author input we include in the process. Sometimes it makes for a more arduous process as we invite more sets of eyes in. But I think it keeps things fresh in terms of images. Many authors have a strong visual idea for their book, and in the best instances, the image is very arresting. The whole process is directed in-house by our editorial director Katie Dublinski. She has a great understanding of each book's character and how it fits into our list. She also has an awesome mix of patience and good sense with which to juggle the sometimes competing demands of marketing, editorial, and author wishes. Although we value author input tremendously, they are not always right, and need to be steered away from certain ideas. Katie works with a team of freelance designers, who come up with brilliant "solutions" when presented with starting images, and, just as often, they suggest new, equally powerful images that they find on their own. My views on design have probably changed over the years, but like one's own accent changing (I came here from Britain) it's not a conscious process. I can say that I dislike photo-collages much more than I used to, and like original artwork more. I think the latter always ends up looking more singular. I also went through a period some years ago when I wanted everything to look misty, like the early Vintage paperbacks. Not very original of me. It's a great adventure, though, starting with a title and a manuscript and ending up with a design that seems inevitable. Frustrating at times, to be sure, but certainly worth it. A good cover is very important for a good book.

Rodrigo Corral, cover designer

My design philosophy with regard to books is that a good cover design should use an appropriate piece of art, combined with well-designed typography, to illustrate a concept or idea from the book—not necessarily a literal moment—which will give hints to the potential reader about the story inside, and which can also be interpreted in multiple ways. The first goal of the cover is to be seen as an object and to be wanted, but the real intention is for it to become a part of that relationship between story and reader, and to stay there even once the book is finished.

Sunandini Banerjee, cover designer

A book cover must attract one's attention in the marketplace. Sometimes with a scream. Sometimes with a whisper. It could interpret or comment upon or simply hint at the content. There are no rules (for I have absolutely no training in the arts) and there are no limits. A cover is not only a window into a book's world but also into my own. My people, my relationships, my literature, my music, my cinema, my food, my dreams, and my nightmares have resulted in me, a specific personality. And elements of this personality are allowed to find their way into everything I create.

Emanuele Ragnisco, cover designer

I approach each cover design as if it were a "small manifesto," one whose goal is to communicate to the potential reader that this book contains something that concerns him directly. The second goal is to distinguish the cover in question from every other cover. We address the first question by individuating the most appropriate language. By "language" I mean the language of signs. In the choice of a particular sign, we posit our response to the first goal. The problem of making each cover stand out from others is more complicated. The solution lies in carefully studying what is currently out there. At certain times, color dominates jacket design, and so a cover that is pure white is likely to stand out. At other times, covers with an abundance of design particulars are predominant, and the intelligent choice in terms of visibility may be a simple, pure design.

Rick Landesberg, cover designer

The first thing I always do in designing a cover is to gain a deep understanding of what the book is really about. Ideally it's good to design the cover after developing the design of the book's interior, as the cover should reflect the interior. The cover shouldn't describe the book; it should represent the book. And we shouldn't forget that the cover should also sell the book. All the physical and graphic aspects of a book, the paper, the typography, even the color of the headband (that bit of cloth we see where the pages meet the binding) should all operate in concert.

Steven Seighman, cover designer

A good book cover is an abstract idea—something that gets people to pick up the book in order to find clues as to what it means. When I'm designing a book, I try to read the entire thing instead of relying simply on press sheets. For my process—when I haven't been assigned artwork to use—that's the only true way I can understand what the cover should convey. I try to collect an overall tone from the book and find a way to give that a face—sometimes using literal elements from the book, and sometimes just hinting at things in order to leave them open to interpretation.

Atticus Waller, cover designer

When designing a book cover, I have six ideal goals: 1) A cover should communicate the book's content, be that the story or simply the mood. Reading the book first is important. 2) The graphics should convey only one conceptual statement about the book, which should nest neatly with the imagery. Avoid graphics with no conceptual reason for being. 3) Cover text should be cohesively incorporated into the imagery. 4) The cover should attract those who'll enjoy the book once drawn in. 5) The cover should stand out amongst many books from across a room. 6) The cover should satisfy the client I'm designing for and the author of the book.

Discussion of Specific Covers

Cover designer Lynn Buckley on David Mitchell's *The Thousand Autumns of Jacob de Zoet* (Random House)

This historical novel focuses on the only bridge of contact Japan had with the outside world in the eighteenth century: trading with the extremely corrupt Dutch East India Company. I began by researching bridges depicted in the gorgeous Japanese woodcut prints from this period, and discovered that these now highly prized prints were then so commonplace they were used as protection for shipping goods to other parts of the world. Perfect image for this book! I wrapped a book with a photocopy of a print, as if it were being shipped; and then photographed it. Unfortunately, that idea made the design much too complicated. So I used the art as is, but played with cutting the print and layering it with old woodcut type—to suggest the layers of intrigue in the novel, and to suggest the very modern way Mitchell writes. I can only hope the cover might bring new readers to David Mitchell, whom the *New York Times* called "a genius."

Cover designer Sunandini Banerjee on Thomas Bernhard's *Prose* (Seagull Books/University of Chicago Press)

In *Prose*, each of the seven protagonists is slightly at odds with the world. There's a man who kills women and then wears their clothes. Another comes down to dinner after having casually shot his wife's lover in the woods. Yet another stumbles upon a cap and then begins to obsess about finding its owner. The cover is a digital collage of elements from the stories—the tree from the one with the forest, the woman's skirt and shoe from the one with the murderer, and so on. The collage seemed to me a very effective form for conveying the madness, the askew nature of the cast of characters. The sunset background draws us into a world where telephones hang in mid-air and men's bodies taper off into women's feet. The world of Thomas Bernhard.

Poet Paul Muldoon on *Maggot* (Farrar, Straus and Giroux; cover designer Quemadura)

The cover of a book is almost as important to me as its contents and I try to play as active a role as my publishers will allow when it comes to design. I'm glad that both my U.K., and, in this case, U.S., publishers, have always been very open to such meddling and I'm grateful to them for it. I've been a fan of the great Irish artist, Dorothy Cross, for many years. I find myself very much in sync with her wondrously unconventional vision. Her 1995 photographic representation of what is, in essence, "a brainchild," seemed to give the perfect visual support to the unconventional contents of the book. Indeed, one way of thinking about a "maggot" is as "a brainchild," a fanciful idea, a whimsy. So I'm really proud to have this Dorothy Cross image as a cover, and really grateful to her for allowing us to use it at all.

Poet Charles Simic on *Master of Disguises* (Houghton Mifflin Harcourt)

How many books, records, and movies were we drawn to in our lives because of a striking title, cover art, or poster that made it impossible to ignore them? Who can forget carrying such a special book or record home in anticipation of an evening and a night spent in their company? It goes without saying that they often turn out to be disappointments, but that doesn't prevent us from doing the very same thing the next time we have an opportunity. I always wanted the appearance of my books to seduce the reader with an air of mystery by juxtaposing the title and the image on the cover in some unconventional way. Over the years I have used photographs, drawings, and cartoons striving to avoid anything visually obvious or familiar, preferring the minor, quirky pieces by artists who were sometimes friends, like the late Saul Steinberg. His old series of thumbprint portraits gave me the idea for the cover of *Master of Disguises*. Of course, without the aid of a great designer like Michaela Sullivan, it would have remained just that, an idea in my head, and not this beautiful cover of the new book.

Cover designer Michaela Sullivan

I was delighted when I saw the Steinberg art that Charles had suggested we use for his cover. Steinberg has always been a favorite of mine. There are so many ways to look at this art. Is this some ominous everyman? But then you get the whimsy of the "man" being made from his own unique fingerprint. I wanted to balance the quirkiness of this surreal image with a very classic type treatment and added a thumbprint-like border along the bottom edge as a complimentary flourish. The reader gets a nice surprise when opening this book to see the bright-red colored flaps, a contrast to the quiet elegance of the cover.

Poet Benjamin Alire Sáenz on *The Book of What Remains* (Copper Canyon Press; cover designer Phil Kovacevich)

One hot summer day, I took a walk in my neighborhood and took some photographs looking for an image for my new book of poems. I took a picture of these steps that once led to the front of a house. The house was long gone—and these steps are what remained. But from the vantage point from which I took the photo, the steps lead toward the sky. There was promise in the ruins. I photoshopped the image so the clouds appeared to be emanating from the steps. I very much liked the results—and so did the good people at Copper Canyon. With the spare and simple lettering, the cover has a very contemporary feel to it so that the cover as a whole represents not only the past, but the present. It is as if the design refutes a nostalgic reading of the photograph which is totally consistent with my work.

Poet Ange Mlinko on *Shoulder Season* (Coffee House Press; cover designer Linda S. Koutsky)

At the time *Shoulder Season* went into production, I was moving my family to Beirut, Lebanon; book design was the last thing on my mind. But Linda surprised and delighted me by going back to Josh Dorman, the artist featured on my last book, *Starred Wire*. Dorman is a painter of intense colors and reveries, and the image for *Starred Wire* was abstract and dreamy; this new image has a kind of "wonder cabinet" look to it, lively and playful. She had managed to convey a message about the content of my new book vis-à-vis the old one, picking up on the change of tone while maintaining continuity. The detail is from a series of map paintings Dorman did, and I can't think of a better metaphor for my work: the irreducibility of geography underlies the lyric—often comic—artifice. Place-names retain their implacable identity through the watercolors; I'd say that's where the poetry happens.

Author Paul Kameen on *Re-reading Poets: The Life of the Author* (University of Pittsburgh Press)

The cover image for my book was created by Bridget Kameen, my daughter, a young artist and photographer. She explains: "The photograph was a gift for my father, a motivational gesture while he was writing his new book, to show what it might look like on shelves. So, the idea of hope is wrapped up in the image itself. The strips of newspaper wrap around my arm, holding their own words, but also rising toward something better: knowledge, aspirations, wisdom, or perhaps a yet unattained dream. I wanted the image to be striking, something that would stand out among the cramped shelves in bookstores. Individuals do judge books by their covers (and, possibly, rightfully so.) A beautiful cover says 'something worthy lies beneath'; all you have to do is open that front cover to find it." Bridget's image is an ideal embodiment of my book's ambition to reach for the life-affirming possibilities of poetry. When she submitted it to the press's design department, they loved it, much to my delight.

Author Andrew Ervin on *Extraordinary Renditions* (Coffee House Press; cover designer Linda S. Koutsky)

Extraordinary Renditions is in large part about political transition and the repetition of history, so I love having three different eras represented on the cover. There's a classic, old-world building, a communist-era automobile, and then some current, America-style graffiti. Those seemingly disparate elements work beautifully together. The book is made up of three distinct novellas, so I even like that there are three windows on that building. I found the image myself on a photography website and was thrilled that Coffee House's designer Linda Koutsky liked it too and was willing to work with it. She did an amazing job, clearly. And of course I've always adored those old Trabants, which sound like lawn mowers. They were all over Budapest when I lived there (1994-1999), but nowadays seem relegated to the countryside.

Cover designer Karen A. Copp on Marilene Phipps-Kettlewell's *The Company of Heaven: Stories from Haiti* (University of Iowa Press)

When the press learned that Marilene was a painter as well as a writer, we were eager to see her paintings. She sent us a sheet of slides, and suggested that *Sunday* would be her first choice. Marilene describes the painting: "The painting shows women of the earth, mothers in the company of daughters. The people have the reddish brown color of the earth of which they are issued. But in the deep hues of green and blue color they choose to paint their houses, they bring some of the sky down and pull some of the Caribbean sea in. In the light blue color of dresses worn by women here, it is as if people enshroud their earthbound bodies with heaven, and make visible their spiritual aspirations. They are wearing their Sunday best that day, but it seems that within their souls, it must always be Sunday." The press loved Marilene's paintings and we were very happy with the way that Rebecca Low's design suggested an island surrounded by ocean.

Cover designer Rodrigo Corral on Qurratulain Hyder's *Fireflies in the Mist* (New Directions)

The cover design of *Fireflies in the Mist* illustrates the transformation of political rule in India, with a viewpoint suggesting a lurking rebellion, but not without hope or an oracle-like bright spot. The illustration is class-driven, and conveys the initial isolation of the main character, and her own transformation into a kind of permanent displacement. The art itself feels twentieth-century while modern at the same time, which I think turned out to be a great solution for a book with its sociological themes. It's both literal and symbolic, two important (if obvious) features of cover art that works.

Cover designer Rebecca Wolff on Martin Corless-Smith's *English Fragments: A Brief History of the Soul* (Fence Books)

I always start with an image or design element that the author chooses or approves of. In this case the image is one of great and inherent significance to the author: It's a fragment of an angel's face from an early thirteenth-century mural in Worcester Cathedral, in Worcestershire, England—Corless-Smith's childhood home and the birthplace of his philosophic concerns. The book is an intricately haphazard admixture of modernity and antiquity, and I wanted the cover to reflect that confluence, so I devised a geometric surrounding for the ancient face. I originally had been working with a concept that involved setting the fragment inside a little embossed, glossy window, but Martin and I at the last minute found it too fussy, and too centralized, symmetrical. The cover stock is beautifully thick, and textured, and gives the airy blue shadow of the angel's fragment a density that is marvelous to behold, and hold in the hand.

Cover designer Rick Landesberg on Tina May Hall's *The Physics of Imaginary Objects* (University of Pittsburgh Press)

I was designing the entire book and not just the cover, so the task was to determine the physical and graphic form for the entire book physically and graphically. My reading of the book plus conversations with the publisher and input by the author suggested what I would call "northern" images. My first approaches were a series of collages juxtaposing pine forest images with analytical diagrams, but it wasn't right. Well into the process, I thought of the evocative work of photographer Zeke Berman. The book is non-linear, somewhat quirky, and in some ways dark. The language is rich and intense. Berman's photographs share these qualities. Seeking them out, I realized that any number of his images could make a strong cover for this book. The mirror (Berman later told me it was a piece of glass) reflects a forest. There's a nature/culture tension in the photograph. It seemed fitting. The typography is expressive but not ornamental. The limited color palette is sophisticated and deep.

Editorial director Michael Dumanis on John Bradley's *You Don't Know What You Don't Know* (Cleveland State University Poetry Center; cover designer Amy Freels)

John Bradley was already a fan of the artist Katherine Ace and gave us a selection of her artwork to choose from. Thinking about the way John's poems often went on a striking rampage across the page, subverted the reportage of various current events, and challenged the notion of how a text communicated, I selected the image of Ace's, *In the Beginning*, that to me best illustrated the book, and John agreed. This cover proved challenging. The image was too large and I wanted the focus to be on the newspapers. The designer, Amy Freels, used details from the artwork, which she layered to enhance the color. Because this involved changing the image, she worked closely with Katherine to produce the cover in a way that satisfied both her and John. I am particularly pleased with how John's name comes through in the smoky light over the newspapers, and how the black of the background and the red of the title font serve to visually complement the artwork.

Cover designer Kerrie Kemperman on Jerome Rothenberg's *Concealments & Caprichos* (Black Widow Press)

Jerry Rothenberg and publisher Joe Phillips agreed that Nancy Tobin's painting, *Waiting for Seurat*, should be on the cover of *Concealments & Caprichos*. Jerry had seen one of her exhibitions, I believe. I liked the collagey look, the way the shapes overlap and seem to move. The challenge was in balancing the art with the text; I wanted to honor the image while still allowing space for the type to announce itself, and room for the cover to breathe. I approached it sort of like a tapestry, pushed the art off-center and draped it over the top edge. I liked the spiky tree branches hovering above while the more dense shapes rose up from below. Old Claude and Granjon were my typefaces of choice because the shapes of the letters and symbols mimicked the shapes in the collage. To me, the Tobin painting seems to emerge from the darkness and dance.

Cover designers Percolator Graphic Design on Peter Paik's *From Utopia to Apocalypse: Science Fiction and the Politics of Catastrophe* (University of Minnesota Press)

University of Minnesota Press is a wonderful publisher to work with, from a designer's perspective. We meet with them to discuss the initial design direction for each book and they also provide us with a detailed design brief to refer to. A prevalent theme in Peter Paik's book is violence. In the various books and movies he examines, he shows how violence is used to create utopia. Our charge was to communicate a grim feeling on the cover without it looking too dark. We settled on the idea of an eye to communicate the feeling of fear that comes with violence. We found the perfect comic book-style eye at iStockphoto.com, which we manipulated to suit our needs for the front cover. We carried over the bold shapes and line work to the spine and back cover and used a comic-book font for the endorsement attributes to further add to the graphic novel feeling.

Cover designer Kimberly Glyder on Mark Slouka's *Essays from the Nick of Time* (Graywolf Press)

From the design brief, the title references Thoreau, who wished "to improve the nick of time...to stand on the meeting of two eternities, the past and future." I originally provided several different cover directions, including type only and photo-driven (one which was a photo of the author in the woods), but in the end, it was decided in-house and by the author that this painting was the most effective. The final artwork used on the printed cover is by Tina Mion, entitled *Joan of Arc*. It was obvious upon seeing *Joan of Arc* that even God couldn't save her. The painting was sent to me by the author who felt it had a strong connection to his writing. For this particular design, the art really led the way. I tried to find typography that complemented the image and used colors drawn from the painting.

Cover designer Jeff Clark on Charles Bernstein's *All the Whiskey in Heaven* (Farrar, Straus and Giroux)

For ninety percent of the books I work on, I design and compose both the interior as well as the cover/jacket of a book. I begin with the former, which is the only way that book design makes sense. A book whose cover is designed without relation to its interior is bound to be either a design failure or a transgression against the text. I read a manuscript—in this case, Charles Bernstein's selected poems—with an eye to determining a short list of what text typefaces would be appropriate. I then experiment with the setting, sizing, and leading of poems. When I've chosen a typeface for the writing, I then move on to try to pair it with complementary display (titles, heads, subheads, etc.) typefaces. When I've chosen the three or so faces I want to use, I then handle every unique element in the book, and from this work, slowly or quickly, comes the overall design of the inside of the book. Once this design is finished, I extrapolate it to the exterior, in this case a jacket for the hardback edition. The artwork originally stipulated for the *All the Whiskey in Heaven* jacket I found faintly suitable, but uncompelling, so I experimented with generating artwork that had the feeling tones of the poems; these directions were rejected by the author, who then sent to the publisher some photographs by his daughter Emma, who had just died. When I saw her photograph of blue sky and white clouds through steel bars I felt a burst of emotion. Here would be a way for me to give something to the author in place of what I hadn't been able to directly (because I felt that a note of condolence would be inappropriate coming from a virtual stranger), having felt sorrow at reading that his own child had died. I had a high-resolution color print made of the photo. I then scored and tore it at its left edge, and taped it to a sheet of watercolor paper I mostly covered with black ink; and then printed and cut out the title, subtitle, and author name, and quickly taped those down. If the finished design conveys anything extra-emotional, it suggests that death, heaven, and selecteds are provisional.

Cover designer Jill Breitbarth on Orhan Pamuk's *The Naive and the Sentimental Novelist* (Harvard University Press)

Pamuk, early on in his book, describes Anna Karenina sitting dreamily on a train, trying to read, but all the while distracted by real life. He was drawn to a depiction of Karenina reading for the cover. I took this suggestion and started to look for late eighteenth-century paintings of women reading. When I came across the image by the Catalan painter Ramon Casas i Carbó, I was struck by the woman's pose. What rich and sensuous places can be reached through books! it seemed to say. The dramatic painting inspired a type treatment that is both bold and reflective.

Editor Michael Barron on Anne Carson's *Nox* (New Directions; cover designer Rodrigo Corral)

Anne Carson's *Nox* is a facsimile of a book she originally crafted by hand. In Ms. Carson's own words, "When my brother died I made an epitaph for him in the form of a book. This is a replica of it, as close as we could get." Designer Rodrigo Corral used a spot-laminate type for the title and author, rendering it into a nearly invisible border for the arresting and slimly ripped cover photo of her estranged brother Michael. This barely perceptible type successfully highlights the distance Ms. Carson felt from her brother who ran away in 1978, and to whom she spoke with only a handful of times before his death in 2000. The photo of Michael in a bathing suit and goggles is coupled with a strip of brown paper, and set against a grimly colored book cloth background. The complete image is, in effect, a moment of silence.

Author Gina Ochsner on *The Russian Dreambook of Color and Flight* (Houghton Mifflin Harcourt; cover designer Clare Skeats)

I'm a big fan of Kazuko Nomoto's artwork and I feel incredibly lucky that she was assigned to this title. I'm astounded at her use of color and metaphoric images. It just drew the breath out of my lungs because her use of color and image was so rich, so cathedral. Leaves on trees become stain glass windows of miniature churches, snow falling from a midnight sky becomes letters of the Cyrillic alphabet. And yet, there's a sense of human presence not only implied by the act of her making this art, but the very humane representation of the human figure in the art.

Cover designer Kyle G. Hunter on Thomas Sayers Ellis's *Skin, Inc.: Identity Repair Poems* (Graywolf Press)

The cover design for *Skin, Inc.* was very author-driven. Thomas Sayers Ellis supplied the photos and the font was inspired by a favorite cover of his. I selected this particular photo from a set of four or five. This was the best composed and perhaps the least "aggressive" of the options. And there just aren't enough people with straws on covers nowadays! In addition to the novelty factor, it works well as a kind of low-fi metaphor for the movement between insides and outsides. Within the parameters set forth by the author, I provided some options. We tried several different treatments of the photo—full color; a more illustrative, posterized version using blocks of color; and then the final black-and-white option.

Director John Donatich on Adonis's *Selected Poems* (Yale University Press)

Prior to the Frankfurt Book Fair, I was invited by the Wissenschaftskolleg in Berlin to give a talk and meet with scholars. When I described the Margellos translation series and how excited I was about the *Selected Poems* of Adonis, the Director whisked me away to his office to see these amazing collages that lined the walls. Using varied materials with an uncanny sense of placement and kinetics, the collages integrated the beautiful Islamic calligraphic script of Adonis himself. I was so excited, I whipped out my iPhone and took pictures of each of them. When I brought them back to the office, the book's designer, Jim Johnson, was also taken with them; you can see the results for yourself.

Author Ron Rash on *Burning Bright: Stories* (Ecco; cover designer Allison Saltzman)

When I handed in the completed manuscript of *Burning Bright,* I believed an effective cover would help set the tone for these stories. After a couple of ideas that pleased neither my editor nor me, this cover came to us from the graphics department. I knew instantly it was the right cover. The weathered wood and collapsed furniture certainly reflect the landscape but also connect to the characters themselves, almost all of whom are scarred and battered by life. However, the bright-colored paint on the wood is what I love most about the cover, because, like the book's title, it evokes so much of the human need to find beauty and light even in the darkest and most impoverished circumstances. These were the major considerations, but I also love how the cover stands out on the shelf—how, without the stories, the photograph tells its own story.

Cover designer Robin Bilardello on Ben Greenman's *Celebrity Chekhov* (Harper Perennial)

The design was an evolution. We started with the contrast of what Ben had created in the stories—the old and the new, with the new being flashy—and tried different treatments to poor Anton to update him to 2010. We gave him a beautiful set of gold teeth, grillz if you will. We put his head on the body of a sweaty rapper with a six-pack stomach and plenty of bling to make Diddy proud. We put his name in lights and bombarded the cover with paparazzi. Ultimately, less is more and the subtle mirrors added to his spectacles did the trick, kept it classy while adding a glimmer of humor. When I got down to working on the type I used MT Walbaum and added lots of scrolls and swirls that like stories are a reimagining of the authentic creation.

Poet Gillian Conoley on *The Plot Genie* (Omnidawn)

I am extremely happy with the cover because it seems to function as an extension of the book's contents, as a working part of the book itself, instead of "a cover." *The Plot Genie* is a book suggested by a plot-generating device of the same title published in the 1930s. The blue indigo drawing on the cover's left side is part of the original device writers were supposed to spin in calculating a plot. The device was so visually evocative that I sent a scan of it to Jeff Clark, thinking it was something he could use. I remember asking Jeff to come up with something that would balance the arcanity of the spinning device, that would bring it into the contemporary—but that was really my only input. When Omnidawn let me know Jeff was the designer for the book I was thrilled because he is not only a gifted book designer, but also a gifted poet. He reads the work, and then works to bring the book forward and alive. He's like Pinocchio's Geppetto.

Cover designer Sara T. Sauers on Michele Glazer's *On Tact, & the Made Up World* (University of Iowa Press)

I did this book design, cover and interior, in collaboration with the author. (Glazer took the original photo.) When an author has a particular vision for their book, and most poets do, I definitely like to hear about it. I read closely the text of every book I design and choose the fonts and images based on content. For Glazer's book I kept the cover typography tactful, allowing the altered photo to do the work of the "Made Up World." I teach courses in typography and book design at the University of Iowa, and I stress learning the traditional rules and technologies (even working in hot type!) because that gives students a solid footing as they face their future print and digital work. There is plenty of room to improve e-book design, so I encourage them to be a part of that.

Author Dawn Raffel on *Further Adventures in a Restless Universe* (Dzanc Books; cover designer Steven Seighman)

The drawing was done by my younger son, Sean Evers. I picked him up from the Art Student's League one day when he was eleven years old, and he had done a version of this. At the time, I had not yet finished writing the collection and didn't have a title: *Further Adventures in the Restless Universe* was one of a few I was toying with. I made up my mind as soon as I saw the drawing, and although there's no title story, I ended up adding a story that referenced the restless universe. The original drawing was horizontal, as you usually see the solar system, and I worried about how that would work on a book cover. Leave it to a child to recognize that there's no reason, other than convention, that the planets can't be stacked vertically. He redid the illustration and suggested running the title through the asteroid belt. Then he gave me a shooting star! Steven Seighman designed it with colored type, carrying the planets around to the back, the flaps, and the title page. I was thrilled with the way it came out.

A Manifesto Against Authors Writing for Free

Authorship is in mortal danger today because its meaning is being redefined in many different ways that are inimical to authors' historical interests; we're being told, by entities ranging from publishers to agents to magazines to internet platforms, to bend over backwards to do precisely the kinds of things that will harm our future viability. I will take up each of the arguments typically advanced in favor of writers offering their work for free, and show that these all amount to nothing more than crass exploitation of our irreplaceable time and energy.

If authorship is to have any chance of surviving in something resembling its traditional form, one of the very first things authors need to decide to do is to *stop writing for free*. It might appear that the floodgates have already been opened and it is a losing proposition to go against the trend, but in the history of writing that is not how things have worked; a few writers decide to take a stand and if they're forceful and articulate enough, things have a chance of shifting in a different direction. At least we have this against the corporate gatekeepers: they only have the power of what they call the cloud or the anonymous herd behind them, while we have the power to decide whether or not they ever get to play on the cloud.

1. Demeans Authorship, Why Should It Be Free?

Who else works for free? *Completely free?* We're not talking minimum wage here—say, $100-$200 for a smart review, or something similar for a poem or short story—but *nothing, just nothing at all.* Zero compensation. Write for the pleasure of writing, and expect to be a corporate slave elsewhere to scrounge up money to eat and live (or teach writing, which is a new form of corporate slavery).

If you worked in a kitchen and agreed to labor for free—with the rationalization that you might get to see a good chef in operation or experience a variety of patrons or be up close to the ingredients and mechanics of food preparation—you'd legitimately be considered insane.

Suppose you were a doctor in training and instead of enlisting in a residency leading to full-time practice you were asked to hang around hospitals for the chance of being exposed to different diseases and seeing how treatment regimens worked over time. You'd have a job on the side to feed your physicianly temperament, and you'd spend the rest of your life shuttling from hospital to hospital taking care of patients—and a few paid doctors' massive egos—for free.

You get the point; any other professional would consider it the most demeaning thing to be asked to work for free, especially in vocations that are typically considered the most noble. People aren't nurses for free, people aren't teachers for free, people don't save lives for free.

What writing for free—in whatever form it occurs—does is to make authors look down on their own profession as something lacking importance to such an extent that it can't even compete with fast food service or telemarketing or cleaning toilets (all of which, by the way, earn more than a typical literary writer does today). Why should writing be the only vocation considered immune to the reinforcing tendencies produced by the quality and quantity of remuneration?

We're supposed to be above and beyond normal considerations, even though we are recruited to give the best of our minds and bodies, like slaves of yore. And if we squeak a word in protest, we're called privileged elitists who don't show enough gratitude for the assignments coming our way.

I realize this is a general condition in the arts these days, not just writing, but I see its force most starkly in writing, perhaps because other forms of art are more tangible and physical and can be marketed as such (or rather cater to commodity fetishism), whereas writing is an abstract rendering of the creative human mind and therefore always finds itself in the worst situation when it comes to fairness in the marketplace.

2. Helps Blur Quantity vs. Quality, Makes Excellence Indistinguishable.

You, a serious literary author, are writing for free for Publication X, with a great masthead and serious financial backing. Someone else—perhaps barely literate—may be writing for the same publication, competing with you on equal terms; that other person has the equal right to express himself or herself, and because of the democracy of no-compensation, which unites opposites, he or she can lay equal claim to validity. Who can tell who's a better writer, who's making better points, who has paid the dues and earned the right to claim authority for the written word? Readers, you say, who are smart enough to distinguish quality from junk and will simply not read (or click on) the trash; the marketplace will decide who gets to be popular, based on quality alone, because by definition the free marketplace functions by rewarding quality. If you're bad, no one will read you, you will simply disappear.

Is that really how we think the literary marketplace (even in its internet manifestation) works? Is it that utopian out there? Does quality naturally rise to the top? Of course that's not the case, it's institutional arbitration that typically decides these matters.

It's more likely than not that the writer getting the most readership is the one catering to the lowest sensibilities, rather than aiming for quality. Kitsch will typically rate higher than anything aesthetically demanding, but there is a bigger issue here. Serious writers give legitimacy to the pretenders by being present on the same field; when we participate in the economy of free, we legitimize and empower the trashy, who will undoubtedly leave us in the dust, since they will play up the inflation of their own reputations, based on nothing, for the sake of publicity, and their form of publicity inevitably wins.

I'm using publicity in its darkest sense here, whereas our game is something else altogether. We must not compete on turf that's oriented toward publicity or it will empower the enemy—bad writing—to the point where we really will become peripheral to the culture.

3. Sets off Negative Loop Affecting Books, Compensation for All Forms of Authorship.

As with all art, clear separations between categories of work are not possible, or easily break down over time. One might rationalize, "This is just a short piece I'll offer for free, it has nothing to do with how I get paid for a book," but of course it has everything to do with it. Serious literary writers are typically expected, except for the few superstars, to get nothing—that's right, nothing!—in return for years or even decades of labor on a book. Perhaps a token advance, amounting to not even the cost of paper and printing over the years. Writing for free in any form, in any venue, exerts incredible downward pressure on writing in every form, including books.

This is not the only explanation for the phenomenon of more or less free books—another explanation is the recruitment of literary writers into academia en masse, so that compensation for teaching is how writers are expected to survive, not compensation by publishers profiting from them in the market-place—but it is consistent with the overall direction: move the expectation of money out of the equation, so that free becomes the norm. It's much more difficult to justify not paying someone for a book compared to a shorter piece of writing, but once the expectation sets in it spreads like a virus into all inter-actions between the writer and his buyers.

This means that writers are expected to rely on forms of institutional and state patronage for their livelihood, with all the familiar results whenever such a transformation occurs. We tend to think of the bad old days of Soviet socialist realism as something unprecedented and unrepeatable, but in the U.S. today a different form of rigid institutional patronage has led to severe political con-straints in written expression, all passing off under the most noble-sounding intentions of course. So next time you wonder how it could hurt to deliver a little extra piece of writing for free, consider the fact that you're yet again reit-erating in buyers' minds that it's okay for writers to have no connection with the marketplace.

I believe that writing is always better off when there is a legitimate, fair, transparently functioning marketplace (for a marketplace to exist means at the very least that there should be free play of supply and demand and that the supplier should be getting paid for services rendered), rather than patronage, which after all constituted the whole struggle of authors in the early modern era.

4. Nothing Positive That's Claimed for Free Writing Makes up for the Losses.

So what would be some of the claims made in lieu of monetary compensation as rewards? That the writer will become better-known; that the prestige of the platform rubs off on the writer; that it is valuable experience; and that one's writing will get better as a result of exposure and feedback (actually, this last one I've never heard, I just made it up, no one takes free that seriously). I think I've pretty much run out already of the claims offered instead of money. It's pretty thin ice, isn't it?

All of it is utter rubbish, anyway, it doesn't hold up to scrutiny for a second. If you want to be better known, should you indulge in competition for free stuff, set yourself up as a vassal happy enough just to be asked by publication X to write for their web spin-off (they won't let you appear in print, of course, because that's where they have to pay their favored writers)? How does that enhance your prestige? How does that inspire you to strive for better? But if your goal is to compete for evanescent popularity with the new content pickers, then you're well on the road to being convinced by such a shallow argument.

The association with any particular venue is fleeting and temporary anyway, it does not pass along with you, it stays with the originator; they are like the robbers, in the current publication climate, who polish off the gold in you, while leaving you pauperized. If you want to get experience in writing, the kind of experience you'll gain by writing for free is not what you want anyway; if you're aiming to compete with the best minds, you cannot do it by having a self-conception of yourself worse than the most cheaply compensated occupations.

None of the arguments advanced in favor of compensation other than money holds water. The situation is exacerbated by what I perceive as the impending death of the internet; partly this has come about because a few monopoly corporations have risen to the top, sucking up all the democratic energies that were in embryonic evidence in the late 1990s and early 2000s, and converting the internet into a vast wasteland that enriches the few, impoverishes the many (in ways that are still not clearly understood or articulated), and leaves *everyone* worse off intellectually. Do you want to write for free and contribute to this degradation? Or do you want to do something—perhaps even nothing—other than this debased form of pseudo-participation?

5. Platform Is Bullshit, Doesn't Sell Books, Social Media Is Oversold.

So we get to the most vociferously advanced argument in favor of writing for free, that it provides you a platform, which is supposed to enrich you in ways that mere monetary compensation never could. Platform will make your name known and will establish your brand, so that you can form a niche within a vast, amorphous, shifting marketplace that otherwise provides few permanent loyalties and few ways to distinguish yourself from the crowd. Platform will make it possible for you to go on to bigger and better things (meaning contracts paying you to write books). Platform will generate feedback effects that will make your writing responsive to what the reading public actually wants rather than writing in a vacuum.

Even on the face of it, none of these arguments have any truth. But if we accept them at face value, they work only if the platform is *you*, the author, to begin with, and not some subservient relationship with an entity that has no loyalty to you, whose very interest, in fact, is to suppress your own brand as Author X and promote its brand as the platform on which you've momentarily been given space. These interests are by definition in contradiction, not mutual cooperation.

Authors have lately become caught up in the illusion that having a wide followership on various social media, interacting with readers and responding to their needs, is somehow tantamount to authorship itself. It is not. Social media has in fact become a *substitute* for writing (real) books. To the extent that there is followership, it is—at least for literary writers—limited mostly to fellow authors, or at least wannabe authors; which means that one is not expanding the marketplace but rather contributing to its increasing contraction by indulging in this collective illusion. Platform serves only the entity that's hosting you: they make infinitely more out of your servitude than you will ever get back from the unpaid slavery.

If you really believe there is something to platform, then at least create your own platform, dissociated from a large corporation. You will soon realize, of course, that with the coming end of the internet (because it already reflects the brutality of end-stage capitalism rather than the expansive frontier it used to be in the early days), creating your own platform is not so easy; and if it's an incredibly convoluted way to getting to write your books, you might as well get to the main task at hand, rather than be diverted—and it's often a diversion with no way out. These feel-good, mutual admiration mini-societies are just that; they have no cultural significance, and if that's where you want to be, flattered that you're doing something worthy of the pursuit known as authorship, then that's fine, but don't pretend that you're being an author when all you're doing is glad-handing—i.e., doing social media.

6. Media Conglomerates Benefit While Creators Are Impoverished.

Consider the internet circa 1995 or 1998 or 2001 or 2004, and then consider the situation now: a handful of monopolies control everything, they have engineered the situation so that readers go to, for example, certain news aggregators, certain established brands maintained by gatekeepers just as assiduous in keeping out the unwelcome as in the old days of print media collusion.

In these twenty years, in various distinct stages, nearly all the power has been diverted from individual entrepreneurs to powerful actors who are interested in exploiting intellectual labor—of a very diminished form, admittedly—for their own financial motives, while preventing individual voices from finding independent legitimacy. Who will pay attention to your blog, one among hundreds of millions, even if you have something important to say, when you're competing with others hiding behind gatekeepers and willing to contribute pseudo-writing for free? Your individual effort doesn't stand much chance of being seen, the way the internet is hierarchized now.

There are of course the examples of corporations who make millions of dollars—even hundreds of millions of dollars—off the back of sincere platform-seekers while refusing to share a cent of these massive earnings with those who created the brand in the first place; this should tell us all we need to know about how these media giants think of free intellectual labor, what utter disrespect they have for those who earn them the big money. Don't write for such outlets. Don't contribute to their wealth, don't contribute to your own impoverishment, don't make it more possible for other authors never to make writing pay for them.

The power of these brands magnified over the years precisely because writers thought it harmless to write for free, yet we now find ourselves in the cold, unable to seek audiences, because the corporate brands helped by us have become so large that they are the only things visible.

I had a most disconcerting exchange recently with the founder of a West Coast review outlet, which was launched with much fanfare a few years ago, who refused to pay anything for contributions or even divulge if and what he paid some of his favored contributors. Does this editor pay himself? Does he pay his associates? Even if there is no direct salary involved—which I doubt very much—this founder and his associates are being enriched in ways that his stable of writers aren't. There are tangible benefits, accruing from visibility and prominence, leading to financial rewards for the owners; there are many ways to spin off fame built on the labor of others and marketize it for the corporation's benefit, and, trust me, each of these benevolent-sounding enterprises are using these resources to the hilt. I will never write for that journal, and I hope that when my fellow authors see hypocrisy and contradiction at such a level, they won't do so either.

At the very least—with those who profess literary intentions—there should be transparency about what they are earning, what they are paying themselves and their staff, and there should be ways of tying compensation directly with the value of contributions; this is a technical, logistical problem with easy solutions, and it is incredible that it is not even part of the discussion, let alone already being pervasive.

7. Affects the Quality of Writing Itself When You Do It for Free.

Perhaps, putting aside all the above arguments, you think you can write for free and just not care about the money because you have some overriding motives beyond the legitimate arguments not to write for free. You think you can gain a foothold, use the medium for your purposes, exploit different platforms that seek free writing and turn it to your own ultimate advantage, without your writing suffering in any way. But it will. You will write differently when you write for free, I can assure you of that.

Why does this happen? It's because you come to a different understanding of authorship when you do it for free, and it radically effects your work at the very level of conceptualization. Again, if you're happy with being a content serf, extracting from the rough soils of popular paranoia whatever can pass as writing, then this doesn't apply to you, so please carry on. But if you think you can write for free and preserve your writerly innocence, think again.

Over time, the effect will be noticeable. Your intended audience will have shifted, your goals toward writing will no longer be as absolute, you will find yourself living more in the moment (free also always means instant and accessible and fleeting) than you ever thought possible—all of which will hinder real writing. You will be drained of energy in ways you never imagined. You will—after a certain amount of time—give up autonomy itself. And don't think for a moment that this isn't exactly the result desired by those who want free writing from you, whether they're traditional publishers of books and magazines catering to the new sensibility of making nothing happen, or whether they're cutting-edge platforms peddling all the bullshit about branding.

They want to destroy writing itself so that the freestanding, unpredictable, status quo-threatening endeavor that has always been writing is assimilated into something more amorphous and conducive to the new collectivist direction: an updated assimilation of totalitarian tendencies which have always been the twin of liberal humanism, but which used to be easier to get a grip on because they stood outside individual agency whereas now they are presented as the sum of agency itself. Writing for free is one part of this collectivization that is crushing independent thinking; writing for free means not just altering the parameters of rewards and motives, but altering writing itself. Free writing has a different quality than writing that comes from traditional notions of authorship. It can't be any other way.

The proof is in the pudding. The promise of the internet—free writing—was that there would be room for criticism of a far more expansive and honest nature; the opposite has actually happened. It amounts to vast terabytes of ideological drivel and the art of criticism has mortally suffered despite the theoretical options available. Instead of serious political commentary there are only endless series of pseudo-outrages, with writers enlisted to perform their roles in the never-ending drama. Free writing finds its natural atmosphere in performance and theatrics, not serious deliberation.

8. Feeds into the Notion of Authorship as Extraneous to Culture.

This is a somewhat different point from the first one, which was about demeaning authorship, assuming that the writer has conventional notions of authorship to begin with and is not just a happy platform builder, satisfied with all that that implies—a ghostwriter really, a conveyor of sentiments and pseudo-profundities that are already rotting the collective mind.

This point is about pushing authors squarely outside the centrality of culture-creation, where they have been for at least five hundred years, since the unraveling of the medieval consensus. It is about undermining their key role as formulators of democratic solidarity authors have found themselves performing—as secular heroes—for half a millennium. Now, under the current form of capitalism, this role is no longer needed; what we have, with new technology, is a pervasive pseudo-democracy, where everyone is a potential author. That is the false promise of the new technology, and it is meant to put to pasture anyone inclined to be a real author. That is what this whole thing is leading to: authors who come up with original ideas do not have a role in the new economy.

What we used to know as culture is now created almost entirely by institutional arrangement, within very well-defined matrices of recruitment, performance, mentorship, and security. If we see free writing in this context, then it becomes something far more insidious than just giving you a platform and everyone automatically being better off. Big authoritative forces are compelling writing to be free and simultaneously putting it outside the framework of culture—any kind of culture that matters, that molds the middle mind, that has a say in the distribution of power and resources. Again, free has its own philosophical orientation; what is free will not be a partner in the future in the ultimate material decisions. It will be beneath contempt, let alone being central to the ideas ruling society.

Let me say that despite the pessimism of the logic of the above points, I do not mean that writers should unilaterally disarm themselves. At the practical level, writers can start affecting the pernicious situation currently existing by taking certain simple steps. Stop writing for free! This applies with special force to writing for entities that are making plenty of money, and whose editors also get paid well, but who ask you to write for fame and experience alone.

Many forms of fair compensation can be imagined, from generous payments dependent on readers brought in, to straightforward lump sums that must meet the comparable definition of a living wage (I hate to say minimum wage) in the rest of the real world; each writer will have to figure out for herself what that basic floor for a particular job will be, but it cannot be something ridiculous (like $20 or $50 for a review), otherwise it beats the purpose. If you write steadily for a whole month and at the end of it you don't have enough to easily survive from your labors, then the least you can do is *not* contribute anymore to the economy of exploitation.

So mine is not some utopian manifesto with no chance of realization; we are the ones with the power, and we can do no less than try to shift the playing field more in our favor. In the longer run, we can think beyond being better compensated by existing forces to engineering entire new formats where serious authorship reigns supreme and earns a fair reward and the monopolists are bypassed.

Real authors don't do it for the money, it goes without saying; but if we don't bring money back into the equation, then, for all the reasons stated above, we can't be authors anymore. The parallels with the rest of the economy—in terms of the insecurity of indentured servitude—are direct and clear; we authors ought to take up arms, one at a time, against an injustice that is sugarcoated in benign intentions but actually is the deepest insult to the freedom we seek to find in writing in the first place.

I would be the first to admit that over the years my own views on this subject have evolved—soured, you might say—as I have failed to see fairer compensation models for writers develop and have instead noted a general degradation of the new technologies writers were so hopeful about only a few years ago. My allegiances, when the rubble of the new writing economy has cleared, stand as they did in my early years, mostly with those honorable print literary quarterlies who strive to compensate writers in accordance with their resources, and who publish, not coincidentally, much of the best writing in the country.

Do you want me to write for you for free? I have one question for you. Are *you* doing it for free? If not, in the immortal words of Dick Cheney, Go fuck yourself.

Acknowledgements

My thanks to the *Huffington Post* for publishing some of these essays, particularly to Amy Hertz, and also to Jessie Kunhardt, Sammy Perlmutter, and Zoe Triska. My deep thanks also to Richard Burgin at *Boulevard*, David Leavitt at *Subtropics*, Sven Birkerts at *AGNI*, Laurence Goldstein at *Michigan Quarterly Review*, Robert Lewis at *North Dakota Quarterly*, John Matthias at *Notre Dame Review*, Robert Fogarty at *Antioch Review*, Jane Ciabattari and Rigoberto Gonzalez at the National Book Critics Circle blog, Brad Tyer and David Duhr at the *Texas Observer*, Brad Listi at *The Nervous Breakdown*, Daniel Honan at *Big Think*, Lucas Wittmann at *The Daily Beast*, Tom Lutz at the *Los Angeles Review of Books*, David Daley at *Salon*, Bob Hoover at the *Pittsburgh Post-Gazette*, John McMurtry at the *San Francisco Chronicle*, Jody Seaborn at the *Austin American-Statesman*, and Colette Bancroft at the *St. Petersburg Times* for being consistent supporters of my work.

"The Function of Criticism," originally appearing in *Subtropics*, received special mention in the Pushcart Prize XXXVIII anthology, for which I thank editor Bill Henderson. "A Manifesto Against Authors Writing for Free," originally appearing in *Boulevard*, received special mention in *Best American Essays 2015*, for which I thank guest editor Ariel Levy.

Above all, my deepest gratitude to Paul Ruffin, publisher of the press and a stalwart defender of Texas letters, who was always a fearless supporter of my critical work. He was a man of imagination who knew how to take hold of reality and bend it according to his vision rather than the other way around. It was his idealism that brought Texas Review Press into the world. And thanks to Kimberly Parish Davis for enthusiastically picking up the baton, and also Nancy J. Parsons, Claude Wooley, Mike Hilbig, Catherine Smith, Elizabeth Evans, and everyone else who worked diligently on this book at Texas Review Press.

My warm gratitude also to the hugely diverse participants in the various symposia and interviews included in this book, representing poets, fiction writers, critics, editors, publishers, designers, booksellers, and others involved in every aspect of the literary venture. Thank you, all of you who participated, for offering your vigorous insights from years of experience in the writing world—from whichever side of the literary divide you belong to!

About the Author

Anis Shivani is a fiction writer, poet, and literary critic living in Houston, Texas. His critically acclaimed books include *Anatolia and Other Stories, The Fifth Lash and Other Stories, Karachi Raj: A Novel, My Tranquil War and Other Poems, Whatever Speaks on Behalf of Hashish: Poems, Soraya: Sonnets*, and *Against the Workshop: Provocations, Polemics, Controversies*. His work appears widely in such journals as the *Texas Review, Yale Review, Georgia Review, Southwest Review, Boston Review, Threepenny Review, Michigan Quarterly Review, Antioch Review, Black Warrior Review, Western Humanities Review, Boulevard, Pleiades, AGNI, Fence, Denver Quarterly, Volt, Subtropics, New Letters, Times Literary Supplement, London Magazine, Cambridge Quarterly, Contemporary Review* (Oxford), *Meanjin, Fiddlehead, Dalhousie Review, Antigonish Review*, and elsewhere. He has also written for many magazines and newspapers including *Salon, Daily Beast, AlterNet, CommonDreams, Truthout, Huffington Post, Texas Observer, In These Times, Boston Globe, San Francisco Chronicle, Kansas City Star, Pittsburgh Post-Gazette, St. Petersburg Times, Baltimore Sun, Charlotte Observer, Austin American-Statesman*, and elsewhere. He is the winner of a Pushcart Prize, and a graduate of Harvard College.

CPSIA information can be obtained
at www.ICGtesting.com
Printed in the USA
FFOW02n2141080617
36517FF